WOMEN AND CONTEMPORARY SCOTTISH POLITICS

To bissums wi' smeddum

© editorial matter and organisation
Esther Breitenbach and Fiona Mackay, 2001.
© in individual chapters as indicated.

Polygon at Edinburgh
An imprint of Edinburgh University Press Ltd
22 George Square, Edinburgh

Typeset in 11 on 13pt Goudy Old Style
by Hewer Text Ltd, Edinburgh, and
printed and bound in Great Britain by
MPG Books Ltd, Bodmin

A CIP record for this book is available from the British Library

ISBN 1 902930 24 X (paperback)

Contents

Contributors

Morag Alexander is Director of the Equal Opportunities Commission's Office in Scotland. She is a member of the Scottish Executive Women's Issues Research Advisory Group and was a board member of Scotland Forward, the all-party and civic organisation which campaigned for a 'Yes, yes' vote in the referendum on a Scottish Parliament. She writes in a personal capacity.

Patricia Bell was a development worker with the Women's Support Project in Glasgow when the article was first published. She has since gained a doctorate and now works as an academic researcher at the University of Teesside.

Esther Breitenbach is the author of numerous articles on women and gender inequalities in Scotland and has been active in the women's movement for many years. She is a Teaching Fellow in the Department of Social Policy at the University of Edinburgh, and is currently on secondment to the Scottish Executive as Women's Issues Researcher. The contributions in this book have been written in a personal capacity.

Alice Brown is Professor of Politics and a Vice Principal at the University of Edinburgh. She was a founder member of Engender and the Scottish Women's Co-ordination Group. She was also a member of the Scottish Constitutional Commission and was active in drafting the electoral agreement on gender balance for the Scottish Parliament and the Labour party's 'twinning' mechanism. She participated in the Consultative Steering Group on the Scottish Parliament. She has published widely on women and Scottish politics and constitutional change.

Catriona Burness (formerly Levy) currently works as an adviser to Catherine Stihler (formerly Taylor), MEP, in the European Parliament, Brussels. She has held several academic posts including the Glenfiddich Research Fellowship in

This includes: public education; support for women whose children have been sexually abused; training and consultancy; developing multi-agency responses to male violence, including developing services for women abused in prostitution.

Tom Nairn is an author, journalist and Fellow of the Research Institute in Irish and Scottish Studies at the University of Aberdeen. Recent publications include *After Britain: New Labour and the Return of Scotland* (Granta Books, 2000) and *Faces of Nationalism: Janus Revisited* (Verso, 1997).

Judith Robertson is Poverty Programme Development Officer for Oxfam in Scotland. At the time of original publication she was a member of the Woman's Claim of Right Group and worked as a campaigner for Oxfam. Currently, she is a member of the Scottish Women's Budget Group.

Anita Shelton is an active trade unionist and campaigner for racial equality. Born and educated in the United States, she holds degrees in information science and sociology. She has been involved in the civil rights and labour movement since the early 1960s and considers the documentation of the lives of black women in Scotland an integral part of the country's social history. She lives in Glasgow.

Lesley Sutherland is a full-time union official and a long standing campaigner for gender equality. She convenes Women's Forum Scotland and is a founder Board member and former Treasurer of the European Women's Lobby. She was involved in the campaign for a Scottish Parliament and is active in promoting an enhanced public role for civic groups. She has recently been elected as a Vice Convener of the Scottish Civic Forum.

Forewords

– WENDY ALEXANDER MSP –

Minister for Enterprise and Lifelong Learning

There really couldn't be a better time for a book on women in Scottish politics to be published. The last ten years' important, hard work by many made it possible for 37 per cent of the elected Members of the Scottish Parliament to be women. We know that we stand on our mothers' shoulders. But this is not the end of the campaign for women's representation, rather it is the beginning of a new phase in women's participation. The opportunity to change Scottish society in a way that recognises the needs, hopes and aspirations of woman today.

Moving forward means understanding where we have come from. This book is an important and timely contribution to that process.

The increase in women's representation is of historic importance, and we must hope others will learn from us as we have learned from them. It is early days to start analysing the impact the presence of women in the Scottish Parliament is having. But even at this early stage I believe a number of key areas can be singled out where women are making a difference to the way politics in Scotland is being conducted as well as influencing the issues that are being debated.

We face both short and long term challenges. In the long-term category are decisions such as the setting up of the Equality Unit and ensuring that equalities will be at the heart of policy making in general, similarly the work underway on women-friendly budgeting, co-operation with Scottish Enterprise on women into business; the review of family law, the changing of the public appointment system. These are about ensuring different long-term structural foundations are laid and the establishment of the Scottish Parliament has been key to this.

There are also the short-term policy decisions – the essential steps that shame us that we haven't done them before. The pre-eminent one is on domestic abuse and the support that has been provided to start to address the shortfall of refuge

that the concerns of women in Scotland are represented more generally. But this will not be the end of the story and much needs to be done by women in the women's movement and more generally to maintain and continue the progress in achieving economic, social and political equality for women. The vision of 'difference' was one of the mobilising forces for women active in Scottish politics and in the campaign for a Scottish parliament. With more women in the Parliament it was argued that there was an opportunity to address the 'double democratic deficit' which some perceived, to change a predominantly male-dominated political culture and political behaviour, to bring a women's perspective to the parliamentary process, and to make better policy and have different policy priorities which can make a difference to people's lives. There is much work still to be done to translate this vision and these high aspirations into reality. Getting women into the Parliament was, after all, not just an end in itself but a means to other ends. Effecting change will require the continuation of alliances that have been built up over the last 20 years in order that women inside and outside the formal political arena continue to work together. It is vital, therefore, that women know their history in order to understand the present and, crucially, to influence the future. Reading this book will equip them well in this process.

Introduction: Women and Contemporary Scottish Politics

ESTHER BREITENBACH AND FIONA MACKAY

Women have an unprecedented voice and a place in Scottish politics with the advent of the new Scottish parliament. Women make up 37.2 per cent of Members of the Scottish Parliament (MSPs), amongst the highest proportions in national and/or devolved parliaments in Europe.[1] In addition, under the 'power sharing' model endorsed by the parliament, new opportunities exist for women's organisations and women as individual citizens to be consulted and involved in policy making. As such, Scotland is arguably at the cutting edge of gender politics and democratic practice.

The campaign for gender balance in the Scottish Parliament and the role of women within the new parliament is also attracting growing interest, not only in Scotland but also from commentators, researchers, students, and activists elsewhere in Britain and internationally as they become aware of the significant changes taking place in the British political system through current constitutional reforms. In short, people are awakening to the fact that something has been going on in Scotland.

As Alice Brown notes in her foreword, the election of a significant number of women MSPs did not happen by chance but as the result of sustained campaigning by women activists in political parties, trade unions, and women's groups. Many women in Scotland had, of course, hoped for more, especially those who had campaigned for 50:50 – equal representation of women and men. Nonetheless, this is an achievement, and an important symbol of the development of a new kind of polity in Scotland – one that aims to be more representative, more inclusive, more democratic, and more modern, at least in the sense of reflecting better the composition of the population and contemporary social structures.

The level of women's representation and the presence of a number of women in top political positions in the Scottish Executive is only the most visible sign of a process of change in the balance of power between men and women. The

are those of women's representation in political and public life, and campaigns against violence against women. The latter theme is also prominent in the second section of the book on the local politics of sex equality. Women's representation and access to decision making of course also feature here, and new material drawing from recent research gives an overview of policy development on a range of equal opportunities issues at the level of local government.

The third section of the book discusses the campaign for equal representation in the Scottish Parliament, how women have mobilised to increase their representation, and how they have challenged conventional ways of doing politics. It also offers explanations for the emergence of political representation as an issue around which a coalition of women's organisations came together. This section contains perspectives both from academic commentators and from prominent women activists in the campaign, categories which, contrary to popular stereotypes of academics, are far from being mutually exclusive.

– THE WOMEN'S MOVEMENT IN SCOTLAND –

Like second wave women's movements in many countries the women's movement in Scotland emerged in the late 1960s and early 1970s. There is, of course, an issue of definition of the 'women's movement'. Should this be applied only to groups and individuals who have consciously identified themselves as part of the Women's Liberation Movement, or, subsequently, as feminist? Or should it be a broader definition including all those attempting to improve women's status in contemporary society? Though this book as a whole encompasses the broader definition, within the first section it is concerned with self-consciously defined feminist organisations and activities.

In Scotland, feminist ideals and critiques of male domination have inspired the formation of a host of groups, have been the basis for campaigns, and have found expression in writing, drama, and other art forms. Over the period since the late 1960s a great deal of ephemeral material has been produced – newsletters, conference papers, leaflets, posters, campaigning materials, badges, postcards, and so on – some of which has been collected by Glasgow Women's Library and other women's centres, but much of which must still be in cupboards, attics, basements, and other homes for forgotten ephemera, where, like Marx's manuscript for *The German Ideology*, it is being nibbled by the mice. A few Scottish feminist journals and magazines have had a short-lived existence, such as the *Scottish Women's Liberation Journal*, *Msprint*, and *Harpies & Quines*. Some newsletters have survived over a much longer period, including *Scottish Women's Aid's Newsletter*, and, more recently, the *Engender Newsletter* has appeared. *Grit and Diamonds* (Henderson and Mackay) published in 1990, provided a snapshot of the range and diversity of the projects and activities of the women's movement in Scotland at the end of the 1980s, but source material that is accessible or in the public domain remains very limited.

There are few accounts which attempt to analyse the wider political and social context in which the women's movement has developed and the politics, strategies, and organisational strengths and weaknesses of the women's movement itself. However, recent research carried out into women in political parties, women in Scottish politics and in local government has an important bearing on questions such as the impact of feminist ideas, and the extent to which women activists in political parties identify themselves as feminists. Much of this material is included in or referred to in this book, and we argue that there is indeed evidence of significant feminist influence in Scottish politics.

Journals, newsletters, and publications such as *Grit and Diamonds* give a sense of the scope and diversity of the women's movement in Scotland. By contrast, articles that attempt to provide a more in-depth or analytical account have tended to focus on feminist campaigns against violence against women, and this theme is prominent both in the section on the women's movement in Scotland, and in the section examining local government and gender politics. Brought together here is a small number of previously published articles, some of which provide narrative accounts of campaigns or the genesis of specific organisations such as Engender, and some of which contribute to wider debates about the nature of feminist politics, or both. In addition to these, the section on the women's movement includes several contributions on important aspects of the movement in Scotland that were invited specifically for this collection – on Women's Aid, the Rape Crisis movement, and on black and ethnic minority women and black feminism in Scotland. While these have helped to fill some of the gaps, they cannot give the full picture.

What continue to be missing, and what we might therefore argue are the gaps that most urgently need to be filled, are accounts and discussions of the range of feminist politics – radical, liberal, socialist, lesbian, black, peace campaigners, and environmentalists – and of the action, campaigning and debates in which these strands of feminism have engaged. The lack of a record of feminist action must not be taken to demonstrate a lack of action in fact. As has been noted elsewhere, the 'argument that there is a lack of research and serious study of the experience of women in Scotland, either in general, or of the experience of particular groups of women, whether black, lesbian, rural, or working class, is not intended to imply that there are no means of self-expression or political organisation for these groups. This is far from being the case' (Breitenbach, Brown, and Myers 1998: 49).

It has been argued elsewhere (Breitenbach 1990) that the pattern of development of the women's movement in Scotland has paralleled that of the movement in Britain as a whole, particularly in its spontaneous development focusing on consciousness raising in the early stages, its hostility to hierarchical

Key developments which Christianson and Greenan document are legal changes, and changes in attitudes by the police and judiciary, changes in the funding climate that made more funding available to rape crisis centres but also shifted them more towards service provision in contrast to their initial radical campaigning stance. From the outset the Rape Crisis movement was clear about the specific legal context in Scotland within which they were operating, and their campaigns were directed towards Scots law and the Scottish legal system. Research carried out for the Scottish Office validated their views on women's treatment by police and the courts (Chambers and Millar 1983, 1986) and exposed the way in which women complainers continued to be subjected to questioning about their sexual histories, despite legal changes intended to prevent this (Brown, Burman and Jamieson 1992). Writing in 1990, Breitenbach noted with optimism this legal change. That it did not fulfil its promise serves only to emphasise the importance of research in monitoring change. Related to the movement's focus on Scottish legal change was a growing frustration amongst rape crisis centres at the lack of parliamentary time allowing Scottish legislation to be enacted, and hence their support for the creation of a Scottish Parliament.

A significant point to emerge from Christianson and Greenan's discussion is the unintended consequences of policies for the Rape Crisis movement, some beneficial some harmful. Christianson and Greenan write that, paradoxically, the law and order agenda of Conservative governments allowed a greater breadth of discussion on issues of violence against women, which they contrast with the more narrow focus on domestic violence by the Labour government. The Community Care Act, through facilitating funding for rape crisis centres, fostered a service provider role, which has sometimes sat uncomfortably with a challenging feminist agenda rooted in a recognition of gender power imbalances. Last but not least, local government reorganisation has had a detrimental effect on the Rape Crisis movement through its restructuring of the funding framework on which centres depended.

Part of the argument in this book is that there is evidence of feminist influence – sometimes direct, sometimes diffuse – on Scottish politics and political institutions. While some groups have campaigned consistently and worked strategically to achieve their goals, for example, Women's Aid and the Rape Crisis movement, this cannot be said of all groups nor of the women's movement as a whole. Thus some of the influence that is apparent seems to have exerted itself through a process of osmosis – or a diffusion of feminist ideas and values into the 'mainstream' – rather than by self-consciously directed action. However, examples of the latter do exist, where groups have set out specifically to introduce a feminist analysis and ways of working into mainstream organisations and service providers. The Women's Support Project provides just such an example. This Glasgow-based project developed from the Rape Crisis Centre, with the aim of bridging the gap between feminist organisations and professionals in education, social work, community education, and so on. Their work has been informed by a feminist analysis of male violence, which draws links between domestic violence and child sexual abuse, and implicitly challenges male power, particularly within the family.

As Macleod, Bell and Forman note in Chapter 2, although there was a growth of organisations in the 1980s, these still could not meet the demand for their services. Despite the evidence of how extensive this demand was, there was 'unfortunately little evidence that mainstream and statutory organisations have acknowledged or responded to the extent of violence against women'. Since the article was first published there has been further change, though the evidence is that responsiveness to the issue of violence against women is still very varied across service providers (see, for example, Henderson 1998). More resources for specialist agencies and services may be seen as essential, but Macleod, Bell and Forman sound a warning that channelling resources into specialist services and changing nothing else 'allows everyone to collude with abuse'. The strategic approach to changing mainstream services adopted by the Women's Support Project foreshadows the approach of mainstreaming of equality that has emerged as dominant in current debates. However their orientation to working with and challenging mainstream providers led to the Project often being in the uncomfortable position of being criticised and condemned by both the establishment and the feminist community simultaneously. This echoes the discussion above on the difficulties of being a 'thresholder', which opens individuals and groups to accusations of 'selling out' or compromising their principles.

Leslie Hills, in 'Why Engender?', published 1994, describes how Engender came into being, and why it was felt that a new feminist campaigning organisation was needed. Engender was set up as an explicitly feminist organisation which put the gender balance of power relations in Scotland at the centre of its concerns. It was an organisation 'for all women who want to change the way power is distributed and wielded in Scotland'. Hills' article is a blast against continuing gender inequalities, and against the impact of Thatcherism in increasing women's burdens as carers through increasing poverty, and through the threat to services and organisations which supported and provided security to women. Written in the same passion and anger that fuelled the creation of Engender, the article provides an indictment of the continuing sexism of Scottish society, and of the failure of the media to take women seriously. It sets out the role Engender defined for itself of making women visible, 'putting Scottish women in the picture' as the Gender Audit[3] declares. The provision of information was seen to be crucial to promoting women's visibility, as well as publicising the continuing gender inequalities in Scottish society. This initiative was undertaken in the knowledge that it would be a long-term project. Seven years on it is clear that it has had an impact and helped to get across the extent to which gender inequalities persist.

In this early phase of development, all the committees in Scotland were set up by Labour councils. Of the other parties, the Scottish Liberal Democrats have shown support, though they sometimes showed a preference for equal opportunities over women's committees, (it is interesting to note that more recently there has been a general trend towards generic equal opportunities committees). Conservative councillors demonstrated considerable hostility initially, and in some cases did as much as they could to undermine the work of committees. While the work of women's and equal opportunities initiatives can still be contentious and the butt of public criticism by Conservative councillors, there have been some shifts in attitudes as evidenced by cross party support for the Zero Tolerance Campaign and other initiatives tackling violence against women (see Mackay 1995).

The theme of feminist influence in local government runs through much of the writing on gender and local government in Scotland. The consensus is that this influence has had a demonstrable impact, most notably in the emergence of the Zero Tolerance Campaign. Not surprisingly, this, and the wider issue of violence against women, has been the focus for several commentators, both those writing about the women's movement and those writing about local government (see, for example, Dobash and Dobash 1992; and in this collection Macleod, Bell and Forman; Cuthbert and Irving; Mackay; and Cosgrove). Campaigns against violence against women, and policy development and service provision for women who have experienced domestic abuse, provide the clearest example of explicitly feminist ideas shaping action in the local state. The point has also been made that such initiatives effect a process of democratisation, through the participation of women in forming policy (Dobash and Dobash 1992).

In this context the capacity of some women's organisations (as distinct from the women's movement as a whole) to act strategically to influence local government has been significant, but equally the role of women inside bureaucracies, so-called 'femocrats', has been essential to success. Above all the development of alliances to achieve sufficient levels of support for campaigns, strategies and policies, has been a key factor. These alliances have extended across feminist and other women's organisations, equal opportunities specialists and other local government officers, councillors – across parties and including male supporters, as both Cosgrove and Mackay point out. These authors stress the importance of local authority support for the Zero Tolerance campaign in giving it both weight and authority, and thereby reaffirming women's rights. The existence of women's and equal opportunities committees and staff provided a structure through which such feminist intervention became possible. The significance of Zero Tolerance lies not only in the campaign itself, but in the shift it represents in the scope of local government action, and in the adoption of feminist values. As Mackay argues, the fact that the anticipated backlash to Zero Tolerance from within councils did not materialise marked a contrast with the early hostility to women's committees, and provides evidence that a shift had occurred.

Despite such successes, the under-representation of women as councillors and in senior decision-making positions within local government bureaucracies has been consistently raised as an issue for concern. In Scotland the proportion of women councillors is 22 per cent, is lower than in England, though higher than in Wales. Ellen Kelly, writing in 1992, had expressed the hope that women would mobilise to take the opportunity of local government reorganisation in the mid-1990s to increase their representation, but in the event this was not to be. Indeed the results of the 1999 local government elections provide a cautionary tale: for, despite the intense interest in gender balance at Scottish parliament level, there were no gains for women in local government. Women were 22 per cent of councillors in 1999, the same low proportion as in 1995.

Women councillors and activists have identified a range of practical, structural and psychological barriers to political participation including family responsibilities, lack of time, lack of resources, lack of confidence, and discriminatory attitudes. In many cases the view remained that it was a man's right to be a councillor but that being a councillor was seen as a hobby for women (Martlew et al. 1985; Mann 1993, Mackay, 1996). In addition the structures and culture of political parties and councils were perceived to be rigid, inflexible and 'macho'. These factors all contributed to 'the creation of an atmosphere that women don't feel comfortable in'. Chapman's work (1993) on recruitment practices within the main political parties concluded that women were disadvantaged.

Changes in the position of women as councillors in Scotland are occurring very slowly. Bochel and Bochel (1998) noted that over time the proportion of women who were councillors had increased, and that the proportion chairing committees was increasing, and the range of types of committees was also broadening. Nonetheless, they comment that from the evidence of surveys in 1977, 1985, and 1993, women in Scotland 'held a disproportionately low number of positions such as leader, chair or committee chair in relation to their presence on councils'. A survey, which they conducted in 1996, revealed that women councillors were more likely to be first elected at a later age than men; were more likely to consider themselves full-time councillors than men, and less likely to be in full-time employment; more likely to serve on committees with 'caring' remits such as Education, and Social Work as against against Planning and Economic Development remits. They were also more likely to serve on Equal Opportunities committees than men. Election to office at a later age is likely to reduce political career opportunities. Paradoxically, however, women's greater commitment to full-time council work appears to be less rewarded than men's lesser commitment in terms of hours put in.

Ellen Kelly has argued that the presence of women in positions of influence – as elected politicans or as senior managers – makes a difference to local government and is likely to lead to services which are more sensitive to the

continued to take different positions on the appropriateness of special measures to achieve equal representation, and what these measures might be. The 50:50 demand, however, quickly became a rallying cry for many women activists, and the official title of a broad-based campaign.

Several chapters chart the growing awareness of and better information about the nature and extent of political under–representation and how the Scottish situation compared unfavourably with many other countries (Galloway and Robertson; Lindsay, Levy; Brown; McDonald et al.). Women campaigners in the 1990s explicitly drew lessons from history and from contemporary academic research and the experiences of women activists in Europe and elsewhere. These lessons fed into demands for electoral systems, recruitment and selection procedures, and institutional practices to take women into account. So, for example, the campaign for women's representation specifically addressed barriers to participation and drew upon research by Brown (1996) and others. For example, support for proportional representation was based not only on the idea of fair representation for parties, but also on the recognition that proportional representation systems can offer the opportunity to achieve wider representation. Selection procedures, which research shows have an important role to play, came under scrutiny. This was specifically, if controversially addressed by the Labour Party, and selection procedures adopted by the SNP are also thought to have contributed to a greater number of candidates being selected[4] (see Brown et al. 1999).

One of the defining features of the broader campaign for constitutional reform in the 1990s was the way in which gender equality became a significant part of wider debates on devolution and democratic renewal. Brown argues that opportunities were not just practical and political but also operated at the level of discourses – that is, the way that people think, talk and argue about politics and democracy. Like Tom Nairn (Chapter 15) she underlines the symbolic importance which the issue of gender balance gained in wider constitutional debates. The 50:50 campaign for gender equality became a shorthand for a desire for a new sort of politics. What we can also draw from these accounts and analyses is that although there were favourable contexts and opportunity structures, progress was by no means certain. Brown is less sanguine than Nairn who, in his 1994 *Scotsman* essay, declared that 'nothing, but nothing will make the issue go away'. Instead she argues that there were various points at which the issue may have been sidelined and that it was the persistence of women campaigners (working inside and outwith institutions) which kept the issue on the agenda and which maintained pressure on the Constitutional Convention, political parties and trade unions. We see this illustrated most clearly in the intervention of the Women's Co-ordination Group which brokered the Electoral Agreement between the Labour party and the Liberal Democrats.

So why did women decide representation was a key issue? There are a number of explanations that can be put forward. These are briefly summarised here, but are discussed in more detail in Chapters 16, 17 and 19, and elsewhere (see for example, Brown 1998a, 1998b). The key mobilising factors have been as follows. Firstly, the campaign for equal representation in the Scottish Parliament, and for gender balance in decision making in political and public life more generally, has taken place within the context of a broader international movement amongst women for more say in decision-making. In particular the role of the UN Conventions and NGO conferences has been important. Secondly, the negative impact on women of Thatcherite social and economic policies brought together women from different perspectives, from inside and outside parties, feminists and non-feminist activists, resulting in alliances to protect the interests of women. Thirdly, over time as women have gained more experience in political parties, trade unions and local government women's committees, more women have come to consider themselves capable of standing for political office. Fourthly, frustration at the ways of working and slow pace of change in the House of Commons has fuelled aspirations for a Parliament that operates in a different way. Fifthly, many women expressed a distaste for the adversarial political ethos and culture which were the norm in the Westminster Parliament and political parties. Sixthly, women believed strongly that they have to be involved directly in decision making if they are not to be marginalised and if policies are going to be responsive to their interests. Lastly, the opportunity of creating a new legislature has made it possible for a political mobilisation of women to occur on the basis of a conviction that a Scottish parliament will be 'different'. In particular it is this vision of difference which has been important in bringing women together in the campaign for a Scottish parliament in a coalition of interests (Brown 1996). This belief in the capacity of women to make a difference is not only evident in the campaigning around the Scottish Parliament, it is also evident in the attitudes of women politicians in local government, many of whom believe that 'the increased presence of women had a transformation potential (Mackay 1998).

The last two chapters, by Brown, and by Sue Innes, update the story to the establishment of the Scottish Parliament. They allow for some provisional assessment of the campaign and raise some questions for the future, as do McDonald, Alexander and Sutherland at the end of their chapter. Brown reports on the final selection procedures used by the four main political parties and the results in terms of women's representation. She assesses the relative success of the campaign. She again notes that the campaign to achieve greater representation was not an end in itself but rather seen as part of a dual strategy involving the representation of women and the representation of women's concerns. Here she distinguishes between symbolic representation (in terms of the presence of women in the Parliament) and substantive representation (the increased opportunities for the concerns and interests of women to be heard and taken into account in the policy-making process). In this respect the key principles recommended by the Consultative Steering Group on the Scottish Parliament and developments such as creation of the Equal Opportunities Committee in the Parliament, the Equality Unit in the Executive and the endorsement of a mainstreaming approach are all seen as important opportunities for progress.

Sue Innes ends our collection with a piece originally written for the UK feminist magazine *Sybil*. She observes that seeing the Parliament in action is 'quietly thrilling' because, unlike most political institutions, 'it looks like the rest of life'. The symbolic importance of women's high visibility in the new Parliament is underlined as a potent shorthand of inclusion and radical difference, although she notes the absence of black MSPs – women or men. She cautions that the partial success of the campaign should be seen as a beginning on which to build – rather than an end in itself.

Finally, brief biographical details are provided on all the women MSPs and the current Scottish women MPs and MEPs.

– CONCLUSION: SUSTAINING THE MOMENTUM –

A notable feature of the 1990s has been the capacity of feminists and other women activists to organise in such a way as to keep the issue of political representation (in its widest sense) on the agenda and to make women and women's concerns visible. It is important to emphasise the inter-relatedness of all these developments, the contact and communication between key actors across a range of organisations and institutions, inside formal politics and the state and outside these.

A crucial enabling condition for the mobilisation of women activists has been the political opportunities created by constitutional change and the establishment of a new institution. The prospect of a new parliament with a different voting system and different ways of working offered a particular set of opportunities around which women could mobilise. Not only did this create the possibility of a new legislature with new members, whose composition did not have to be the same as the existing UK legislature, it also created the possibility of change in political styles and ways of conducting politics. That the demand for the Parliament was fed by the frustration of being governed by a party that the majority of the electorate did not support has also been significant, and this has engendered a wide ranging debate about the nature of democracy, participation and consultation. Consequently, getting more women MSPs into a Scottish parliament is regarded as only one aspect of achieving political equality: it is also recognised that there is a need to give individual women and groups of women greater access to government and the policy making process. Additionally, the campaign in Scotland has been influenced by the development of wider campaigns by women for a greater voice in decision making at European and global (UN) level. These broader campaigns have helped to raise awareness and increase the legitimacy of the case for gender representation in the Scottish context.

We have noted that the belief that more women in parliament would make a difference has been one of the catalysts. These perceptions of difference are shared by women activists in many countries, but have not as yet been adequately scrutinised, theorised or empirically tested. However the election of a substantial proportion or 'critical mass' of women MSPs – operating under new parliamentary arrangements – offers a particular opportunity to test the extent to which the presence of more women does indeed 'make a difference' in terms of: legislative and political conduct and styles; policy priorities and processes; internal and external relationships between women; and new ways of working. There are potential difficulties, for example, that women MSPs may be incorporated rather than included, and may not be afforded the same opportunities in their political careers as men. The way in which the relationship between women inside and outside the Parliament develops will also be significant. There is still considerable anxiety and scepticism that the Parliament will be able to meet the expectations of women activists (see Brown 1998b) and concerns, in turn, that women MSPs face unrealistic expectations.

Much is written in this book about what has been achieved through a series of loose and relatively informal alliances, though both new and existing organisations have also been essential to developing focussed work round specific aims, whether provision of refuges, raising public awareness, or publicising information about gender inequalities. But whatever the degree of success of these achievements, undeniably women in Scotland still have a distance to travel to reach an equal position with men. Existing structures and forms of organisation may have been at least sufficient to carry the movement thus far. But there are still questions to be posed about whether opportunities were missed, or whether momentum for change can be maintained. The context in which the women's movement is now operating has changed considerably with the creation of the Scottish Parliament.

We have argued that political opportunity structures in Scotland provided women with access to the new political institutions. The development of new institutional mechanisms and policy machinery to promote gender equality, and equality for other groups such as people from black and ethnic minority communities, disabled people, and lesbians and gay men, is an ongoing process, but already major changes have taken place. The principles which the Scottish Parliament seeks to embody include that of equal opportunities; the Parliament has adopted different working hours and practices that are intended to be 'family friendly'; there is a standing Equal Opportunities Committee of the Parliament; there is a duty to promote equal opportunities and legislation is required to make a statement about equal opportunities impacts; the Scottish Executive has made a commitment to mainstreaming equality, and has created an Equality Unit to take this strategy forward; various consultation mechanisms are being developed, including the Women in Scotland Consultative Forum, and the Scottish Civic Forum.

Devolution, and the agenda of modernising government shared by the UK government and the Scottish Executive, are already contributing to greater accessibility and openness, and it is only to be expected that women's organisations will benefit from this greater access. In the past, as Lovenduski and Randall argue, feminist mistrust of the state may have meant that opportunities have been lost (Lovenduski and Randall 1993). In the context of the creation of new political institutions and a shift in political culture, it is crucial that feminist and women's activists review their attitudes to the state, and devise strategies that maximise access to policy making machinery. This is not to say that autonomy should be forfeited. On the contrary, like Lovenduski and Randall, we believe 'that feminists inside a system are more likely to be effective and motivated if there is a strong feminist movement outside the system' (Lovenduski and Randall 1993: 13). Part of the strategy, therefore, should be to address systems of effective communication and mutual, though not necessarily uncritical, support, building upon the links built up during the campaign for constitutional change. We may learn from the experience of women's organisations and women politicians elsewhere. Research in the US (Carroll 1992) has demonstrated the importance of ongoing links between women politicians and women's organisations. Women's organisations provide support, expertise and a gateway to other women; female politicians support and promote women's concerns on the inside and facilitate access. Whilst there is a recognition that female politicians are often 'caught between a rock and a hard place', women's organisations see part of their role as acting as their 'consciences' – maintaining the momentum for action and change.

In conclusion, we suggest that the developments of the 1990s demonstrate the women's movement's capacity for lesson-learning and strategic action, although it is important not to overplay these features nor to underplay the missed opportunities and fragmentation that have co-existed with this. The period has brought relative success in both the symbolic representation (of women as elected representatives) and substantive representation (of women and their policy concerns). There is however a danger that the momentum – and loose alliances – built up around the common goal of gender equality of representation in a Scottish parliament may now dissipate. In order to sustain progress and make full use of the new opportunities created by constitutional change the women's movement needs to embark upon a conscious strategy of capacity building and strategic working. Communication, dialogue, support and alliances are all crucial to ensuring that those on the inside and on the outside, and on the threshold, can sustain the transformative project of feminism.

– Notes –

1. Following the first elections to the Scottish Parliament, held on 6 May 1999, women make up 37.2 per cent of Members of the Scottish Parliament (MSPs). This takes Scotland to near the top of the international league in terms of women's representation, just behind Norway and Sweden at 39.4 per cent and 40.4 per cent respectively, though it should be acknowledged that there are differences between 'national' and devolved legislatures, and that therefore an exact comparison cannot be drawn. A higher proportion of women (40 per cent) was elected to the Welsh Assembly which does not have legislative powers.

2. These were:
   equal pay for equal work;
   equal opportunities and equal education;
   free contraception and abortion on demand;
   free twenty-four-hour childcare;
   legal and financial independence for all women;
   an end to all discrimination against lesbians and the right of women to determine their own sexual orientation;
   freedom for all women from violence, or the threat of violence, and sexual coercion, regardless of marital status, and an end to all laws, assumptions and institutions that perpetuate male dominance and men's aggression towards women.

3. Since 1993 Engender has published annually the *Gender Audit*, which provides a statistical picture of women in Scotland, together with commentary and analysis on a wide range of topics.

4. This view was publicly stated by MSP SNP Fiona Hyslop at a meeting organised by Engender, 17 May 1999.

– References –

Arshad, Rowena and Mukami McCrum (1989), 'Black Women, White Scotland', in A. Brown and D. McCrone (eds) *The Scottish Government Yearbook 1989*, Edinburgh: Unit for the Study of Government in Scotland, University of Edinburgh.

Bochel, Catherine and Hugh Bochel (1998), 'Scotland's Councillors 1974–1995', *Scottish Affairs*, No. 24 pp. 29–44.

Breitenbach, E. (1990), '"Sisters are doing it for themselves": The Women's Movement in Scotland', in Alice Brown and Richard Parry (eds) *The Scottish Government Year Book 1990*, Edinburgh: Unit for the Study of Government in Scotland, University of Edinburgh.

Breitenbach, E., A. Brown and F. Myers (1998), 'Understanding Women Scotland', in *Feminist Review*, No. 58, pp. 44–65.

Breitenbach, E., A. Brown, F. Mackay and J. Webb (1999), *Equal Opportunities in Local Government in Scotland and Wales*. Edinburgh: Unit for the Study of Government in Scotland, University of Edinburgh.

Brown, A., D. McCrone, L. Paterson (1996), *Politics and Society in Scotland*, Basingstoke: Macmillan.

Brown, A. (1996), 'Women and Politics in Scotland', *Parliamentary Affairs*, 49(1).

Brown, A. (1998a), 'Representing Women: The Tactics of Gender', *Parliamentary Affairs*, July, Vol. 51, No. 3.

Brown, A. (1998b), 'Women and political culture in Scotland', in A. Howson and E. Breitenbach (eds) *Gender and Scottish Society: Polities, Policies and Participation*, Edinburgh: Unit for the Study of Government in Scotland, University of Edinburgh.

Brown, A., A. Jones and F. Mackay (1999), *The Representativeness of Councillors*, York: Joseph Rowntree Foundation.

Brown, B., M. Burman, and L. Jamieson (1992), *Sexual History and Sexual Character Evidence in Scottish Sexual Offence Trials*, Edinburgh: Scottish Office Central Research Unit.

Bruegel, I. and H. Kean (1995), 'The moment of municipal feminism: gender and class in 1980s local government', *Critical Social Policy*, 44/45, Autumn.

Bryson, V. (1992), *Feminist Political Theory*, Basingstoke and London: Macmillan.

Carroll, S. (1992), 'Women State Legislators, Women's Organizations, and the Representation of Women's Culture in the United States', in J. Bystydzienski (ed) *Women Transforming Politics*, Bloomington, IN: Indiana University Press.

Chambers, G. and A. Millar (1983), *Investigating Sexual Assault*, Edinburgh: Scottish Office Central Research Unit.

Chambers, G. and A. Millar (1986), *Prosecuting Sexual Assault*, Edinburgh: Scottish Office Central Research Unit.

Chapman, J. (1993), *Politics, Feminism and the Reformation of Gender*, London: Routledge.

Cosgrove, Katie (1996), 'No Man has the Right', in Chris Corrin (ed.) *Women in a Violent World*, Edinburgh: Edinburgh University Press.

Dobash, R. Emerson and Russell Dobash (1992), *Women, Violence and Social Change*, London: Routledge.

Edwards, J. (1989), 'Local Government's Women's Committees', *Critical Social Policy*, No. 24, Winter.

Edwards, J. (1995), *Local Government Women's Committees*, Aldershot: Avebury.

Galligan, Y. (1998), *Women and Politics in Contemporary Ireland*, London and Washington: Pinter.

Halford, S. (1988), 'Women's Initiatives in Local Government: Where do they come from and where are they going?', *Policy and Politics*, 16 (4).

Halford, S. (1992), 'Feminist change in a patriarchal organisation: the experience of women's initiatives in local government and implications for feminist perspectives on state institutions', in A. Witz and M. Savage (eds) *Gender and Bureaucracy*, Oxford: Blackwell.

Henderson, S. (1998), *Service Provision to Women Experiencing Domestic Violence in Scotland*, Edinburgh: Scottish Office Central Research Unit.

Henderson, S. and A. Mackay (eds) (1990), *Grit and Diamonds*, Edinburgh: Stramullion.

Hills, Leslie (1994), 'Why Engender?', *Chapman*, 76, Spring, pp. 45–50.

Kelly, Ellen (1992), 'The Future of Women in Scottish Local Government', in *Scottish Affairs*, No. 1, pp. 66–77.

Lieberman, S. (1989), 'Women's Committees in Scotland', in A. Brown and D. McCrone (eds) *The Scottish Government Yearbook 1989*, Edinburgh: Department of Politics, University of Edinburgh.

Lovenduski, J. (1995), 'An Emerging Advocate: The Equal Opportunities Commission in Great Britain', in D. M. Stetson and A. Mazur (eds) *Comparative State Feminism*, London: Sage.

Lovenduski, J. and V. Randall (1993), *Contemporary Feminist Politics: Women and Power in Britain*, Oxford: Oxford University Press.

Mackay, F. (1995), *The Case of Zero Tolerance:Women's Politics in Action?* Edinburgh: *New Waverley Papers*, Department of Politics, University of Edinburgh.

Mackay, F. (1996), 'Getting There, Being There, Making A Difference?: Gendered Discourses of Access and Action in Local Politics', unpublished PhD dissertation, Edinburgh: University of Edinburgh.

Mackay, F. (1998), 'In a different voice? Scottish women local politicians and the vocabulary of care', *Contemporary Politics*, 4, (3).

Mackay, F. and K. Bilton (2000), *Learning for Experience: Lessons in Mainstreaming Equal Opportunities*, Edinburgh: Governance of Scotland Forum, University of Edinburgh.

Macleod, Jan, Patricia Bell and Janette Forman (1994), 'Bridging the Gap: feminist development work in Glasgow', in Miranda Davis (ed.) *Women and Violence*, London: Zed.

Mann, L. (1993), *Public Policy and Participation: The Role of Women in the Highlands*, Report to Barail, Easter Ross: Lorraine Mann Research and Consultancy.

Martlew, C., C. Forrester and G. Buchanan (1985), 'Activism and Office: women and local government in Scotland', *Local Government Studies*, 11/2.

Stedward, Gail (1987), 'Entry to the System: A Case History of Women in Scotland', in J. Richardson and G. Jordan (eds) *Government and Pressure Groups in Britain*, Oxford: Clarendon.

Turner, E., S. Riddell and S. Brown (1995), *Gender Equality in Scottish Schools: The Impact of Recent Educational Reforms*, Glasgow: EOC.

SECTION I

The Women's Movement in Scotland

CHAPTER 1

Why Engender?

LESLIE HILLS

'Why Engender?' *Chapman* No. 76, Spring 1994: 45–50.

Engender is an organisation founded and funded by women for women to research women's lives and their histories and to use information and research networks to campaign to improve women's social, economic, personal and political lives. It is for all women who want to change the way power is distributed and wielded in Scotland. Engender works in a complementary way with other women's organisations.

In 'Woven by Women', Margaret Bain, accounting for the lack of prominence of women in Scotland, wrote, 'in a society which is essentially repressive and lacking in confidence, the weaker sections will be even more repressed and their achievements even more ignored'. The intervening years have seen little change.

The British political establishment, of both the left and right, continued to act as though the interests of women could be effortlessly elided with those of men. Policies were set forth as preserving the rights of men, their wives and their families. As Esther Breitenbach wrote in the *Scottish Government Yearbook 1989*, 'if we are to ask the question whether women in Scotland have made progress towards equality in the decade since Mrs Thatcher came to power, then the short answer is that they have not. The overall picture for women in Scotland is that in terms of work, income and housing their position relative to men's remains grossly unequal.'

Issues of particular concern to women were not merely ignored: their existence was not recognised. Such specific policies as tax measures may have helped a few, but only a small number of the relatively advantaged.

Under John Major's premiership women in Scotland have fared no better. His much-trumpeted Opportunity 2000 initiative, energetically prosecuted by Lady Howe, is aimed at helping a small group of women crack the 'glass ceiling'. Women's representation in top jobs in industry and the professions and in public life remains derisory. The initiative ignores those women struggling at and below the poverty line. For them life has become far tougher. Women still suffer the effects of occupational demarcation; in a time when the state and society are withdrawing rapidly from any concept of communal responsibility for the care of the elderly, the young and the disabled, women's burdens as carers have grown enormously. While funding for women's refuges is threatened, violence by men against women and their children increases.

Women form the biggest percentage of the poor, the old and the low-paid – groups particularly hard hit by recession and cuts in social services and forming the weaker sections of society to which Margaret Bain refers. With deregulation in the labour market, low-paid and part-time workers, the majority of whom are women, have lost the protection of employment legislation and in particular of Wages Councils. Two thirds of workers protected by Wages Councils, destined for abolition, are women.

The destruction of what little provision there was for adequate childcare has meant that many women who want to work are unable so to do and are caught in the poverty trap. Scotland has the lowest provision of childcare in the EC. Low wages will not cover the costs of private childcare. Many fall back on benefits and are again at the mercy of the punitive social security system.

Concentrating power in the South East has particularly negative effects on women, who tend to exercise their politics at local levels. Privatisation and centralising 'rationalisation' further weaken women's control over their own lives. There are few women on the newly appointed Boards and fewer still are feminists.

There are many women journalists now working for Scottish newspapers, and many make an attempt to mirror and analyse the lives of women in Scotland. But they are vastly outnumbered by their male colleagues and only a few, notably Sue Innes in *Scotland on Sunday*, are able to state the feminist case, consistently, week in, week out. Maria Fyfe, MP for Maryhill, says 'I find all the time that the political reporters are typically not the slightest bit interested in issues like childcare. They are only interested in women's issues when they are to do with sex – so it is an uphill struggle to get women's issues taken seriously.' This quote appeared in *The Herald* on International Women's Day 1993 on the Women's page. On the general news pages there are a few column inches, which do not mention the astonishing variety of meetings, conferences, seminars and work-shops held by women across Scotland to mark the day. Instead there is a large colour photograph. The picture, all cute and pink and ruffles, is of a fashion show. *The Scotsman* printed a picture of that same fashion show, captioned 'Three Little Maids', as its only nod towards International Women's Day.

One of the few glimmers of light in the media is the success of *Harpies & Quines*, published by a collective in Glasgow. This splendid, controversial, feminist magazine gives a platform to women who have something to say which cannot be said elsewhere. It is irreverent, informative, entertaining, welcome, and answers a deeply felt need.

Eleven years ago Margaret Bain wrote that if any child were asked to name famous national women the reply was unlikely to extend much beyond Mary Queen of Scots and Flora McDonald, and ascribed this to a fault in the system which has failed to compile and evaluate the significant deeds of Scottish womanhood. 1992 saw the publication of *Chambers Scottish Biographical Dictionary*. The index of contributors lists 69 men and seventeen women. And it is interesting to note the great imbalance between the institutional status of the male contributors and the description of the majority of the women as freelance. Needless to say, the overwhelming majority of the biographical subjects are men. Subjects are chosen from fields of endeavour such as arts, sport and the military. Interestingly there is no literature field, which might have gone some tiny way to redressing the balance. There are many glaring omissions. How, for example, can the omission of Judith Hart, long-serving MP and Cabinet Minister, be justified?

In 1992 Chambers also published an *Anatomy of Scotland*. There were eleven contributors, ten men and one woman. The Foreword states that this book 'is about how Scotland works. It is about who runs it, where power lies, and the way in which power is exercised.' And indeed it is. In its detailed description of patriarchy, in terms of its stated intention, it cannot be faulted.

In the introduction Peter Jones discusses 'the set of myths and assumptions about the nature of Scottishness that have over the years . . . coalesced to form the character of the nation as it sees itself today'. He is using the definition of myth set out by Gray et al. in *Reconstructions of Secondary Education; Theory, Myth and Practice since the War*:

> We do not mean by myth things that are thought to be true, but that are in fact always false; nor do we mean things that are valuable but are, in fact, beyond human attainment or consent. Instead we use the term myth to refer to a story that people tell about themselves, and tell for two purposes. These purposes are, first to explain the world, and second to celebrate identity and to express values.

The problem for women in Scotland is that these dominant myths which have 'coalesced to form the character of the nation as it sees itself today' are at best gender-blind and at worst totally exclusive of women in Scotland. The history of women, their struggles and triumphs, has not been absorbed by the dominant Scottish myth.

If women, realising the deeply negative effect that straining to accommodate themselves to the dominant myth has on them, their choices and their capacity for autonomous action, reject the myth, they are left in a very exposed position. Women also need to 'celebrate identity and express value' to construct a myth which will incorporate women's stories and women's histories.

Attempts to celebrate identity in Scotland fall foul of a deeply misogynist society – a society demonstrating its misogyny in its press, its public life, its politics and the daily lives of women. The incidence of sexual assault, even of very young girls, is very high, as Richard Kinsey (1992) has recently shown. Most women learn very young to keep their heads down, to placate, to ignore sexist 'jokes' and degrading songs and to avoid trouble as far as is possible. In a brilliant evocation of an experience every woman in Scotland will recognise, Janice Galloway writes:

> But I still hear something like him; the clink and drag from the close-mouth in the dark, coming across open and derelict spaces at night, blustering at bus stops where I have to wait alone. With every other woman, though we're still slow to admit it, I hear it, still trying to lay down the rules. It's more insistent now because we're less ready to comply, look away and know our place. And I still see men smiling and ignoring it because they don't give a damn. They don't need to. It's not their battle. But it was ours and still is. I hear my mother too and the warning is never far away. But I never could take a telling. (Galloway 1991)

In 1993, the 75th anniversary of the winning of the vote, women in Scotland are largely invisible. An archaic and corrupt political system affords the electorate little or no say in the way it is governed. Women are doubly disadvantaged by their gender and by the system of government.

After the April 1992 election, women recognised wryly the protests of their male friends that they had no autonomy and were at the mercy of a small group of men for whom they had not voted and who did not have their best interests at heart. For many women the election merely confirmed a growing alienation from the existing political parties and structures. The political parties in Scotland do not have a good record in their treatment of women and gender issues. Only 22 women have been elected to parliament since 1918 when women were first eligible. For many, especially for women on the left, the realisation that any change in the culture of Scottish politics was at best cosmetic, was bitter, disorientating and sad. It was also, however, energising. Energies which in the past had been channelled into electing men into a parliament hampered by grotesque procedures and fruitless combative rituals were now set free.

Before the April 1992 election, the 'Changing the Face of Scottish Politics' conference held in Glasgow had more than two hundred participants, three of them men – and one of these, an MP, stayed only one hour, having remarked that one had to attend these things as the party needed to attract more women voters. The conference was about empowering women by getting more women into parliament and about the implications of more women MPs for the lives of Scottish women. After April, the conference organising committee held a recall conference in Edinburgh. It was a lively and, under the circumstances, relatively optimistic affair and led to the setting up of a group to co-ordinate efforts to advance women's representation and access to political and public life.

It was in this context that the organisation and purpose of Engender was hammered out. The women who set out to form Engender looked at the patchwork that is the women's movement in Scotland and saw that what was missing was a mechanism for researching women's lives and gathering and disseminating information. If this sounds a dry affair, it should be said that Engender was born in passion, in anger and frustration. And there was much sport in its making.

It is an organisation formed and funded by women for women in order to collect and use information about and for women; to research women's lives and their histories; to use information and research networks to campaign to improve the lives of women in Scotland; to work with other women's organisations and to make a distinctive contribution which will complement their efforts.

The provision of information is crucial for the work of promoting greater visibility and representation and of changing the very nature of the moribund power structures and relationships which blight the lives of women in Scotland. We need information to make our case, to focus our work and to make ourselves heard. We need to recover and consider our history to celebrate our identity and express values.

Over the past year a small group of women have formulated Engender as a company and have taken the first steps in putting in place the structures needed, keeping in touch with members by newsletter and local meetings and by liaising with other women's organisations and participating in conferences and the Women's Co-ordination Group. There are working groups on finance and funding, membership, publicity, research, communications, planning, and information technology. Local groups have been formed to pursue local issues.

In February 1993 Engender was launched as a membership organisation. Membership is made up of a diversity of women, geographically, socially and politically. There have been many comments on the lines that not only was it high time but that the time was ripe. Members are participating in four ways. Some want to help fund activities which they value but are at present unable to pursue; others are working in local groups; others are contributing to and benefiting from the research and information function and others help in the running of the organisation. That is how it looks at the moment, but it will and must evolve, responding to the needs and at the behest of its members.

The first major project has been in response to the Women's Co-ordination Group's recognition of a need for much more and better information. The task of monitoring the progress, or lack of it, of women has been hampered by the absence of relevant data. Information is neither readily available nor accessible. That which is available is often difficult to locate, based on UK figures which are not broken down by country, region or gender, and often hopelessly out of date.

As one of Engender's main aims was to establish an information network, we took on the task of collating information which is presently available, and of producing a *Gender Audit*, which surveys the position of women in a broad range of areas of public and political life. The *Gender Audit* has been extremely popular – the first print run has sold out and it is now being reprinted.

However, the function of the *Gender Audit* is to go beyond issues of representation and equality and to examine the position of women in relation to such issues as housing, health, domestic violence, the arts and poverty. It is only the beginning of a long-term project in which information will be gathered over time and monitored.

This work draws on information already available. One of the ongoing tasks of Engender will be to improve access to existing research on the lives of women and on gender issues. There is a considerable body of research scattered in libraries and filing cabinets across the country and needing to be liberated and used. Another ongoing task will be the creation and maintenance of a database of women with expertise and, crucially, experience that will be of help to others.

The experience of women in Scotland, very different from that of men, has been a well-kept secret. This experience must be described and analysed until through time it becomes part of the dominant myth and ensures that our children do not have to re-form the women's movement year after wearisome year.

In becoming part of the dominant myth it must change it. Engender is quintessentially about change. Women in Scotland are deeply dissatisfied with the society that men have made and the culture they have formed. It neither acknowledges women nor answers their needs and often is inimical to them. It causes a great deal of pain.

We are beginning to write our story. Every year a few more books are published, a few more plays performed and a few more songs sung. But the women who research and write and play and sing do so against tremendous odds, underfunded, underpaid, laden with responsibilities for dependants and at work, and against entrenched interests and extraordinary complacency. And who heeds their words? Sometimes it seems we are talking to ourselves. But we also need to talk to men, and not only to the many men who support us and who also wish for change. There are many who see no need for change. Last year the Scottish Law Society opined that the moves towards equal opportunities being made by their fellows in England were not wanted here and that guidance or rules on discrimination for the legal profession in Scotland are not necessary. A working party report urging positive action on equal opportunities by the Scottish Law Society has been gathering dust for more than a year. Meanwhile the Glasgow-based Association of Women Solicitors has formed a sex discri-mination committee and a working party. They are in for a tough time. But then as women in Scotland they must be used to that.

May they flourish.

– REFERENCES –

Bain, Margaret (1980), 'Woven by Women', Chapman 27/28, Edinburgh: Chapman.

Breitenbach, Esther (1989), 'The Impact of Thatcherism on Women in Scotland', in A. Brown and D. McCrone (eds) *The Scottish Government Year Book 1989*, Edinburgh: Unit for the Study of Government in Scotland, University of Edinburgh.

Galloway, Janice (1991), 'Fearless', *Blood*, London: Secker & Warburg.

Gray, J. M., et al. (1983), *Reconstructions of Secondary Education: Theory, Myth and Practice since the War*, London: Routledge & Kegan Paul.

Kinsey, Richard (1992), *Survey of Young People*, Edinburgh: University of Edinburgh.

CHAPTER 2

Bridging the Gap: Feminist Development Work in Glasgow

JAN MACLEOD, PATRICIA BELL AND JANETTE FORMAN

'Bridging the Gap: feminist development work in Glasgow', in Miranda Davis (ed.) (1994), *Women and Violence*, London: Zed.

Traditional images of Glasgow include shipbuilding, engineering, heavy drinking, left wing politics, great good humour and friendliness, and macho men. In the 1950s, large numbers of families were moved from overcrowded inner-city areas to newly built housing schemes on the outskirts of the city – 'deserts with windows', as described by one comedian.

In 1993, the shipbuilding and engineering have all but gone and the city has high unemployment, particularly in the peripheral housing schemes. Glasgow has also gone through a public relations exercise, presenting itself as a centre for cultural activities, and working hard to change the hard, often violent, image associated with the city. Unfortunately, however, the macho attitude remains firmly in place, at all levels of society. Glasgow does not come out well when a close look is taken at women's experiences, for example of domestic violence and rape in marriage.

However, whilst the 'macho man' image is well known, what is less well publicised is the strength of Glasgow women. It has been common for community organisations and activities to be led by women, and for women to lead political actions, one of the best-known examples of which would be the Glasgow rent strikes of 1917.

The political commitment of Glasgow women is also reflected in the existence of a number of voluntary, feminist women's organisations. These offer both services for women who have suffered male violence, and work against the attitudes that condone and encourage such violence. They include Women's Aid, organisations working on issues of child sexual abuse, and the Rape Crisis Centre, from which the Women's Support Project developed.

In 1981 the Rape Crisis Centre was overstretched and under-resourced – not an unusual position for voluntary and feminist organisations. In among the individual counselling, administration, volunteer training, talks and fund-raising, we spent hours agonising over two main points. First, what did we have to offer the many women who, with great courage, were coming to us to talk of their experiences of sexual abuse as children? What on earth could we do to meet this 'new' demand? Second, why were we so often left to pick up the pieces after abused women had been to the police, courts, GP or social worker? Why did women have to suffer secondary abuse through the unsympathetic attitudes they often had to face? How could we influence the few specialist services provided within statutory organisations, and so try to avoid the further abuse of women by the system? Why, when we had so few resources, were we supporting field workers who were in contact with abused women and children, whilst their own departments had nothing to offer them? The Women's Support Project grew from these concerns.

In the Centre, crisis work had always gained priority at the expense of educational and development work. We felt that we had the ideas and the experience to back them up, if only we had the time and resources to implement them. We decided to attempt to bridge the gap between ourselves and similar feminist organisations, and the professionals; we began to plan the Women's Support Project.

The Project, which opened in 1983, was funded by Urban Aid for the first seven years. We now receive a grant from Strathclyde Regional Council, which covers wages, and we have to raise money for running costs and development work. The project now employs two development workers and two information workers.

The style and direction of the project had to change considerably over its first two years. A main initial aim was to 'encourage women to make greater use of locally available services'. However, we found that a vicious circle existed: women did not feel comfortable using local services because they did not receive an appropriate response, the usual initial reaction being to try to refer on as soon as violence or sexual abuse is mentioned. At the same time we were often told by workers that 'violence is not a problem here', or 'women never tell us about violence', because women were not using the services.

We had thought that we could offer some individual counselling and advice work, but it became clear that to advertise this service would swamp the project and repeat the situation of the Rape Crisis Centre. Our job became to stimulate the development of services, to produce educational material, and to work at keeping women on the agenda of services which at worst have women-blaming responses and at best are prepared to refer women on. Since we were not offering a counselling service we worked to provide a first-class information service. Our resource library developed from this work, and is now in great demand, not only in Glasgow but throughout Britain. We have over 700 books and videos available for loan, all dealing with different aspects of male violence, and many unavailable elsewhere.

The main thread of our approach has always been a feminist analysis of male violence, maintaining strong links between the causes and effects of rape, domestic violence, incest and child sexual abuse. We have been prepared to use any openings, and to jump on most (but not all) bandwagons in order to 'bridge the gap' and put our views across.

For example, people can easily persuade themselves that domestic violence is a private, family matter and that battered women choose to stay in a violent relationship. We often have to point out that domestic violence abuses children, too, before people will take the issue seriously. We build on discussions of domestic violence before talking about incest and child sexual abuse. This is partly to minimise the mother-blaming which goes on whenever child sexual abuse is raised, but also to give workers a social and political framework within which to make sense of the day-to-day problems women face. In addition, people feel more comfortable discussing domestic violence since it is a more familiar area than child sexual abuse. This enables us to draw crucial links between the two areas, implicitly challenging male power, particularly within the family.

Our experience of training has convinced us that what is needed is not just clearer guidelines or more procedures but changes in attitudes. To put it bluntly, there is no point in giving people procedures if they don't believe male violence happens or think it is not their job to deal with it. Workers find it difficult to admit that, as 'professionals', they feel deskilled and unable to cope. In trying to isolate themselves from the painful issues, they often separate themselves from the clients who have this problem.

Child sexual abuse, domestic violence and rape are not easy areas to work in. The issues involved challenge our personal beliefs and attitudes. Even with the most concerned and sympathetic of adults there is a great pressure to shy away from the possibility of abuse. A great many adults have been sexually abused themselves as children and, whilst personal experience can make you alert to the signs of abuse, carrying painful memories can be an added pressure against raising the issue. Our training aims to break down these professional barriers to enable people to face their feelings.

We often begin by getting workers to do an exercise on 'burn out'. They are asked to look at their own work situations and answer the following questions: what do you feel, what do you say, what do you do, and, finally, why do you stay? This brings out points such as feelings of inadequacy, exhaustion and failure and, at the same time, a sense of commitment to some areas of the job, the need for money and workers' fears of making changes. The last heading is then changed to 'why does she stay?' and the point is made that the feelings identified by the workers themselves are very similar to those expressed by battered women. The exercise is extremely effective in making people realise that it is not easy to leave a situation, even when you know it is not doing you any good, and so makes workers less quick to condemn women for staying in a violent relationship.

We also role-play a disclosure of child sexual abuse to make workers look at the way they are treating people, how they would want to be treated, and how the service they provide could be more appropriate and responsive to the needs of women and children. In the words of the Incest Survivors' Campaign, we are asking people to look at what they offer and ask at every stage, 'Who benefits and who has to pay?' There is no doubt that this approach to training is very effective. People are less likely to blame incest on the mother, alcohol, children, unemployment or overcrowding and more likely to face up to the position of women and children in our society. Once this has happened, workers can then look at alternative responses to the problem, such as supporting mothers, working with the child within the home and removing the abuser.

Violence against women and children, whether in or out of the home, is not a minority problem. The social position of women and children encourages their daily exploitation. Child sexual abuse exists on such a scale that we need a totally new approach to the problem. Voluntary services cannot meet the need and neither can limited specialist projects run by a handful of experts. In order to respond adequately, we need a community-based response which recognises the relative powerlessness of women and children and does something to address this. This may involve people in reviewing their whole approach to their work, and facing difficult choices. For example, staff in a community-based project backed away from a campaign on domestic violence in case it upset their relationships with local community activists who were overwhelmingly men. What does this say about the value placed on women in the community?

As part of our education work we developed a series of posters. These highlighted the fact that acts of violence against women are crimes. The posters are unusual in that they were not aimed at women who had suffered violence, but at the public in general. They were intended to provide information that would promote discussion about the whole issue of male violence, and most important, to challenge men's perceived right to abuse.

The Project has also worked to make our services and materials accessible to as many women as possible. For example, we have been involved in the development of women's self-defence work. A main aim of this work for us has been to create opportunities for women to discuss experiences and fears of violence in a safe and supportive environment. Classes are not based on physical strength and fitness, but on a mixture of discussion, mutual support and simple, practical physical techniques, including use of voice. We have worked hard to make these classes open to a wide range of women, and have for example offered courses to girls' groups, black women's groups, survivors' groups, and pensioners' groups.

In order to address the increased vulnerability of women with physical disability, and to increase our skills in working with women with disability, we organised a training course with Lydia Zijdel, a Dutch self-defence instructor very experienced in this area of work.

The Project has also looked at services available for profoundly deaf women. This work was initially undertaken in conjunction with workers with deaf people, and then with a group of deaf women. This collaboration has been very effective and has resulted in a series of education meetings, production of a video in British Sign Language, and a series of information leaflets aimed at deaf women.

Although there are now more resources identified for abused women, for example more organisations offering counselling for adults abused as children, these organisations cannot meet the demand. There is unfortunately little evidence that mainstream and statutory organisations have acknowledged or responded to the extent of violence against women. This also still applies to some voluntary organisations; for example, we often find that drug and alcohol counsellors are offered little training or support on violence, although they report that this is a common problem for women using their services. Instead of training on male violence being seen as an essential component, it still tends to be added as an extra, often being dealt with in one session. All too often a first response is still to refer women on to specialist services.

Channelling resources into specialist centres and individual treatment whilst changing nothing else allows everyone to collude with abuse. It avoids challenging the power of men in families, the power of professionals over clients, the power of adults over children. It particularly ignores the fact that many existing services for children condone, ignore or in some cases actively encourage an environment which is in direct contradiction to any claim of prioritising children's needs or encouraging their development. For example, workers involved with teenagers in care wanted to start self-help groups for girls who had disclosed previous sexual abuse. They encouraged the girls to talk, but had no way of explaining to those same girls why they had to put up with male staff touching them, making sexual comments and remarking on their dress and appearance. Again, teachers involved in the 'preventive' work of encouraging children to be assertive and to stand up to potential abusers decided not to let the children use role-play because it would 'undermine discipline'.

It is clear that child sexual abuse is an area in which theory greatly influences practice and this is why much of our work concentrates on making people look at their attitudes. It is also important to offer practical suggestions for ways in which workers can build up confidence and skills and develop support networks both for themselves as workers and for those who are suffering abuse. It is common for people to feel so overwhelmed by the scale of the problems that they don't know where to start. We have found it important to point out that very small steps can make an impact. For example, having leaflets and posters on display helps women to realise that sexual abuse is a subject that they can discuss. Having relevant books or games available helps workers to raise the general issues with children in a non-threatening way. And, of course, workers feel more confident in approaching women and children if they are aware that back-up support and information are available for themselves, and so are reassured to hear of the work of voluntary organisations such as Women's Aid, Rape Crisis and Action Against Incest.

Towards this we have built up a wide range of books, videos and resource material. We have developed links with local community groups, offering information on violence, health and regular self-defence courses, mainly with social workers, health centres and nursery staff. This often involves producing new material, as there is little available.

We also offer regular training days which are open to workers from statutory and voluntary organisations, as well as interested individuals. Issues covered include: supporting women whose children have been sexually abused; working with incest survivors; introduction to child sexual abuse; and group work with abused women. Feedback from these days is consistently positive. One aspect workers really appreciate is the inter-agency approach, the opportunity to meet with workers from other fields, and to share concerns over working with abuse.

Another way in which we try to break down professional barriers is in encouraging different agencies to communicate and work together more, and in developing inter-agency contacts. No one agency can deal with all aspects of a child abuse case. If each agency has a different theory, approach and level of 'proof', how does this appear to the child? Can you think of any way to justify this situation to a child?

Previously, for example, in conjunction with Glasgow Women's Aid we organised 'local information initiatives' on the problem of male violence. These brought together interested workers from a variety of backgrounds and provided a useful forum both for examining local social work practice and for highlighting gaps in information and service provision. Following these events a multi-disciplinary working party made up of local field workers met regularly to share and develop ideas and experience. This group brought together nursery nurses, teachers, health visitors, social workers, community workers and workers from voluntary organisations to discuss issues around violence against women and children, and to look at local service provision. This group also produced a brief information pack on dealing with child sexual abuse. Although the group no longer meets, the information pack is still in print and has been greatly appreciated for the simple, practical information contained.

The work we do is often exhausting in every sense, but it can also be very exciting. Individual crisis work is largely invisible, but with development work the results are more tangible and easier to build on. More and more resources are now being released to tackle the problems of child sexual abuse. It is important that feminists have the opportunity to do more development work, using the experience gained through individual counselling work, so that developing services are appropriate and begin to tackle the real needs as identified by the women and children themselves.

The Project provides an opportunity for experience gained through involvement in feminist collectives to be used in helping field workers gain confidence in dealing with the problem of male violence. In doing this the Project does walk a tightrope and has frequently been in the uncomfortable position of being criticised and condemned by both the establishment and the feminist community simultaneously. Opportunities to discuss this problem and share experiences are limited, as we do not know of many other groups doing similar work. We hope to see more of such projects, and would appreciate hearing from women anywhere who are involved in, or interested in, similar areas of work. We believe that the only effective way to tackle the many manifestations of male violence is to stimulate a community response equal to the scale of the problem.

CHAPTER 3

A Liberating Event for Scottish Women

SUE INNES

'A liberating event for Scottish women', *Scotland on Sunday*, 13 March 1994.

It was a great party, and a historic event for women in Scotland. No-one was saying anything as grand as that, but the opening of the Maryhill Women's Centre, the first purpose-built women's community centre in Scotland and one of the very few in Britain, is as significant a milestone in the uphill trek towards equality and – it's an awkward word, but the right one – empowerment, as any I can think of.

This is no shabby portacabin or gloomy basement, the sort of drab, cheap spaces women's groups are used to meeting in, but shiny, clean and new, an unextravagant but ideal small building with a meeting room, small library, workshop, kitchen, counselling room and cheerful crèche.

Sheboom, the women drummers, rapped a strong, exuberant rhythm; a wide circle of forty women, dressed in suffragette colours. The atmosphere was great: sun shining through wide windows, music, kids scrambling about, a high clatter of talk and laughter, lots of women of all shapes and sizes, ages and backgrounds. No men.

Which was the only aspect of it that the rest of the press paid any attention to. The complaints of one disgruntled local councillor that he had not been invited to the opening ceremony drew a predictable ration of column inches repeating 'outrage', 'discrimination' etc. No-one bothered to report the actual event, the culmination of nine years of work by a lot of women, including councillors. Regional councillor Neelam Bakshi reminded us that it wasn't because councils or the Scottish Office are loving and giving but because 7,000 women had made their voices heard that the centre now existed, that there had been years of effort and a lot of resistance by men – though other men had given support. In a climate of cutbacks and institutionalised sexism this was a triumph.

This is the 'worthy feminism' which has been much-derided – developing services for women in a deprived area. Perhaps it is guilty of 'puritanism' and 'whining and complaining about men', and the even worse sins of 'innocence, a faith in human potential and idealism' and 'naiveté', to quote a recent *Guardian* editorial on the failings of British feminism. One woman called the Maryhill Women's Centre 'the theory of the Women's Movement in reality'. That sounds more like it to me.

It is important that there are places for women to meet as women for two reasons: the first is that men continue to casually and habitually dominate public space just as they dominate public life; the second is that there are strengths that women can build together that are important both in the wider fight against inequality and in recognising and challenging the ways women's position in society reinforces poverty and isolation and marginalises our concerns. Women-only spaces and meetings can be a stepping stone to women taking a more active role in the local and wider community; they can also be an end in themselves, a valid and valuable way of working. So much that makes women's lives better, from activities like art classes and aromatherapy to sensitive issues like violence and sexual abuse, starts with the freedom to be at ease together. (And never forgetting the crèche.)

The experience of the group that set up the Centre is that it is hard for women to get space in mixed community centres, especially space that feels secure enough to deal with sensitive issues. They also found that there was very little on offer specifically for women except for Mother and Toddler groups and Keep Fit. Women-only groups and organisations are no panacea. I hope the Maryhill Centre will continue to be as welcoming to all women as it seemed on Saturday, but it will not always be easy. There are real problems of working across differences between women and respecting them – and some differences get more respect than others. The Centre has a particular role to play in seeking to support the high numbers of unemployed women, lone mothers and women pensioners living alone in parts of Maryhill, as well as working on domestic and sexual violence, tranquilliser dependency and mental health issues. But, importantly, it mixes that with a merry assortment of art, drama and DIY classes, confidence building and job search skills, and occasional music and performance events.

Also important is supporting women's role in community life: community campaigning is dominated by women, at least in numbers if not always in leadership, and women deal with and consequently understand better more of the day-to-day issues. When someone has to run the playgroup, or someone has to see the school about children skiving off, or answer the door to the social worker or explain why the rent is late, it's usually a woman. In community regeneration women's roles are crucial, and can be reinforced by enabling women to develop new skills of campaigning and organisation and to take up more active roles, yet that is rarely given any real focus or encouragement.

Anything that is woman-only attracts a wearily predictable fuss. Men display not the slightest interest, until you say they can't come in. It's not as if there are many places or occasions or times that are women-only, yet each attracts a disproportionate attention, all piqued ego and hurt good intentions. Why is even a little autonomy in women so threatening to some men? Then they cry discrimination, a subject on which the same chaps have usually otherwise been remarkably quiet.

Another example is the defensive and disproportionate response to the proposal from the Labour party's Scottish Executive that all candidates for vacant Labour seats and key marginals should be women. Oh yes, we want more women, they say piously, but we don't want to do the thing that would really ensure it. The careers of a whole generation of able young men would be blighted you see – especially those of black men. As Maria Fyfe, one of the three women out of forty-nine Scottish Labour MPs said, the dashed hopes of women aspirants for years hadn't brought so much tears and heartbreak.

The central reason why there are so few women in Parliament is that they have had less chance at the winnable seats. Between my copy deadline and you reading this on Sunday the proposal is likely to have been defeated at the party conference: the big boys, plus a few henchwomen, have descended in all their horrified might. Yet a scheme that sounds so radical, would, because of incumbency, be quite modest in its results. At the last election there were only nine new faces from all the parties together in Scotland; it has been estimated that on Labour's fifty per cent plan the next election would still deliver only a maximum of eighty women out of 370 at Westminster. To rephrase: Why is even a little progress for women so threatening to some men?

CHAPTER 4

Black Women's Agency in Scotland: A View on Networking Patterns

ANITA SHELTON

In discussions with black ethnic minority women in preparation for this chapter, the question of whether or not there is a black feminist movement in Scotland was answered with a decided 'no!' Population size and fragmentation, along with funding difficulties, were reasons usually provided for this negative response. Other factors cited were opportunism among individual women and a generalised political apathy.

Questions as to the existence of networks among black women, however, elicited hesitation and ambiguous responses. There was general acknowledgement that they do exist, however faulty or dysfunctional. Lack of time to develop these communications channels fully and inaccessibility of relevant decision-making processes were felt to be overriding issues. Nonetheless, the co-operative, empowering interaction among black women which does take place was felt to be more than a response to a shared history of struggle against injustice.

The discussion which follows is an overview, a preliminary exploration into black women's agency in Scotland, be it collective activity in membership organisations or through networking. It concerns women who may or may not share a common political ideology or purpose but who do communicate and exchange information for professional and social purposes. It demonstrates the need for further research and systematic analysis of the collective activism of Scotland's black women.

– SCOTTISH CONNECTIONS –

At the time of the 1991 Census, black and ethnic minority women made up 1.1 per cent (29,910) of the total female population of Scotland, and were primarily resident in urban areas. The largest black ethnic group is that of females of Pakistani origin, followed by Chinese women.[1] It is noteworthy that the population concentrations of both black and white women are in the Central Belt of the country. This enables women to interact in significant numbers in this area but works to disadvantage women in other parts of the country, especially north of Inverness and the southern areas of the Borders and Dumfries and Galloway regions. In addition to financial considerations, geographical distance, the lack of an integrated public transportation system, and general environmental factors, such as climate and personal safety, pose additional difficulties for black women living in rural areas of the country.[2]

The experience of black women in Scotland cannot be said to be different in all contexts from that of white women or black men. Neither can it be said to be different in all respects from that of black women in the rest of the UK. Black women's experience, nonetheless, is distinct and particular. It is mediated through factors such as race, class and gender and is further differentiated by ethnicity and national origin. Collective action among black women, generally, therefore, has varied according to time and necessity.

The pervasive use of the term 'black' in Britain, and the interchangeability of 'multi-cultural' and 'anti-racist', obscure the distinctiveness these terms ostensibly define. In short, this practice serves to confirm the invisibility of non-white people (Bhavnani 1994). In membership organisations and networks, Asian and black women of Afro-Caribbean origin have usually worked jointly, in Scotland as in other parts of the UK, as an expression of solidarity against the shared experience of anti-black racism. For many, this expression reflects a change in political consciousness: unlearning British colonial divisions of class and colour (Braham et al. 1992).

Women-only groups are often found as informal networks among black females throughout Scotland. These are comprised of groups of women with shared interests, operating without formalised structures, providing support and advice to one another. In the context of language improvement groups, co-operative nurseries, social, community, or cultural/religious groups, they come together. For participants, these networks are channels through which the experiences of an often-alienated population are validated and rewarded.

Among single-sex networks also are groups of Muslim women, black and white, for whom the integration of issues of faith in a Christian or secularised society presents challenges. They express a wish for safe places where there exists an ability to mingle with others who share a collective view of womanhood, which is likely to differ from that prevailing in Scotland.

A review of the Scottish Ethnic Minorities Directory (Positive Action in Housing 1999) shows that twenty-six organisations are classified as 'Women's Groups' in seven cities or regions in Scotland. The Directory confines itself to voluntary organisations but is an important source of information on established groups concerned with minority issues. Generally, the women's groups listed provide information and support to women and their families on issues relating to health, housing and welfare; education/training/personal and social development and employment; and cultural and religious matters. These patterns of activity compare similarly with those observed by Sudbury in the United Kingdom as a whole (Sudbury 1998: 36).

Aberdeen is the only city/region included in the *Directory*, outside the Central Belt, where formally established women's groups are located. Long-established groups such as Shakti and Hemat Gryffe Women's Aid, and Meridian, which have assisted black women in the Central Belt are now joined by informal Asian and African women's groups in Aberdeen and Dundee. Indeed, the growing number of ethnic minority community and cultural groups in the country's northern areas may be indicative of women's developing networks. In Aberdeen, as in other areas of Scotland, funding is a crucial issue. As a result of the inability to secure a satisfactory level of funding, one organisation reports that service provision has been reduced to around 12 hours each week. In Edinburgh, another organisation specifically supporting victims of domestic abuse has undergone a radical reduction in its provision of service, again due to a lack of sufficient funding. In Glasgow and Dundee, the continuous search for financial assistance, staffing and necessary material resources for black women's aid and advice services has resulted in 'burn out' of existing personnel and concerns over the maintenance of quality standards.

– RACIAL EQUALITY OR EQUAL OPPORTUNITIES? –

Looking further at networking among black women, it is useful to consider additional aspects of their experience in Scotland. Issues of immigration, child-care, poverty and violence are ongoing struggles around which black ethnic minority families coalesce. With the exception of refuges or shelters, black women's organisations have not universally viewed co-operative engagement with men as negative or unhelpful (Sudbury 1998). Indeed, unity in the fight against racism has required the participation of both sexes.

By and large, black women in Scotland have declined full membership in what are viewed as white feminist groups. Sisterhood between black and white women *en masse* has failed to materialise, with the definition of 'feminism' and the primacy of gender or class over race remaining unresolved issues.

For many black women in 1990s Britain, the possibility of developing sustained coalitions with white women becomes an abstraction when issues of funding and power-sharing are at stake (Sudbury 1998). Others view co-operative action as most successful through networking or ad hoc arrangements, where objectives are more clearly defined, and opportunities for divisiveness are lessened. Razia Aziz has concluded, 'Black women bring to feminism lived realities of a racism that has marginalized and victimised them in the wider world' (Aziz 1997: 70). Their focus is on a feminism that acknowledges agency and struggle in black women's lives and does not promote and sustain a white perspective.

The Commission for Racial Equality (CRE), established by the Race Relations Act of 1976, and the ensuing regional Racial Equality Councils have been important enabling agencies for networking among black women in the UK as a whole, including Scotland. As part of their statutory obligation to build equality of opportunity and assist in the achievement of improved race relations, women have been able to influence programme development and implementation. Likewise, the Equal Opportunities Commission (EOC) has contributed in a significant way to the change in public attitudes about issues that affect women in general.

The inability of the EOC to pursue racial matters with regard to the issues of double discrimination faced by black women is unfortunate. The limitations of the Race Relations Act and the Sex Discrimination Act leave a gap, which neither the CRE nor the EOC is presently able to overcome, but which must be addressed to ensure a greater level of legal redress for black women experiencing discrimination based upon both gender and race.

Campaigns sponsored by the CRE and the EOC hold promise as networking opportunities for minority women in Scotland. While there is criticism that national initiatives undertaken are too often focused on cultural issues rather than on the socio-economic status and political profile of black women, they nonetheless provide opportunity for engagement and progress.

– Networking: the labour market context –

Black and ethnic minority workers in Britain are disproportionately concentrated in low-wage employment and experience lower rates of pay than do white workers in the same jobs. In Scotland, black ethnic minority females experience different rates and patterns of participation in the labour market from white females. They are more vulnerable to unemployment and economic uncertainty than are white women. This also applies to young women, who are consistently less likely than their white counterparts to obtain employment or to secure places in training programmes such as Modern Apprenticeships (CRE 1997:17). According to the Equal Opportunities Commission, there is a far higher rate of self-employment among black women in Scotland than in England. This may be a result of the limited employment opportunities available to them (EOC 1994).

In response to the need for trade unions to improve the visibility and representation of black workers 'North of the Border', the General Council of the Scottish Trades Union Congress (STUC) endorsed a move to make structural changes within the organisation. In Scotland, there has been general consensus within trade unionism that black women's involvement in committee structures, especially in women's committees, has not been sufficiently realised and that they, along with white women, remain at the margins of decision-making. Change was brought about by the establishment of a Standing Committee of Black Workers, nominated and democratically elected by the various STUC affiliates. The Black Workers' Committee (BWC) began work in 1997, and black female members have been integrally involved in the range of activities undertaken to mainstream racial equality, strengthen advocacy of black workers and promote trade unionism.[3] In Scotland, there is general consensus that black women's involvement in trade union committee structures has not been sufficiently realised, especially in the women's committees.

The STUC has been successful in promoting minority representation on Scottish Executive advisory groups and other public bodies and committees. BWC members have been involved in consultations with government ministers and agencies on issues and programmes as diverse as mainstreaming racial equality and the social inclusion agenda, the New Deal employment and training initiative, the Commission on the Future of a Multi-Ethnic Britain, amendment of the Race Relations Act, and the possible establishment of a human rights commission in Scotland. These activities have taken place alongside ongoing BWC work on mainstreaming racial equality and on employment-related issues. In May 1999, the BWC formed the Black Workers' Network, which aims to support individual members on employment-related workplace matters (STUC 1999).

– POLITICAL MOBILISATION: OPPORTUNITIES FOR CHANGE –

The opening of the Scottish Parliament on 1 July 1999 was by far the most important recent political event in the life of the country. The involvement of women in the long campaign to fulfil this end was in the hope and expectation that the Scottish Parliament would 'reflect the needs and circumstances of all the people of Scotland regardless of race, gender or disability' (Scottish Office 1997: vii). In the new political environment, where issues of social inclusion were foremost on party agendas, it was a bitter disappointment that no black ethnic minority members – male or female – became Members of the Scottish Parliament (MSPs).

Overall, networking among black women around the establishment of the Scottish Parliament took the form of participation in civic and party-sponsored campaign activities. The candidate selection process, viewed by many blacks as flawed, and inadequate support to black candidates by their respective parties, removed any realistic chance of success for black candidates. Black women's efforts, therefore, were in areas of wider concern and interest, including the increase in women's representation in Scottish political and public life.

Black women have also been involved in the Women in Scotland Consultative Forum, established by the (then) Scottish Office in 1998, and the Race Equality Advisory Forum which was established by the Scottish Executive in 1999. The work of the Race Equality Advisory Forum will include forming action plans to eradicate institutionalised racism in all areas of Scottish life and advising on the best way for the Executive to consult people from ethnic minority backgrounds.

The Scottish Parliament will play an important role in promoting equal opportunities, even though equality legislation covering gender and racial discrimination are among the reserved powers of the UK government. Schedule 5 of the 1998 Scotland Act, however, exempts from reservation the encouragement of the observance of equal opportunity requirements. Further, the Act imposes duties on public bodies in Scotland to ensure that functions are carried out with 'due regard' to the need to meet the equal opportunity requirement. An Equal Opportunities Committee has been established in the Parliament with a race equality sub-group and an Equality Unit has been formed in the Scottish Executive. Furthermore, the Parliament and the Executive have both made a commitment to 'mainstream' gender, race, disability and other equalities perspectives into the policymaking process. Despite the absence of black MSPs, the ability of black people in Scotland to inform and influence policy development would appear to have been enhanced. In particular, black women are in a position to reorganise and to develop new civic and political relationships.

Research has emphasised the evolutionary nature of black women's organisations in Britain (Sudbury 1998). They have not been static but have changed over time; newly organised networks, such as Black and Ethnic Minority Infrastructure in Scotland (BEMIS) and RoSA!! (Racism on the Scottish Agenda) are two such examples. Both organisations aim to empower ethnic minority communities and to promote inclusiveness. While BEMIS intends to address issues affecting support for the black and ethnic minority voluntary sector, RoSA!! is focusing on the attainment of equality through institutional change. Strategies involve the promotion of black participation and representation in Scotland's governing bodies and service providers (RoSA!! 1999; BEMIS 1999).

A study, commissioned by BEMIS to explore the needs of the black and ethnic minority voluntary sector in Scotland, identified the need to set up black-led organisations for several reasons, including: satisfying unmet needs; developing culturally sensitive services; providing advice, support and information; and maintaining cultural heritage (BEMIS 1999). While use of new, low-cost telecommunications technology, including the Internet, will be helpful in building alliances across sectors and interest groups, the difficulties in responding to the needs of an ethnically diverse group are enormous. Ultimately, the growth and development of networks among black women depend upon the commitment of participants to respond to new opportunities which currently exist in Scotland.

– NOTES –

1. OPCS/GRO(S) 1991 Census, Table 6. The ten ethnic group classifications used in the *1991 Census of Population* serve to define the categories 'white' and 'black' used in this chapter. Also see Shelton (1999) 'Black and Minority Ethnic Women' in the *Gender Audit 1998/99* (Engender 1999).
2. For references to research on Scottish women in rural areas see Engender (2000) *Gender Audit 2000*, Edinburgh: Engender.
3. In 1994, approximately a third of black employees were trade union or staff association members. While total trade union membership declined between 1989 and 1994, black membership fell at a slower rate of fourteen per cent as compared to nineteen per cent for whites (*Labour Force Survey* 1994). The historical commitment to trade union membership by black workers has been noted by commentators such as Phizacklea and Miles (1992).

– REFERENCES –

Aziz, Razia (1997), 'Feminism and the Challenge of Racism: Deviance or Difference?', in Heidi Safia Mirza (ed.) *Black British Feminism*, London: Routledge.

Bhavnani, Reena (1994), *Black Women in the Labour Market: A Research Review*, Manchester: Equal Opportunities Commission.

Black and Ethnic Minority Infrastructure in Scotland (1999), *Listening to the Voice* (executive summary), Glasgow: BEMIS.

Braham, Peter, Ali Rattansi and Richard Skellington (1992), *Racism and Antiracism*, London: Sage.

Commission for Racial Equality (1997a), *Annual Report*, London: CRE.

Engender (1999), *Gender Audit 1998/99*, Edinburgh: Engender.

Engender (2000), *Gender Audit 2000*, Edinburgh: Engender.

Equal Opportunities Commission (1994), *Equal Opportunities for Black and Ethnic Minority Women in Scotland*, Conference Report, Glasgow: EOC.

General Register Office for Scotland (1993), *1991 Census*, Edinburgh: HMSO.

Office of Population Censuses and Surveys/General Register Office for Scotland (1993), *1991 Census of Population*, London: HMSO.

Phizacklea, A. and R. Miles (1992), 'The British Trade Union Movement and Racism', in Peter Braham, Ali Rattansi and Richard Skellington (eds) *Racism and Antiracism*, London: Sage.

Positive Action in Housing (1999), *Scottish Ethnic Minorities Directory*, Glasgow: Positive Action in Housing.

RoSA!! (1999), *Speaking for Ourselves* (pamphlet), Glasgow: Racism on the Scottish Agenda.

Scottish Office (1997), *Scotland's Parliament*, Cmnd. 3658, July, Edinburgh: The Stationery Office.

Scottish Trades Union Congress (1999), *General Council Report*, Glasgow: STUC.

Shelton, Anita (1999), 'Black and Minority Ethnic Women', in *Gender Audit 1998/99*, Edinburgh: Engender.

Sudbury, Julia (1998), *'Other Kinds of Dreams': black women's organisations and the politics of transformation*, London: Routledge.

CHAPTER 5

Women's Aid in Scotland: Purity versus Pragmatism?

JEAN CUTHBERT AND LESLEY IRVING

'If I had known it was going to be like this and I would have peace of mind I would have left my man years ago.' ('Linda')[1]

– INTRODUCTION –

The Women's Aid movement in Scotland grew from the 'second wave' of feminism in the early 1970s. Women who were meeting and organising to discuss women's liberation wanted a practical focus for their politics. Violence against women was raised as an early and pressing issue and feminists were in the forefront of campaigning and practical support. Refuges were clearly needed and were an immediate way of offering women support in leaving their abuser, an option not previously available (see 'Linda's' words heading this piece). Today, over 25 years after the first Women's Aid (WA)[2] refuges were opened in Scotland – in Glasgow and Edinburgh – refuges remain an enormously significant resource, which transform women's lives. In addition to providing direct services to women and children, WA also works locally and nationally to raise awareness about domestic abuse through publicity, education-work and training.

Women's Aid in Scotland, as elsewhere, has engaged with the state from a relatively early stage. The organisation received initial Scottish Office funding towards establishing a national co-ordinating office in 1976 and local groups have had to negotiate routinely with local authorities for financial support towards establishing and maintaining refuges. Little has been written about how the organisation engages with political structures and adapts to changes and pressures outside the movement, with the exception of Gail Stedward's article 'Entry to the System' dating from 1987. Stedward argued that there was a tension between the service provision role and the organisation as a political movement: these different orientations resulted in the organisation being a 'thresholder' group – neither entirely 'in' policy communities nor entirely excluded (see the introduction to this collection). She also noted that, by the mid-1980s, the feminist ethos, working methods and collectivism of Women's Aid were coming under increasing pressures of 'professionalisation' and 'bureaucratisation'.

We aim to look at some more recent developments in the 1990s. Ten years on from Stedward's article, the Scottish Women's Aid (SWA) *Annual Report* for 1996–97 took stock of some of the network's achievements and the positive and negative aspects of adapting to a shifting political climate over the years. It identified five main aspects: pressure for workers to have externally validated qualifications; developments in work with children and young people; the implications of a multi-agency approach to tackling domestic abuse; the introduction of service agreements between local Women's Aid groups and local authorities; and the development of the quality of refuge provision. Underlying these five themes is a sixth strand: the pressure to change or develop WA's original collective form of organising, which was identified by Stedward as a key issue, and which still plays a vital role in shaping interactions with all those in contact with the organisation. This is considered at different points throughout the present article. We end with an overview of Women's Aid's achievements and how it has engaged with the changing political process, particularly with the advent of devolution.

All six areas identified above could be seen as relating to a gradual pressure from outside the organisation, and from the insiders, to force Women's Aid collectives, as thresholders, to conform to professional bureaucratic norms. This has meant a constant struggle between ideological purity and pragmatism within the organisation. We argue that, in many respects, WA therefore remains a classic thresholder.

– TEN YEARS ON: PURITY VERSUS PRAGMATISM? –

The first and second strands, qualifications and children's work, are closely linked. Funders have sometimes been unwilling to accept that an organisation can run effectively without a hierarchy, wage differentials or compulsory qualifications. WA sees the value of qualifications but wants women's experiences to be valued and hopes to work towards a point where women have greater access, through their work, to routes to formal and informal training, should they want it. WA still insist all women working with WA, whether paid or unpaid, are 'workers', not 'officers', and women remain 'women' rather than 'clients'. WA workers remain 'women helping women helping women', as they see abuse as not just 'out there' with a client group, but 'in here' as well (see SWA 1992). One option WA hopes to explore is the accreditation of women's work experience with the organisation into a cluster-type award, but it would never want women to feel devalued or excluded because they had not had access to gaining formal qualifications. There has been a pressure from funders to insist that workers, particularly children's workers, have formal qualifications. In the last ten years, work with children and young people, who form two-thirds of refuge residents, has become more formalised. This work remains severely underfunded and most WA groups are constantly applying for money for children's workers. With more funding, and other developments such as the publication of the *Cullen Report* (1996), has come the impetus to modify our previous idealism, where a women's experience was valued more than any paper qualification.

However, not all the pressure to formalise or standardise work practice has come from outwith the organisation. In 1990 a Code of Practice was nationally agreed. This was finalised after extensive consultation, is constantly being debated and added to and is generally regarded as a positive initiative. The WA Code of Practice states that groups should work collectively, both locally and nationally. One the one hand, the Code of Practice has proved particularly valuable with the introduction by many local authorities of service agreements with voluntary agencies in the mid-1990s. Most local WA groups' funding is now dependent on the negotiation of such an agreement. Local government reorganisation in 1996 meant that many aspects of the service we offer had to be, sometimes extensively, re-negotiated, particularly where the new authority might have more than one WA group within its redrawn boundaries. On the other hand, it has sometimes been the case that WA's insistence on remaining collective has been seen by local authorities as problematic or 'unprofessional'.

Belief in the necessity of retaining a collective form of organisation both locally and nationally is still a deeply held and fiercely defended position. While it might be fair to say that there is increased awareness of the problems sometimes arising in this way of working, the majority of the WA network remain fully committed to this philosophy. Collectives are still viewed as a way of attempting to address power imbalances in society. Problems in collectives are viewed as partly, at least, stemming from hostility to such forms from those outside the Women's Aid movement. It can be argued that this stand on collective working acts to entrench – or at least contribute to – WA's continuing position as 'thresholder'.

Local groups affiliated to the network of Women's Aid in Scotland are autonomous collectives because of a wish not to reproduce what are seen as traditional male hierarchies of power. The ideal was always to develop a way of working which valued equality and gave the most scope for skill sharing and development. As Arnot has written, working collectively is 'giving power and the ability to people to allow them to control what is happening to them . . . Women can start to redress the balance of power, personally and in their organisation, by learning how to use it for the benefit of all women' (Arnot 1990: 78).

– MULTI-AGENCY WORKING AND SERVICE AGREEMENTS –

Turning to the third and fourth strands identified in the introduction to this chapter – multi-agency working and the introduction of service agreements between local Women's Aid groups and local authorities – which are closely interlinked. Both heralded a new type of interaction between thresholder groups like Women's Aid and state agencies and other policy insiders. For multi-agency working to be successful all agencies have to be clear about the service they offer and develop common understanding about the appropriate service response to an issue. WA has gained credibility as the lead agency providing services to women, children and young people who have experienced domestic abuse, not only in the eyes of women who need to use our services but in the eyes of other agencies as well. Perhaps most importantly, it has established that domestic abuse is a serious and prevalent social issue, which requires to be addressed. This has not been achieved alone – the work of many feminist researchers has complemented the anecdotal evidence gleaned from our work supporting women and children.

Multi-agency work is being developed throughout Scotland with the involvement of local Women's Aid groups. Participation in such groups has brought to the fore some of the tensions between direct service provision and the pressure to attend meetings and other liaison or development work. As Hague, Malos and Dear (1995) have shown, the least resourced members of such fora are often the local Women's Aid group. Meetings are often dominated by an insider, often a statutory agency. Local groups have a different status on the fora according to the local political climate, the balance of power and the way the forum is funded, usually as thresholders. The publication of CoSLA's 1997 *Guidance on Preparing and Implementing a Multi-Agency Strategy to Tackle Violence Against Women* has helped move this work forward throughout Scotland.

The need for training for all agencies has been recognised by the multi-agency fora and this, in turn, has led to added pressure and distraction from grassroots service provision. WA's expertise in this area is now generally recognised and it has been particularly successful in gaining access to training the police. One of the recommendations of the 1997 HMI Report on police response, *Hitting Home*, was that training links with Women's Aid both nationally and locally should be extended. Many groups train officers at force level and national workers provide input at the Scottish Police College. Women's Aid has recently (1999) contributed to a review of probationer training at the College.

Health is another area where the organisation has had considerable input. It was a member of the Scottish Needs Assessment Project (SNAP) working party, which produced a report on health service response to domestic abuse. Successful recent work in establishing multi-agency training courses in Lothian in partnership with Lothian Health provides a good model for such work. It is hoped that the implementation of the Scottish Executive's *National Strategy to Address*

Domestic Abuse (see below) will lead to a less ad hoc approach to training provision on this subject throughout the statutory and voluntary sectors.

The fifth strand identified at the start of this chapter is the quality of refuge provision. At time of writing (2000) there are 38 affiliated groups and two groups in the process of forming and working towards affiliation. There is now some level of Women's Aid service in all local authorities except East Renfrewshire and Orkney. Groups have developed around Scotland with considerable differences in funding, leading to some groups being very much better resourced than others, and this has obviously impacted on the number and quality of refuges locally. Usually, groups have formed because there are women in the area interested in providing a service. Once there is a core group, a public meeting will be held to attract more support. This larger group then receives pre-affiliation training from the SWA national office and other local groups nearby to enable them to start supporting women and children. The new group then has to negotiate with their local council for funding to pay for the establishment of an office and refuge.

Research into service provision for women, children and young people experiencing domestic abuse carried out for the Scottish Office in 1998, showed significant gaps around Scotland, with provision being patchy, and pockets of good practice (Henderson 1998). We would like to see these differences abolished, and more consistency established. One of WA's long-standing aims is to achieve one refuge space per 7,500 of the population, which was recommended by CoSLA in their 1991 report *Women and Violence*. There are currently 325 refuge spaces in Scotland; this is quite an achievement given that we started with none in 1972, however, it represents less than half the recommended spaces. Every year WA turns away more women and children than it can accommodate, even with an open door policy (which means that any refuge with a space will offer it to any woman and children who need it, no matter where they come from in Britain).

Gradual depletion in council housing stock has also meant that the time taken for women to be rehoused has increased considerably in the past ten years. The sale of council houses has made the situation worse and only a massive increase in affordable, public rented accommodation will make a real difference. Services for disabled women and children, for black and minority ethnic women and children and for women and children in rural areas are particularly lacking. There are only seven refuge spaces in Scotland that are wheelchair accessible, only one office has a QWERTY phone and there are only two groups providing services specifically for black and minority ethnic women and children. Significant increases in resourcing are needed in all of these areas.

Women have recently identified a preference for an element of shared accommodation. Some refuges have started to provide this and more will be developed through the Scottish Homes element of the Scottish Executive's Domestic Abuse Service Development Fund (DASDF) during 2000. Accessible refuge provision will also be increased in this way during the course of the next two years, and more than 50 refuge spaces will be created or refurbished in various parts of Scotland.

While there is no doubt that both the quality and quantity of refuge provision have improved over the past ten years, new service requirements have been identified by those using WA services in recent years. Specialist refuges for women with additional needs, such as alcohol or drug dependencies or mental health issues, are needed. Women who are abused and who have these additional difficulties can require more support than can be provided in WA refuges, but there is little provision for them, and even less which they can access with their children. There is also a need to provide more follow-on and outreach services for both women and children and more services to meet the particular needs of those in rural areas.

Looking back over the years, Women's Aid in Scotland has clearly achieved much. It has established that domestic abuse exists – which was disputed by many when we started. It has been shown that it can happen to any woman, no matter what her circumstances, age, class, or ethnic background. In the past it has been thought to be a problem only experienced by 'problem families' living in 'deprived' areas. It is now recognised that abuse is not just physical, it has other aspects such as emotional, sexual, psychological and financial, all of them different forms of controlling behaviours used by men to exert power over women and children – people now accept that it is not just about 'battered wives'.

Agencies working with children now acknowledge that domestic abuse affects children, too, not just in experiencing the abuse of their mother, but in being involved in that abuse and having an increased likelihood of being abused themselves; previously it was believed that domestic abuse was simply about men hitting women. So now insider agencies are devoting some resources to this issue, particularly to child witnesses of domestic abuse. But every time WA works with an agency which has just 'discovered' domestic abuse, definitions and boundaries have to be carefully negotiated, as it weaves a path between purity and pragmatism. Some ideals remain non-negotiable, and in many respects WA remains on the threshold of most mainstream policy communities. However, it is now on the fringes of many it was never approached by in the past, and much has been achieved from this vantage point. For example, most local authority children's service plans now explicitly recognise the needs of children and young people living with the abuse of their mother. This has meant more resources have been made available to them through statutory agencies.

How many of the above achievements have resulted from the triumph of pragmatism over purity? It is difficult to say. As with any movement organisation, WA yokes together many feminisms, from eco to radical, socialist to liberal, each with their different slant on feminist purity.[3] It is a tribute to movement women's commitment to the common end of eradicating violence against women that generally consensus has been reached, often with difficulty, about what is negotiable and what is absolute. Differences have to be recognised and accepted as enriching and healthy if WA as a movement organisation is to survive in what can still be a hostile political climate.

ENGAGEMENT WITH THE POLITICAL PROCESS: RECENT DEVELOPMENTS

As mentioned above, as a movement organisation WA's ultimate goal is the eradication of male violence against women, which has obviously not yet been achieved. A lesser goal which also has not been achieved is the securing of stable funding for all 38 local groups. This is essential to ensure that all women and children in Scotland can access the same full range of quality services from Women's Aid, regardless of where they come from. At present, local authorities regularly cut grants, or offer standstill funding year after year. Much of WA work is carried out by unpaid workers, without whom the service could not be provided. Unpaid work is a valuable experience for many women, and can increase skills and confidence, but should not have to be relied on to carry out core work.

Domestic abuse cuts across a number of current social policy areas, including social inclusion, justice, social welfare and crime prevention. As the political agenda has shifted since the advent of the Labour government in 1997 and the creation of the Scottish Parliament in 1999, there have been more opportunities for our issues to be raised and an accelerating pace of change. Similarly, a multi-agency approach has been recognised as the best way forward at a local level.

In our early years, liaison with politicians was an essential part of establishing the need for our services and negotiating funding. In some areas, this was a more productive experience than in others. Male politicians of every political hue have in the past denied that domestic abuse happens in their area, or that it is anything other than a minor problem. Some female politicians have joined them in asserting that women are their own worst enemies and provoke their partners into assaulting them. Women's Aid therefore had to undertake awareness raising with politicians, too, before serious dialogue could take place about what the issues were and how to make progress.

Locally, the aim was to get services established and adequately resourced. This work has continued from the earliest days to date, as new groups form and look for funding. Once the service has been safeguarded, groups work with politicians and officials to ensure that women and children who have experienced abuse have their needs and rights reflected in policy. This has been required particularly with regard to housing, as local practices have varied greatly, in spite of legislation and Codes of Guidance issued by the Scottish Office.

Nationally, WA has responded to consultation on numerous proposed legislative or policy changes affecting women and children who have experienced abuse. This covers a wide range of issues, including housing legislation in 1977 and 1987 and the two Codes of Guidance, a Green Paper on housing, the Matrimonial Homes Act 1981, benefits changes, the poll tax, the Child Support Act, the Children (Scotland) Act 1995, reviews of criminal and civil law, protection of vulnerable witnesses and sexual history evidence in rape trials.

In many of the above instances, extensive lobbying of politicians has been undertaken at all stages of the legislative process to try to improve the final product. The wide ranging implications of domestic abuse are not always recognised, a case in point being the Children (Scotland) Act 1995. This gives parents responsibilities with regard to their children, and confers on them rights as a result of these responsibilities, with the needs and wishes of children and young people recognised as paramount. However, the Act makes no mention of domestic abuse and does not provide specific protection for children and young people from an abusive father who wishes to have contact with them. Although we failed at the first attempt to have this issue taken on board, WA is hopeful that a review of family law undertaken in 1999 may allow improvements to the protection of women and children to be achieved.

Legislation remains a vital area in terms of the protection of women, and Stedward (1987) has written about WA's qualified success in having our concerns taken on board regarding the Matrimonial Homes (Family Protection) (Scotland) Act 1981. At present, the Justice and Home Affairs Committee of the Scottish Parliament is considering extending the legal protection available to women who have been abused by separating it from property rights. WA also hopes to have its views on the working of the Protection from Harassment Act 1997 taken into account.

A Scottish Office *Action Plan on Preventing Violence Against Women* was put out for consultation in 1998, and a detailed response was submitted. WA has two representatives on the Scottish Partnership on Domestic Abuse (SPDA), which was convened in 1998 to develop a national strategy on domestic abuse for Scotland. A *Draft National Strategy* was put out for consultation early in 2000 by the SPDA. Domestic abuse impacts on women's lives in the home, at work, in their use of transport, health and social work services; we therefore continue to press that this should be taken into account in all these areas. Recent Government policy on mainstreaming, under which all developments have to be assessed for their impact on women, should provide the opportunity for more 'woman friendly' legislation and policy in future.

A parallel development to the Action Plan and the National Strategy has been the DASDF. As mentioned above, this has meant the possibility of increased refuge spaces. It is also a sea-change in policy, as for the first time funding has been ring-fenced for services. While it is nowhere near enough funding, it is a start, and this policy shift is surely, at least in part, if not mainly, due to the advent of the Scottish Parliament.

How has WA got this response from the Parliament? Persistent lobbying has been the most frequently employed tactic for getting issues on to the political agenda. WA has been more successful in this respect during the past ten years than previously, and, as noted above, the rise of women's units and committees from the late 1980s on has undoubtedly helped. Although there have always been a wide spectrum of male politicians who have been sympathetic, and some who have been prepared to openly condemn male violence, women have, in the main, been more willing to be seen as supportive. The organisation has always sought support from all political parties, although some have been more sympathetic than others. Liberal Democratic, Labour, Scottish National Party and the Green Party conferences have all passed motions supportive of WA work or offered other forms of support.

Women's Aid has had to be ready to take every opportunity to make contact with politicians and officials, and to keep going in the face of seeming hostility or indifference. Finding a sympathetic individual and working with them on the best tactics to employ has been fruitful, as has bringing issues up again when they have not been accepted the first time. The importance of supportive politicians cannot be over-emphasised, and individuals with a commitment to the issues have initiated many advances. The opportunities which WA have encountered have often come through Women's Committees, which have actively sought to promote women's interests in general and issues around men's violence to women and children as part of that work (see Introduction to this collection). The work of the Zero Tolerance campaign (see Chapters 9 and 10 in this collection) and the current work in local authorities on developing strategies to tackle violence against women emerged from the Women's Committees, now largely replaced by Equalities Committees. Obstacles still remain in attitudes which condone and excuse abuse and blame women. Cuts in funding, projects being abandoned, policies eroding: it is difficult to say how much of this is, in reality, the result of discrimination inspired by personal prejudices, or the outcome of internal party political manoeuvring and power struggles.

On occasion, direct action has been resorted to, notably in Falkirk in 1989 when the council took the refuge from the WA group, and in Midlothian in 1998, when cuts to funding made the group unviable. In both cases, women from all over Scotland marched to show their support and in both cases there were successful outcomes, although Falkirk's new refuge was not provided until some time later. In 1999, the first national march and rally was held in Edinburgh, attended by a thousand women, to raise awareness about the need for a national funding strategy.

Listening to women and children continues to inform all WA work. Although the organisation has obviously adapted and refined its methods over the years, the fundamental core of the work has been fiercely defended – listening to women and children's experiences of abuse. WA still bases its demands on what women and children have told them they want. This is an important point for women's organisations – it is not good enough for a small group of women to decide what all women want. There must be meaningful consultation and a willingness to take on the lessons learned from the process. Some awareness raising may be required to enable women to participate fully in the consultation. It is an essential, if time consuming, process.

Another strength has been the ability of WA to retain a collective structure, in spite of the challenges it presents and in the face of frequent pressures from funders to change. As organisations in the business world increasingly incorporate a more female ethos into their management methods, collectivism could be the favoured approach of the future.

Perhaps a weakness of the approach is that WA has not always been as organised as it could have been. Co-ordinating the opinions of a network of 38 groups is not always easy, and the demands of service provision have often taken priority, and in this respect, as Stedward (1987) has pointed out, some of WA's campaigning energy has been defused. However, energy surfaces wherever possible, whenever it is needed. Some opportunities have not been followed up, and some have not been taken at all because we did not have an agreed position, and could not reach one even after a process of discussion and consultation.

– The impact of devolution –

There is no doubt that the Scottish Parliament will have a considerable impact on the way we engage with the political process, and indeed has already done so through the advent of the DASDF mentioned above. Domestic abuse comes under the portfolios of the Minister and Deputy Minister for Communities, both of whom have shown a commitment to moving the agenda forward. In addition, there are a number of MSPs who have a connection with this issue as a result of previous life and work experiences. One is a founder and continuing member of Ross-shire Women's Aid, another worked for Monklands Women's Aid. Others have been touched by domestic abuse through a variety of work settings or have experience from their personal lives.

Having more women members of the Scottish Parliament, compared with Westminster, seems to have already influenced discourse. There have been two discussions in the Parliament about domestic abuse to date.[4] Both have been notable for the cross-party agreement, the quality of the debate and lack of mere political point scoring.

New technologies have increased WA's access as well. WA can e-mail all 129 MSPs in a few seconds, and have made use of this on a number of occasions. The organisation has been able to contact them quickly in response to items in the news or letters in the newspapers. MSPs have been receptive to detailed briefings about domestic abuse, much of which they have drawn on for use in debate or in committee. MSPs also contacted WA for information in preparation for the two debates.

WA held a very successful lobby of Parliament towards the end of 1999, to raise awareness with MSPs about our funding difficulties. This matched up women from local Women's Aid groups with their constituency or list MSPs. Local information, relevant to each MSP, could be set in the context of the national picture.

Evidence has been given to the Justice and Home Affairs Committee, which, as mentioned above, has been looking at increasing the civil law protection available for women who are abused. WA also intends to monitor the work of all the Parliamentary Committees, and offer to give evidence whenever relevant.

Although WA will still have to lobby locally in the short term, the work of the Scottish Partnership on Domestic Abuse, a multi-agency task force set up by the Scottish Office in November 1998, should ensure more consistency of service provision across Scotland, not just for Women's Aid, but for all other agencies as well.

Now that we have the Parliament in Scotland, our work will develop differently from that in other parts of Britain. Our sister federation in England, WAFE, has had more regular contact with government than we have had in the past. However, as the Scottish Parliament seems to be seeking to present a distinctly different Scottish agenda, and as women's issues seem to be getting a higher profile than at Westminster, we anticipate a great amount of contact with both MSPs and the Executive. The smaller number of MSPs compared with MPs also allows us an increased opportunity for influence. The Scottish Executive, in addition to its research and policy initiatives mentioned above, has also recently funded a widely publicised leaflet about domestic abuse and the Scottish Crime Prevention Unit has funded two parts of an advertising campaign (December 1998 and December 1999) to raise awareness and try to decrease the acceptability of domestic abuse. This could be seen as a major shift, as it is a recognition that domestic abuse is life threatening and that the home is not the safe haven portrayed by previous crime prevention literature.

Welsh Women's Aid will have to continue lobbying Westminster, as the Welsh Assembly has no legislative powers. Northern Ireland Women's Aid is in the same position, but has had some success in lobbying for the implementation of the 1995 government policy document *Tackling Domestic Violence*.

Looking further afield, there are women's organisations working on domestic abuse in many parts of the world, some of the work less well established than in Scotland, and some well ahead of us and whose experience we need to learn as much as possible from. The European Women's Lobby and Women Against

Violence Europe provide a focus for campaigning against male violence on a European basis. In other parts of the world, notably Canada, the United States, Australia and New Zealand, there have been considerable advances, such as dedicated domestic abuse courts, comprehensive multi-agency strategies and increased legal protection for women and children.

– CONCLUSION –

The Women's Aid movement is probably the most successful example in Scotland of a woman's organisation which grew from feminist roots, has encompassed both a local and a national platform, and has retained an explicitly feminist ethos and method of organisation. Retaining its original ideals has not been easy, particularly in a climate of increasing professionalisation of the voluntary sector. We have often felt uneasy, even on the threshold. As a feminist movement organisation, WA will continue to remain a thresholder in most contexts, until the power structures of society change. There have been many positive developments since Stedward wrote her article, but much remains to be done. Women's Aid's original aim was to put itself out of business by eradicating domestic abuse, so we still have some way to go. The struggle between purity and pragmatism will continue for the foreseeable future![5]

– NOTES –

1. Scottish Women's Aid (1999), *Women's Aid in Scotland: 25 Years of Listening to Women*, Edinburgh: Scottish Women's Aid.
2. Women's Aid in Scotland is used to refer to the network of 38 local Women's Aid groups and Scottish Women's Aid National Office, their national office.
3. Often local WA groups will reflect a different slant according to local politics.
4. 22 September 1999 (committee); 27 October (debate).
5. This chapter does not claim to necessarily represent the views of Women's Aid in Scotland.

– REFERENCES –

Arnot, K. (1990), 'Leaving the Pain Behind', in S. Henderson and A. Mackay (eds) *Grit and Diamonds, Women in Scotland Making History 1980–1990*, Edinburgh: Stramullion.

CoSLA (1991), *Women and Violence*, Edinburgh: CoSLA.

CoSLA (1998), *Guidance on Preparing and Implementing a Multi-Agency Strategy to Tackle Violence Against Women*, Edinburgh: CoSLA.

Cullen, The Honourable Lord (1996), *Public Inquiry into Shootings at Dunblane Primary School on 13 March 1996*, Edinburgh: Scottish Office.

Hague, G., E. Malos and W. Dear (1995), *Against Domestic Violence: Inter-Agency Initiatives*, Bristol: University of Bristol.

Henderson, S. (1998), *Service Provision for Women Experiencing Domestic Violence in Scotland*, Edinburgh: Scottish Office Central Research Unit.

HM Inspectorate of Constabulary (1997), *Hitting Home*, Edinburgh: HMIC.

Lothian Health/Scottish Women's Aid (1997), *Evaluation of A Pilot Training Day*, Edinburgh: Lothian Health/Scottish Women's Aid, unpublished.

Northern Ireland Office/Department of Health and Social Services (1995), *Tackling Domestic Violence: A Policy for Northern Ireland*, Belfast: NIO/DHSS.

Scottish Executive (1999), *Domestic Abuse – there's no excuse* (leaflet), Edinburgh: Scottish Executive.

Scottish Needs Assessment Project (1997), *Domestic Violence*, Glasgow: SNAP.

Scottish Partnership on Domestic Abuse (2000), *National Strategy to Address Domestic Abuse in Scotland*, Edinburgh: Scottish Executive.

Scottish Women's Aid (1992), *Women Talking to Women: A Women's Aid Approach to Counselling*, Edinburgh: Scottish Women's Aid.

Scottish Women's Aid (1987–1998), *Annual Report* (1987–1998), Edinburgh: Scottish Women's Aid.

Scottish Women's Aid (1999), *Women's Aid in Scotland: 25 Years of Listening to Women*, Edinburgh: Scottish Women's Aid.

Steward, Gail (1987), 'Entry to the System: A Case History of Women in Scotland', in J. Richardson and G. Jordan (eds) *Government and Pressure Groups in Britain*, Oxford: Clarendon.

Chapter 6

Rape Crisis Movement in Scotland, 1977–2000

Aileen Christianson and Lily Greenan

The first rape crisis centres in Scotland opened in Glasgow, 1977, and Edinburgh, 1978.[1] Since then there has been a changing number of centres.[2] All of them were initially founded on the feminist principles that rape is a violent, not a sexual, crime and that all women are vulnerable to the threat of sexual assault. They combined a commitment to supporting the women who asked for help and campaigning for changes in society that would fundamentally improve attitudes to women and to sexual assault. Since the 1970s, there have been several major legal changes in Scotland brought about by the campaigning of rape crisis centres, linked with a significant shift in society's attitudes. Where the issue of sexual assault was hidden and regarded as 'private' and for the woman to hide and deal with herself, now the issue of violence against women and children is a matter of public and political debate.

The motivation for rape crisis centres' work came originally from anger at the position and treatment of women; the structure of the centres was inspired by the American and then London model of collective working. But the Scottish approach to public campaigning for radical change was based on a clear and careful knowledge of the Scots law and the legal system from early on. When the centres were first opened we were small, unfunded, almost secret, and paranoid because of the strength of feeling that we were tackling radical and unwelcome ideas about women. However, the need to engage with the realities of the law, as it manifested itself in police attitudes and in the law courts, meant that the most effective way of campaigning became one of letter writing, giving talks, approaching MPs, lawyers, police, doctors – any group whose attitudes could affect the way women who had been sexually assaulted were treated.

Retrospectively, the period breaks down into groups of years in which particular issues were focused on, and successes are apparent. For example, the major successes of the 1980s were in the area of establishing that rape in marriage was a crime and of changing police attitudes to women complainers of rape. The Scottish rape crisis centres obviously campaigned on issues similar to those of English or American groups, particularly the commonly held beliefs in society as to who can rape, who can be raped, and what situations can be labelled the crime of rape: what we called the 'myths of rape'. What was looked for was nothing less than a complete change in the attitudes to women by society. These changes were demanded by all campaigning women's liberation groups of the time, for example, the abortion campaigns and women's aid, as well as rape crisis. We became specifically concerned with the differences in Scots law as compared to English law; for example, in cases of rape in marriage where our law, based on precedent, allowed for the possibility that once a case was prosecuted this would establish the principle of it being a crime, while in England and Wales it was necessary to have a legislative change.

The first period of 1977–82 is notable for the public appearance in 1982 of several issues on which the campaigning work of the Scottish rape crisis centres had been concentrated. In January 1982, three coincidental events forced the public to acknowledge and face up to what rape crisis centres had been saying about the treatment of women complainers in the legal system. Roger Graef's television programme featuring Thames Valley Police (part of a fly-on-the-wall documentary series), showing the unsympathetic questioning of a woman reporting a rape; the breaking to the media of a Glasgow rape case (where the accused were let off prosecution because of the supposed mental fragility of the complainer) with its accompanying resignation of the Solicitor General, Nicholas Fairbairn; and the fining in England of a convicted rapist for the rape of a hitchhiker (because of the judge's view that she had contributed to her own rape): all combined to provide the opportunity for centres in England and Scotland forcefully to raise the profile of issues on which they had already been campaigning. Each became an essential reference point in campaigning for changes in police procedures and attitudes to the 'credibility' of women complainers, and in sentencing. This was the clear point at which our view of the way women were treated pushed through into public consciousness and began to become part of mainstream opinion. In April 1982, a rape in marriage case was brought, the judge pronouncing that this was a crime as much as assault. In this first case the man (who was separated from his wife) was found not guilty, but the principle that rape in marriage was a crime in Scotland was now established.[3]

The period 1983–7 was one of movement and consolidation. Previously all the rape crisis centres had been funded by voluntary contributions and small one-off grants in some districts. In 1982 Glasgow Rape Crisis changed its name to Strathclyde Rape Crisis Centre after being given funding for their first (part-time) administrative worker, funded by Strathclyde Council; in 1983 they obtained funding for an Urban Aid project (the Women's Support Project in Glasgow's East End). Edinburgh Rape Crisis was ineligible for Urban Aid as it was not possible to prove numbers of uptake in urban aid areas, and because there was resistance on their part to naming working class areas as being more prone to sexual violence: an example of political analysis clashing with funding bodies' requirements. From 1987, Lothian Regional Council gave Edinburgh some money for running costs. These slow advances in public funding represented the equally slow acknowledgement of the centres' role in providing a service not provided by social work departments.

By 1982, Aberdeen, Central, Dundee and Highland Rape Crisis Centres had been set up, and from 1983 there were joint Scottish Rape Crisis Centre campaigns. Edinburgh RCC began contributing in August 1983 to Lothian police training programmes, and Strathclyde contributed to training at Tulliallan Police College (the national police college). The publication of the Scottish Office research, *Investigating Sexual Assault* (Chambers and Millar), in November 1983 (begun in 1980, in reaction to rape crisis campaigning), confirmed much of what we had been saying about police treatment of women complainers.[4] A slow but definite shift in police attitudes followed, which the publication of *Chief Constables' Guidelines*, November 1985, was an essential formal part. It led gradually to better treatment of women reporting sexual assault to the police. This better treatment was in part helped by the reintroduction of the women and child units (ironically abolished after the Sex Discrimination Act of 1975) which provided more sympathetic dedicated spaces (usually a couple of rooms and a shower) for questioning by specially trained officers and for the gathering of forensic evidence.

The second part of Chambers and Millar's study, *Prosecuting Sexual Assault*, confirmed officially our complaints about the way women witnesses were treated by the court systems. Its issue was followed by a long and dispiriting campaign to get the government and the then Lord Advocate, Lord Cameron, to implement changes in court procedures in rape cases.[5] The government and the Scottish Courts' Administration proved far more intractable than the police in acknowledging and acting on the need for change. In 1982, Edinburgh and Strathclyde RCCs had failed in a campaign to introduce a private member's bill to the Westminster Parliament to make a woman's past sexual history inadmissible in court. (One of the reasons the centres supported a Scottish parliament was the impossibility of gaining time in Westminster for specifically Scottish legal changes.) There followed an official attempt to control (in a more limited way) the questioning of women complainers about their previous sexual history in the Law Reform (Miscellaneous Provisions) (Scotland) Act 1985, clause 36. Its implementation was investigated in a Scottish Office funded research project from 1988, by Brown, Burman and Jamieson; publication of their findings (which found, as we had feared, that it was easy for defence advocates to avoid the protection the legislation was supposed to offer women complainers) was delayed until September 1992. The failure of the legislation and this delay in official confirmation of the failure was to us symptomatic of the half-hearted commitment of the legal establishment to any real change in the legal system where it impacted on vulnerable witnesses, indicating a continuing lack of understanding on their part of the issues.[6]

The major change in both rape crisis and public perception in the 1980s came in the area of child sexual abuse. When they began, all the rape crisis centres found that many of their calls were from incest survivors. From 1982, incest survivor support groups were set up under the auspices of rape crisis centres. But the change in attitude was motivated by the survivors themselves, who increasingly contributed to the campaigns which finally made clear the extent of hidden sexual abuse within the family. Incest survivor phonelines were opened, staffed by incest survivors, from 1985. This strand of our work became a major part of the 1987 Women against Violence against Women Conference, where 300 women from all over Scotland took part in assessing progress and planning directions for future campaigning. The setting up of Esther Rantzen's Childline, in October 1986, produced mixed feelings for us. It was not based on any feminist analysis of male abuse of power through sexual violence. Nonetheless its founding represents another point where a major shift in public awareness was accomplished, prepared for by the courage of incest survivors who had spoken out. Childline also found that a high proportion of its early calls were from adult incest survivors, and the incidence of child sexual abuse could be hidden no longer, despite subsequent attacks on the pursuit of abusers, particularly at Cleveland (the events were in 1987 and the report in July 1988) and Orkney (February 1991 and the report in October 1992).

The years between 1988 and 1993 saw the completion of our rape in marriage campaign, when a case against a husband still living with his wife was brought in March 1989. The appeal court upheld the judgement that this was a crime. That the man was found 'not guilty' (despite much corroborative evidence of his guilt) was evidence of the lag of jury opinion behind judicial. Nonetheless, the principle was now fully established: married women had the same full legal right to protection against rape by their husbands as by other men. Attitudes to women in society had always affected the way juries came to their verdicts, making the incidence of 'guilty' verdicts much lower in rape cases than in cases of violence not involving sexual assault. One of the corresponding effects of our work to change public attitudes was that the number of guilty verdicts increased. Certainly, consistent early campaigning on a woman's right to say no, whether she was sober or drunk, had led to a greater number of guilty verdicts in cases where a woman had been out drinking and was then raped by a man or men that she had met in the pub or night club. But there still remained a higher than average number of 'not guilty' verdicts even when the woman's evidence was substantially corroborated by forensic or other evidence. A small (but essential) comfort for women complainers in Scotland was that often juries found the man 'not proven' rather than 'not guilty', with the implication that there was not enough evidence, rather than that they had not believed the woman. The campaign in 1993 to abolish the 'not proven' verdict, led by the then Shadow Scottish Secretary George Robertson, was, we thought, ill founded and dismaying. Jury education seemed a much greater need than the regularisation of the three Scottish verdicts into line with England's simpler two. The Tory government announced, in June 1994, a commitment to the retention of the 'not proven' verdict. George Robertson continued to campaign within the Labour party against the verdict, opposed by lawyers and other Labour party MPs, particularly at the Scottish Labour party conference, March 1994. June 1995 saw the last Labour party attempt to abolish the verdict. Robertson's departure to a UK ministerial post (and now to the UN) meant, to our relief, that a powerful motivating force for the campaign was lost.

A sea change of opinion in government ranks was encouraged by the speech at a Scottish Tory party conference, in May 1993, by 'Judy', a Tory party worker who spoke in the presence of Prime Minister Thatcher of her own experience of sexual assault and of her anger at the leniency of sentencing and the lack of understanding of judges of violent sexual crimes against women. Again this was a moment when a public event meshed with patient rape crisis groundwork on legal campaigns and with the recent Edinburgh District Council Women's Committee's Zero Tolerance campaign (a powerful poster campaign against violence against children and women). The Scottish Office woman's safety package, *Talking Sense*, was published in May 1993 against this background. Lord Fraser's words in relation to the safety package, 'we must always remember the victim is never to blame' (*Scotsman* 25 May 1993), represented both a breakthrough (that women were never to blame) and one of our failures. Rape crisis centres had never used the word 'victim' to describe women who had been sexually assaulted as we felt it trapped us in a passive stereotype that was unhelpful in the process of recovery from the overwhelming effects at the time of the assault. However, it was always an uphill struggle with the media, who preferred the emotive shorthand of the word 'victim'. While we continue to use the term survivor, society has not followed us.

Another failure was our resistance to the concept of 'counselling' as opposed to the more equal one of 'support', which assumed a greater commonality of experience between women offering support and women contacting us for support. UK society, however, changed in an unexpected way. After two major public disasters in Scotland – Lockerbie and Piper Alpha (both in 1988) – increasingly the public moved to an acceptance of the existence of post traumatic stress disorder and the need for counselling to counteract its effects. This led to an expectation amongst women who contacted rape crisis centres that they would be helped by trained 'counsellors', as well as an assumption on the part of women volunteering for work with rape crisis centres that this is what they would become. Different centres in Scotland took different lines on this, some remaining true to their feminist roots and resisting the 'counselling' mode while others embraced it. The bedrock of rape crisis work had always been the confidential support of individual women. This new expectation of 'counselling' increased the numbers of women contacting the centres, as well as giving them a particular expectation of what rape crisis centres should provide, without that necessarily being connected to what the centres could provide.

Increases in public and political awareness were paralleled by the growth and development of local rape crisis groups, particularly in terms of funding. The period 1992 to 1996 saw an unprecedented flow of money into local rape crisis centres, and this facilitated a more active engagement with both local and national government. The existence of paid workers meant that a consistent daytime involvement was possible for the first time; it also meant that relationships amongst rape crisis centres around the country were able to develop beyond the twice yearly informal meetings. Late in 1992, discussions began on the theme of federating or constituting our links more formally, and in 1994 a statement of common policy was adopted by seven centres. Between 1994 and 1996 a constitution for the Scottish Rape Crisis Network was drafted and approved by the Inland Revenue. We produced a training pack using materials contributed by local groups, ran a press conference to launch the new Network, and appealed for financial support to run a television advert which had been produced for the Network by an independent TV company. This advertisement eventually ran on STV and Grampian for twelve weeks (late 1996/early 1997). It is worth noting that, although a great deal of joint work was undertaken during this period, the focus was on developing our role as service providers, in contrast with earlier joint work which had been very much focused on campaigning for legal and social change.

Throughout this time, the Zero Tolerance campaign played a significant role both in promoting public debate about violence against women and children, and in focusing local authority attention on the need for services for survivors. In some areas, notably in Central Region, this had a very direct benefit to local rape crisis groups in the form of funding to increase service provision. Ironically, the Conservative government, not known for its woman friendly policies throughout the 1980s, promoted a law and order agenda in the early to mid-1990s which had some surprising benefits for the rape crisis movement (see above). By comparison, although the Labour government has implemented some commendable work on domestic violence, their resistance to broadening the debate to include other difficult issues of violence against women is disappointing. The unexpected benefit to women's groups from Tory policies may have been because they never saw us as 'political', and saw our work as consistent, up to a point, with their 'law and order' agenda. The 1970s women's movement slogan of the 'personal is political' thus bore unexpected fruit, because they failed to understand that what we were doing was 'political' in the broadest sense. For some in the Labour party we were perhaps more of a threat, maintaining as we did that violence against women was not about class, social background or economics, but was very firmly about gender inequalities.

Local government reorganisation in 1996, and the requirement laid down by the Government that local authorities must develop partnership working arrangements with the voluntary sector, provided further opportunities for rape crisis centres to influence local government policy. In some areas this focused on incorporating women's concerns into local community safety strategies, in others the need to address violence against women as a specific issue was pushed much further up the agenda. The involvement of rape crisis representatives on the 1997 working group which produced CoSLA's *Guidance on Preparing and Implementing a Multi-Agency Strategy to Tackle Violence Against Women* was an indicator of just how far we had come. A number of local authorities have taken the *Guidance* on board since then, and have involved rape crisis centres in developing local multi-agency strategies.

But local government reorganisation also had a detrimental effect on funding arrangements between rape crisis groups and our local authorities. For some, as in Edinburgh, this has meant a steady reduction in grant, and a need to look elsewhere for funding of what are now recognised as core services for women. For others, in particular in Glasgow, reorganisation had a catastrophic impact on what had been a relatively stable funding base. Based in the city of Glasgow, but providing services across the whole of the former Strathclyde Region, this group have since 1996 found themselves in the position of applying to nine different local authorities in order to maintain the existing level of service to women. The energy that this level of fundraising consumes inevitably affects that service. Across Scotland, funding continues to be an area of great concern for rape crisis centres, and much work has been done at a strategic level, both locally and nationally, to try to draw attention to the dearth of adequate resources to fund services for women survivors of sexual violence.

The implementation of the Community Care Act in 1993 had little immediate impact on the work of rape crisis centres. We saw ourselves, and were perceived by others, as falling outwith the legislative framework it laid down for the care of vulnerable adults. However, the longer term effects of this piece of legislation, and the political and cultural shifts which went with it, cannot be underestimated. The advent of the contract culture – and its more recent manifestation, 'Best Value' – has placed increasing demands on voluntary organisations to demonstrate that they provide good value for money. This raises some serious questions about whose 'values' we are talking about. Rape crisis centres began in the 1970s as small groups of activists working to a radical agenda, providing support to women who had been raped, and later to survivors of child sexual abuse, but always within a feminist framework which was rooted in a recognition of gender power imbalances, and always with a very clear campaigning role. But as rape crisis centres are pushed more into the role of service providers, it is increasingly a challenge to hold on to that radical agenda. It may be that our original campaigns are won. But rape and sexual assault, as well as power imbalances in relation to gender, remain. Awareness of the societal context of sexual violence against women and children is essential for continuing the changes begun twenty five years ago by those women who set up the first rape crisis centres. We hope that Scottish rape crisis centres continue combining support for individual women with a strong campaigning commitment concentrated around the opportunities of the Scottish Parliament, so that the effects of sexual violence are minimised. It seems overly optimistic to think that the twenty-first century could see its complete disappearance.[7]

– NOTES –

1. In both cases the opening followed at least 18 months of preparatory work.
2. At various times: Aberdeen, Dundee, Central, Highland, Ayr, Ayrshire, Fife, Dumfries, in addition to the original two.
3. Our campaign had been supported by legal authorities (for example, Gordon, Gerald (1967), *Criminal Law of Scotland*, Edinburgh: W. Green & Son) but the procurators fiscal had not brought any case to court until we publicly argued the issue.
4. A more radical report had been leaked in August 1983 to *The Scotsman*.
5. For details of this campaign, see Edinburgh Rape Crisis Centre (1988) *Second Report 1978–1988*, pp. 10–11, 45–6, Edinburgh: Edinburgh Rape Crisis Centre.
6. For details of rape crisis campaigns on this issue, see Edinburgh Rape Crisis Centre (1993) *Third Report*, pp. 11–12.
7. This chapter is written by two former members of Edinburgh Rape Crisis Centre (Christianson, 1978–96; Greenan, 1981–8 and 1992–9); their opinions are not necessarily those of the Scottish rape crisis centres or network.

– REFERENCES –

Brown, B., M. Burman and L. Jamieson (1992), *Sexual History and Sexual Character Evidence in Scottish Sexual Offence Trials*, Edinburgh: Scottish Office Central Research Unit.

Chambers, Gerry and Ann Millar (1983), *Investigating Sexual Assault*, Edinburgh: Scottish Office Central Research Unit.

Chambers, Gerry and Ann Millar (1986), *Prosecuting Sexual Assault*, Edinburgh: Scottish Office Central Research Unit.

CoSLA (1998), *Guidance on Preparing and Implementing a Multi-Agency Strategy to Tackle Violence Against Women*, Edinburgh: CoSLA.

Edinburgh Rape Crisis Centre (1988), *Second Report 1978–1988*, Edinburgh: Edinburgh Rape Crisis Centre.

Edinburgh Rape Crisis Centre (1993), *Third Report*, Edinburgh: Edinburgh Rape Crisis Centre.

CHAPTER 7

The Women's Movement in Scotland in the 1990s

ESTHER BREITENBACH

A longer version of this chapter appeares as 'The Women's Movement in Scotland in the 1990s', *New Waverley Papers*, Department of Politics, University of Edinburgh (1996).

– THE INFLUENCE OF THE WOMEN'S MOVEMENT –

The events that have occurred in recent years, such as the 'Agenda for the 90s' and 'Changing the Face of Scottish Politics' conferences, the creation of the Women's Co-ordination Group and Engender, the existence of *Harpies & Quines* (despite its eventual demise), the higher profile of work by women's and equal opportunities committees and the Equal Opportunities Commission, taken together suggest a women's movement in Scotland that is growing both in power and influence. The interconnection between groups and organisations and the way in which their work feeds and complements each other also appears to be growing in strength. Significantly, in carrying out the research which resulted in *Contemporary Feminist Politics*, Lovenduski and Randall found Scotland different from the rest of the UK.

> There is no doubt that the visible national feminist movement has declined. As we travelled to collect the material for this book, everywhere we went, except Scotland, we encountered a sense that activists were fewer, that old networks had broken down . . . Many women questioned whether there was still an autonomous women's movement.

By contrast, in Scotland 'there was an evident resurgence from 1987 onwards and conferences of feminists were being organised throughout the country'. They argue that 'local factors may go some way towards explaining these variations.

During the years of Conservative rule, political activists in Scotland cultivated its oppositional culture and regional identity, providing a milieu in which an oppositional social movement might thrive' (Lovenduski and Randall 1993).

Difficult though it may be to discover or delineate precisely how processes such as changes in consciousness take place, I would argue that the growth in support for Scottish self-government and the debate on women's political representation, and the widespread debate about national consciousness and identity, have been significant factors in creating a basis for the development of a stronger Scottish women's movement. While feminists in Scotland remain concerned about and actively campaign on similar issues as feminists elsewhere in the UK and other western industrialised countries, the interest in developing a specifically Scottish perspective has grown, and has provided a greater cohesion to the women's movement than it enjoyed in the 1980s. In one respect the women's movement in Scotland is significantly different from the women's movement elsewhere in the UK, that is, in its degree of engagement with the issue of political representation.

It is argued that feminism in Scotland has demonstrated a growth in influence, as a new wave of organisational structures has come into being in the early 1990s. This raises questions about the character of these developments, and what kind of politics they represent. In particular, there are continuing debates in feminist literature which it is pertinent to relate to Scottish experience.

– DERADICALISATION –

One of the difficulties confronting commentators on the women's movement is what definition to operate with – women's liberation, feminism, women's movement. While one does not need to be purist or politically correct in the use of such terms, the linguistic shifts and differences of emphases do have significance. Precisely what the significance is may be harder to explain. Elizabeth Wilson and Angela Weir have commented on the change from women's liberation to feminism, arguing that it has a narrower range (Weir and Wilson 1984). This would be consonant with the thesis of deradicalisation advanced by some writers (Dahlerup 1986, Lovenduski and Randall 1993). Paula Jennings and Jennifer Kerr write also of the problem of the change in terminology, and in the change in the movement,

> linked to the equal rights trend is the view that women's liberation is dated . . . Women's liberation is not new any more and is certainly not news . . . The media, 'feminist' and mainstream, have hastened to update feminism in line with values of the 1980s, the glossy mags with their vision of the sexy, well-groomed female executive . . . (Kerr and Jennings 1990).

These writers perceived the term 'feminist' to be less radical than 'women's liberation'. However, even the term 'feminist' remains problematic for many women who may be considered part of the women's movement. Often it would appear to be the case that women espouse 'feminist' views and advance 'feminist' causes, and yet will wish to disassociate themselves from this term as such. Ellen Kelly confirms this from her experience of working in local government:

> Most feminists would identify the role of women councillors as feminist, but the councillors themselves rarely identify openly as 'feminist' and often seem uncomfortable with the term. They do identify as being pro-equality, whether that be in access to council services or to employment within the council . . . (Kelly 1992)

More systematic research currently being carried out would seem to bear this out, and hopefully will be able to provide an analytical framework for understanding this phenomenon. What is interesting about this phenomenon amongst political, trade union, and community activists, is that in other spheres feminism has gained ground and recognition. For example, in academia, at least within the social sciences, it is no longer the case that feminist perspectives, courses and research are treated with suspicion. This is not to say that gender is given its proper place, or that teaching or research as yet adequately addresses this. But it is becoming more and more common for gender to be accorded recognition as a significant category in understanding society, and for feminist work to receive attention.

It seems easier for women to identify themselves as part of the women's movement (significantly 'liberation' no longer figures), than be 'feminist'. This does not seem to be hard to explain, in that such a broad term can encompass a wide range of activities and organisations, some of which would have been regarded by the Women's Liberation Movement of the 1970s as concerned with a very narrow conception of equality. For example, when the Scottish Convention of Women was set up in 1977, activists in the Women's Liberation Movement were on the whole uninterested. SCOW was seen by some as neither feminist nor revolutionary, nor was there thought to be much value in feminists working within it (*Scottish Women's Liberation Journal* 1977). It was argued, however, by the *Scottish Women's Liberation Journal* that it was worth engaging in dialogue with SCOW as a means of raising feminist issues and stimulating wider debate. By the end of the 1980s SCOW and feminist organisations had moved closer together, as can be seen from the fact that SCOW, on its winding up in 1992, urged its members to support the newly formed Engender, an avowedly feminist organisation. This does suggest a degree of convergence between groups that were previously quite far apart. This convergence can also be seen happening in the kind of alliances that have been formed more recently, for example, the Women's Co-ordination Group. It could be argued, then, that there has been movement from both sides into a middle ground. Does this represent deradicalisation, and does it matter?

In order to attempt to answer this question it is necessary to give some examples of the key issues for the women's movement in Scotland at the present time, and an account of who is working together on what. One example would be work on equal opportunities. This can be illustrated in the joint work being done by women's and equal opportunities committees with the Equal Opportunities Commission on local government reform, and the collaboration of Engender with the Equal Opportunities Commission. This certainly represents a much happier and closer relationship than existed between the Women's Liberation Movement and the Equal Opportunities Commission when it was set up. The Equal Opportunities Commission was regarded as a toothless organisation, which was of little use to women. While it might still be argued that the Equal Opportunities Commission is constrained in what it might achieve, both by limitations of the law and of resources, the attitude amongst feminists is a much more supportive and constructive one (see also Lovenduski, 1995, for an account of the development of the relationship of feminists to the Equal Opportunities Commission).

Another important example of changing emphasis in feminist activities is that of the political representation of women. The revolutionary tenor of the Women's Liberation Movement entailed rejection of parliamentary politics, and frequently also of party politics altogether, even of revolutionary parties. The last thing that would have been looked for was liberation through the ballot box. Of course, this is not the argument that is being made now. It is a much more focused argument, based on ideas of equal rights to representation. Because there is a real prospect of change that will improve women's representation, this tends to be a major focus of energy and action in itself, and there is a limited debate about broader issues that relate to the question of women's representation. At the most basic level the demand is simply for more women to be there. However, it needs to be asked who they will be, what they will represent politically, if they will be feminist, if they will bring about a better deal for women generally. If women's representation does improve this will be a consequence of the shift in attitudes and behaviour inaugurated by the women's movement, but how feminist groups and organisations will be able to influence decision making and policy formulation is a question that still needs to be addressed. It could be argued that this process of convergence towards a middle ground and the current emphasis on equal rights and political representation, which might be regarded both as much more focused and more short term goals, do represent a process of deradicalisation, and a much more limited vision of women's future than that envisaged by the Women's Liberation Movement.

On the other hand, ideas produced by the women's movement have permeated society at large in some form. The women's movement is more actively engaged in a process of lobbying and negotiation with representatives of political power at local and Scottish level, taking feminist goals and strategies into these arenas. This may be seen as a process of radicalisation of these institutions. As R. Emerson Dobash and Russell Dobash have argued, using the example of Women's Aid, 'to the struggle for change, women brought skills, insights and enthusiasms, fuelled by an appropriate anger and passion about the violence against women. A significant element in social change, perhaps one of the most significant, is the very act of creating new visions and thinking new thoughts. Once a new idea has become established, it is difficult to imagine how it was ever otherwise.' They characterise social movements, of which the women's movement is one, in the following way:

> Developing a new vision and acting to achieve it is the core of social movements. Forming a vision which truly represents an alternative to the status quo is the core of social change. And struggling for changes which transform the lives of all women is the concrete, constructive core of feminism. All three have come together in the movement for abused women. (Dobash and Dobash 1992)

In this process the state is also democratised through the participation of women in forming policy. Thus feminist action against violence against women offers an example of radicalisation. However, a crucial part of this process is the development of new visions, and insofar as the women's movement has difficulty in finding ways of continuing to develop such new visions, and of formulating further demands and programmes of action derived from these, then there is a danger of deradicalisation, and of an inevitable focus on short term goals.

DEFINITIONS OF POLITICAL ACTIVITY AND POLITICAL STYLE

Grit and Diamonds, published in 1990, illustrates the range and diversity of activities that the women's movement in Scotland is engaged in and also illustrates the broadness of the definition. Given that it can be hard in the absence of 'conventional' structures to get a grip on what the women's movement is, it is useful, not to say essential, to have documentation of the kind that *Grit and Diamonds* provides. Because so often the activities covered are relatively small scale, either because they are locally based or short term, any records of processes, achievements, people involved, and so on are very easily lost. Lack of recording the present, or history, can have serious consequences for groups who have been disenfranchised or disadvantaged. It is not just simply the process of marking, for example, women's presence, but the fact that their absence allows a powerful ideological machine to deny them agency, and this continues to permeate attitudes towards women, and to underpin acts of discrimination. The variety of activity described in *Grit and Diamonds* serves to confirm that there is an issue about definitions of feminism that is no longer being consciously grappled with as it was in the 1970s. It is as if, in reaction to the bitter infighting of the late 1970s, the women's movement has reached a situation in which it is now possible for almost any women's organisation to call itself part of the movement. On the one hand this may happen without much connection between groups – there are parallel activities, which may be similar in content, or overlapping, but which do not actually connect. On the other this desire for the broad all encompassing alliance surfaces in an organisation like Engender, which has defined its aims very broadly, contains women from a variety of backgrounds – political and women's organisations – but has so far been determinedly against having 'lines' on particular issues. This is all right up to a point – it can unanimously support greater representation for women without getting into difficult arguments, it can agree that our knowledge of women in Scotland is inadequate and needs to be improved through publishing documents such as the *Gender Audit* and providing a platform for public debate of feminist issues. But this is only up to a point. Focusing on issues or immediate or short term goals on which there may be easy agreement means that there is an avoidance of discussion of underlying assumptions or of the stance people take on issues like abortion, reproductive technologies, family life styles, pornography, or issues of race and class, which are likely to prove more controversial.

It can be argued that the perceived need for consensus inhibits the type of discussion necessary to formulate theory and programmes of action. Iris Marion Young argues that the inability to find a means of accommodating difference limits the effectiveness of feminism and makes it exclusive.

> Insofar as feminist groups have been impelled by a desire for closeness and mutual identification, however, our political effectiveness may have been limited . . . A woman in a feminist group that seeks to affirm mutual identification will feel and be doubly excluded if by virtue of her being different in race, class, culture or sexuality she does not identify with the others nor they with her. A desire for community in feminist groups, that is, helps reproduce their homogeneity. (Young 1990)

The other side of the coin of placing a high value on consensus politics is the rejection of 'confrontational' politics. Attacks on confrontational, adversarial politics are frequent.

> Women have repeatedly expressed to us deep dissatisfaction and unease at a style which they perceive as adversarial, competitive and careerist. The 'macho tendency' is still alive and kicking in Scottish politics. Women experience campaigning politics, on the other hand as more co-operative and more likely to work by consensus. Campaigns are also more concerned with the issue at

hand than with the carving-out of personal power bases. (Woman's Claim of Right Group 1991)

This statement is, however, instantly undermined by the admission that community groups and tenants associations can also be battlegrounds. However, the Woman's Claim of Right Group continue to assert the consensus line,

A large proportion of women prefer a mode of organising which, while informal and not very structured, is efficient and very much centres on achieving campaigning objectives rather than self-promotion or power-grabbing' . . .

Many women prefer campaigning groups as they are concerned with issues, whereas political parties are more often concerned with obtaining power, as well as generally being male-dominated. Political parties often have particular lines on issues which constrain their membership and which may also change fairly arbitrarily. Many women prefer to be free of this sort of constraint and to form their own view of things . . . (Hersh 1991)

It is arguable whether a mode of organising which is informal and not very structured is efficient; political parties are concerned with issues, and of course they are also concerned with obtaining power – how else would they put policies into action? Party members may feel constrained by lines, but, insofar as these are formulated through debate within parties and at party conferences, they can hardly be said to be arbitrary. The kind of dogmatic position illustrated above leads very easily to a version of feminine essentialism that argues that women's more nurturing, caring qualities will lead to a gentler more consensual politics. Because conflict and confrontation are written off as male there is no attempt to understand the reasons for conflict and confrontation. It seems pertinent to ask how there can be consensual politics when there are so many divisions in society, not least of which is the division between women and men.

It is not being argued here that some, perhaps many, women do not feel distaste for confrontation and conflict, though sweeping generalisations of the kind quoted above should be treated with suspicion. However, there is an assumption about the rightness and moral superiority of this position that has inhibited analysis of political action, and left feminists frequently ill-equipped to deal with power struggles where conflict is unavoidable.

What makes this emphasis on consensus paradoxical, however, is that a significant strand of the women's movement takes a radical and polarising view of male power. Male violence against women is the expression of that power, and it affects all women, through creating an atmosphere of fear, and through policing women's access to public space. The way in which this power is exercised, and fighting back against it, is for too many individual women literally a matter of life and death. Arguably this kind of recognition of the nature of power needs to be brought into relation with strategies for political action across the spectrum of feminist activity, and not just in relation to men's physical violence against women.

The issue of definitions of political activity and political styles is related to the issue of structure and organisation within the women's movement generally. As has been noted, what are regarded as 'male' modes of organisation and style have been widely rejected – confrontational, adversarial, bureaucratic, formal styles. As has also been noted, this is very much a gut response rather than a stance based on reason and analysis. For example, it has not been shown in which ways these characteristics are inherently male, or how they favour the power of men over women, as distinct from the power of some people over other people (while not denying that these tend to be men, nor indeed that this should be a proper matter for examination). For example, criticisms that rituals and jargon are esoteric and exclusive, and entrench power in the hands of an elite, are not just something that can be levelled at political parties, trade unions, or private companies. They can also be levelled at seemingly informal, open and non-hierarchical organisations. In the early days of the women's movement a paper from a North American feminist, Jo Freeman, 'The Tyranny of Structurelessness', was much discussed. This argued that within informal non-hierarchical groups in the women's movement, power still ended up being concentrated in a few hands, but within an informal group there was no way of dealing with this, or calling people to account or replacing them. Hence it was often very destructive. The issues discussed by Freeman remain pertinent, and there has been only limited progress in advancing the debate. What progress there has been is mainly due to the efforts of leading feminists such as Hilary Wainwright and Sheila Rowbotham. As Hilary Wainwright has written,

The modern women's movement developed its democracy *ad hoc,* to suit its needs and to find a political voice. It drew on the ideas of other movements: the direct action of the black civil rights movement, the anti-authoritarianism of the student movement. But its forms of participatory democracy have not been theorised; neither have there been sustained, documented debates about its strengths and weaknesses. (Wainwright 1987)

Sheila Rowbotham elaborates on the danger of failing to theorise,

Our debates have been grounded in real conflicts but it has been difficult to generalise beyond the particular. We have no means of placing them in any context. Experience which is not theorised has a way of dissolving and slipping out of view, even when it belongs to the relatively recent collective memory of a living movement. We can retain attitudes and responses towards forms of organising which we prefer but it is hard to pass them on or give them a more general validity. (Rowbotham, Segal et al. 1979)

It is not necessarily being implied that practice has not changed to some extent, but it is being argued that the debate has not developed very far, and that therefore the women's movement continues to lack a coherent view of democratic organisational principles that would derive from the positive aspects of feminist experience, but also have the capacity for drawing from the positive aspects of other forms of political organisation.

– PATTERNS OF FEMINIST ACTIVITY –

A striking feature of feminist activity, looking at the record of *Grit and Diamonds*, is its evanescence – how many initiatives have a short lived existence. Sometimes this is a feature of the objectives of a group, but more frequently it appears to be because of the inability of groups or activities to sustain themselves. Some of those that have managed to survive on a longer term basis have only done so in the face of crisis after crisis. Nonetheless, it is perhaps too easy to blame the hostile environment of a patriarchal society for feminist failure, and for groups to see themselves as martyrs to a cause.

On the one hand, then, evanescence is a significant characteristic. On the other hand the same or similar activities or initiatives keep resurfacing: the attempt to establish a Scottish feminist publication – *Scottish Women's Liberation Journal, Msprint, Harpies & Quines*; the focus on women's representation which first came to the fore in the Women's Claim of Right, and though this group had a short-lived existence, remains a major focus of debate in the Women's Co-ordination Group and Engender currently; the expressed need for better communication at various conferences and attempts to set this up that never seem to progress very far. There is a cyclical feel to this – in some cases when the cycle recurs a strengthening also appears to take place, even if this does not result in permanency. Thus *Harpies & Quines* represented a significant advance on *Msprint* in terms of production standards and circulation. From the point of view of the feminist activist, progress is always a struggle and always threatened by lack of resources – time, energy, money. It is difficult not to have a siege mentality and be constantly anxious that things are on the verge of collapse. Taking a more distanced view allows a greater optimism. Feminist ideas are more widespread and influential than they have ever been (in terms of the second wave) – evidence of this would be the profile of debates on women's representation in Scotland, in the political parties, especially the Labour party; the impact of Zero Tolerance campaigns; the continuing work of women's and equal opportunities committees; the gradual entry of feminist work into academic disciplines; more publication of feminist work in Scotland; and changing attitudes to working mothers; changing attitudes to rape, domestic violence, and sexual abuse.

The women's movement seems to have the capacity both to expand (albeit very hard to measure, but again the number of organisations and activities covered in *Grit and Diamonds* would suggest this) and to regenerate itself, although it is not clear how these processes are connected. There is, however, duplication, and wheels do get reinvented. It is therefore legitimate to ask what mechanisms the women's movement has for understanding and disseminating the lessons of its experience, what it envisages itself achieving in the future, and how it will do this.

Drude Dahlerup writes in the introduction to *The New Women's Movement*,

> it is suggested that the group-oriented structure, based on the idea that 'the personal is political', in fact was the main reason why it was possible for the new women's movement to release so much energy and to present a radical new way of thinking about women which has influenced public opinion as well as public policy . . . (Dahlerup 1986)

Its openness was essential to its success. Paula Jennings and Jennifer Kerr write in *Grit and Diamonds* about how the ethos of the Women's Liberation Movement of the 1970s has been lost, 'the idea of women getting together because we like each other is not common currency any more and is certainly not considered an intrinsic part of feminism . . . A feminism which is not woman-loving and woman-centred becomes a very limited equal rights movement', and they express the view that something of this nature needs to happen again to bring the women's movement together and re-energise it.

> Feminism will only be effective when there is a *collective movement* of women . . . A viable Women's Liberation Movement could be a reference point for single issue campaigns; a place to keep coming back to first principles, to work out changes of tactics and ways of adapting to changing social circumstances. Without a networked movement, we have also lacked a forum for developing theory, consensus, and plans of action around pressing issues in women's lives. (Kerr and Jennings 1990)

The national conferences of the 1970s permitted the formulation of a programme of demands. Scottish conferences also adhered to these, and did not formulate any separate programme, although Scottish organisations took part in national movements, for example, the Legal and Financial Independence Campaign, Scottish Women's Aid, and the Scottish Abortion Campaign. The key issues debated in the 1980s in any widespread or popular way have focused on violence against women (and also children), and pornography. There has been a fragmentation however, and sense of a lack of a co-ordinating mechanism, even if it is as loosely defined as the national conferences and the seven demands (For details of the seven demands, see Chapter 1 in this collection). In both *A Woman's Claim of Right in Scotland* and *Grit and Diamonds* there are arguments for a re-creation of such a co-ordinating mechanism. Jennifer Kerr and Paula Jennings write that 'women's liberation as a movement has faded', but express the hope that there could be a viable Women's Liberation Movement again, since 'networking and sound coalition-building seem more important than ever' (Kerr and Jennings 1990). It can be argued that recent developments represent a move in this direction, and that there is the potential for the women's movement in Scotland to recreate a co-ordinating mechanism for itself, though this is not likely to be identical to that of the 1970s.

– CONCLUSION –

I have argued that within the women's movement in Scotland there has been a trend for the formation of broader alliances than existed previously, and for more engagement with the state, especially on the issue of political representation. All this may be seen to reflect a concern with liberal equal rights feminism, to be concerned with women's rights as citizens and with their equal representation within Scottish society: in political parties and institutions, at work, and within institutions such as education, the legal profession, health and social services. At the same time, the issue of violence against women has developed a higher profile, and received support for campaigns from local and central government. The growth of Women's Aid, rape crisis centres, and incest survivors' groups has also meant increasing engagement with the state – as funders of refuges, in terms of changing legislation on domestic violence and rape, in terms of changes in police practice relating to these types of violent offences, and in gaining support for public campaigns.

What this means is that many feminist issues are much more widely debated and have reached the agendas of employers, political parties, and others – at least up to a point. Equal opportunities policies have been adopted by a wide range of employers in the public and private sector, though clearly there are real problems about the efficacy of these, and about the slow progress of women in gaining senior positions in the field of employment. Successful litigation on equal opportunities issues is also creating a change in practice, as are EU directives on equal treatment.

The debate on women's representation in a future Scottish parliament, and in the political parties, also indicate the changing climate of opinion. Likewise the public discussion of domestic violence, rape, and child sexual abuse indicates a change in social attitudes towards these issues. Changes in language and attitudes are apparent if hard to quantify. Much harder to assess are changes in behaviour – much statistical evidence would suggest that these are less apparent, whether figures on women's employment and pay, political representation, or crime in relation to domestic violence and crimes of sexual violence. All this has happened while the term 'feminist' itself may still frequently excite disapproval, or be resisted as a label by women activists.

In examining the view that the women's movement has undergone a process of deradicalisation, I have concluded that this may be true in some respects, but in others the women's movement has radicalised ideas and practice within public policy and institutions. Insofar as deradicalisation can be said to have taken place, it raises questions which are fundamentally about what types of structures and organisation allow a renewal of formulation of demands, strategy and theory. These are themes which recur in discussions of and within the women's movement both in Scotland and the UK, but which remain insufficiently theorised, and are therefore weaknesses of the movement. The women's movement in Scotland has continued to expand and to regenerate itself since the late 1980s, and it is moving towards a greater co-ordination of activity, which may create a mechanism that could enable unresolved issues about structure, action and strategy to be more fully debated.

– ACKNOWLEDGEMENTS –

As an activist in the women's movement my views have been shaped and informed by discussions with many women, too numerous to mention individually. More recently my participation in Engender has provided a stimulus for thought, and discussions with other members of Engender have proved helpful to me, and I would like to express my appreciation of this. Responsibility for the views put forward in this chapter, however, rests with me alone.

– REFERENCES –

Dahlerup, D. (ed.) (1986), *The New Women's Movement*, London: Sage.

Dobash, R. Emerson and Russell Dobash (1992), *Women, Violence and Social Change*, London: Routledge.

Freeman, Joreen (1996), 'The Tyranny of Structureless' in *Communities Directory: A Guide to Co-operative Living*, Oxford: Oxford University Press.

Henderson, S. and A. Mackay (eds) (1990), *Grit and Diamonds*, Edinburgh: Stramullion.

Hersh, M. (1991), 'Women in Campaigning Groups in Central Scotland' in Woman's Claim of Right Group (eds), *A Woman's Claim of Right in Scotland*, Edinburgh: Polygon.

Kelly, E. (1992), 'Women's Committees', *Scottish Affairs*, 1 Autumn.

Kerr, J. B. and P. Jennings (1990), 'Scottish Feminism in the 80s' in Henderson, S. and Mackay, A. (eds), *Grit and Diamonds*, Edinburgh: Stramullion.

Lovenduski, J. and V. Randall (1993), *Contemporary Feminist Politics: Women and Power in Britain*, Oxford: Oxford University Press.

Lovenduski, J. (1995), 'An Emerging Advocate: The EOC in Great Britain' in D. M. Stetson and A. Mazur (eds), *Comparative State Feminism*, London: Sage.

Rowbotham, S., L. Segal et al. (1979), *Beyond the Fragments*, Newcastle: Newcastle Socialist Centre and Islington Community Press.

Scottish Women's Liberation Journal (1977), 'The Scottish Convention of Women' in *Scottish Women's Liberation Journal* 3, Edinburgh: Scottish Women's Liberation Journal.

Wainwright, H. (1987), *Labour: A Tale of Two Parties*, London: The Hogarth Press.

Weir, A. and E. Wilson (1984), 'The British Women's Movement', *New Left Review*, 148 Nov/Dec.

Woman's Claim of Right Group (eds) (1991), *A Woman's Claim of Right in Scotland*, Edinburgh: Polygon.

Young, I. M. (1990), 'The Ideal of Community and the Politics of Difference', in L. J. Nicholson (ed.) *Feminism/Postmodernism*, London: Routledge.

Keeping Gender on the Agenda: Feminist Politics and Local Government

CHAPTER 8

The Future of Women in Scottish Local Government

ELLEN KELLY

'The Future of Women in Scottish Local Government', *Scottish Affairs*, 1, Autumn 1992: 66–77.

Not long ago I attended a meeting. There we were, me the solitary woman, and sixteen chaps. We were all attending the agenda meeting of the Policy and Resources Committee. The chaps were the Leader of the Council, the clerk to the Committee, the service directors and Chief Executive. (The agenda meeting, also known as the 'call-over' or pre-meeting is when the Chair/Convener of the Committee whips through the agenda items, with the responsible staff, just to ensure there are no pitfalls to trap the unwary at the actual meeting.)

When I attended the P&R meeting proper, me and the chaps sat at the side of the room, with the exception of the Leader, Chief Executive, and committee clerk, who sat on the top of the table. The elected members, fourteen men and seven women, filed in and the meeting took its course.

After the meeting the decisions were conveyed through the departmental management teams (95 per cent male), actioned by the principal officers (75 per cent male), put into practice by those in administrative (50:50 male/female) clerical (75 per cent female) and manual grades (almost complete job segregation between male and female). Almost every Scottish Council is structured this way. The City of Edinburgh District Council, where I work, has in fact probably more women in senior and atypical manual grades than many others.

'Thus it is, and always has been', would be the comment of many observers. It would be hard to deny that women are under-represented, both in the senior ranks of local authority staff and as senior councillors. There are, however, especially in those authorities committed to equal opportunities, some small but perceptible signs of change.

In this chapter I argue that the quality, accessibility and effectiveness of local authority services can be directly linked to the representation and degree of influence exerted by women within local authority structures, both as elected members and as senior officers. This belief stems from an examination of the role women councillors play within local authorities, and of the motivation of women for serving in local government. I then go on to argue that, given the unique contribution made by women, effort should be made to ensure parity of representation for women within the new local authorities that may result from the current review of local government.

– The gender balance of councils –

In Scotland, the proportion of councillors who are women averages about 20 per cent in the Districts and about 17 per cent in the Regions and Islands. These figures conceal wide variations. Caithness DC and Skye and Lochalsh share the dubious distinction of having no women councillors. In the 1992 district elections Skye and Lochalsh did manage one woman candidate, but even this was beyond Caithness. It is perhaps unfair to draw any conclusions from these two councils, where 32 of the combined total of 35 councillors are independents. Aside from the rural reaches of Caithness, and Skye and Lochalsh, there are six district councils with less than 10 per cent of women elected members.

A discernible pattern emerges within these six. The west coast Labour heartlands of Hamilton, Monklands, Motherwell, and Cumnock and Doon Valley have, in total, 70 councillors, but are able to muster only six women. Only two of these six are Labour members.

The dominance of West Coast Labour Man stops abruptly in Kyle and Carrick, where some 48 per cent (12 of 25) councillors are women. This puts Kyle and Carrick into Scotland's top three districts for achieving representation of women as councillors. The other two – Sutherland, and Cumbernauld and Kilsyth – top the list, with a 50:50 split between women and men.

Though well down the list, the four major cities, with the exception of Dundee, all manage above-average representation of women. Dundee, at only 16 per cent, is low, but redeems itself, to some extent, with the redoubtable Kate MacLean as Leader. From the bottom up, Glasgow manages 21 per cent (14 of 66), Edinburgh 24 per cent (15 of 62) and Aberdeen 27 per cent (14 of 52). (Figures from the Scottish Local Government Information Unit.) Glasgow, of course, has the superbly well qualified Jean McFadden as Leader.

What, if anything, can be drawn from this analysis? Obviously, the male-dominated rustbelt heartlands of the west and most of the far-flung rural districts, although poles apart in their politics, have been equally successful in stifling even a glimmer of equal representation. The major cities make a much better showing, but are still very far from parity.

The trite conclusion would be that macho man is alive and well and enjoys playing politics in Scotland. This may well be true, but it overlooks the underlying issues.

– Explaining gender imbalance –

The first factor is well known, but still needs to be stated. Women still have the primary responsibility for caring, women still do the great majority of shopping, cooking, cleaning, caring for elderly relatives and children. Women have, on average, three fewer leisure hours per day than men. A high proportion of women work outside the home. When women have to combine this with domestic responsibilities it leaves them very little time for other pursuits. Being a councillor is a very time-consuming occupation, which throws strain on relation-ships and demands great support from partners. A recent publication shows how difficult life can be for women councillors:

> In every family in which we were told that the husband had taken on extra chores, the wife was already a councillor. In contrast, none of the politically active women in our recruitment study mentioned that her husband had taken on extra work in the house. On this evidence, it appears that it is only when elected to the council that the enormity of the workload becomes evident; and therefore it is only in the face of the extra workload of public office that the men respond by shouldering a significant proportion of the household chores. Moreover, many of the councillors who had participatory partners felt they were 'lucky' because their husbands were 'good' to them in this way. They believed they had to demonstrate their gratitude frequently, or their husbands would feel their efforts were not appreciated. Even 'allowing' them to carry on with their political activities was valued.

> 'I'm one of those fortunate women who has never had any problem about women's role in life, and my husband has been happy for me to do quite a number of things.' (Jill Finch, Conservative backbencher)

> Only occasionally and indirectly did women recognise that supportive though their husbands might be, they were not getting the same back-up as any man would take for granted. 'I need a good wife – I really do', said one Labour woman, who had recently become Chair of a major committee; whereas Mrs Finch, who is quoted above, went on to say that her husband's acquiescence lasted as long as she kept the home going as well, so 'I've always thought you do two jobs'. Although these women recognised that their husbands were not providing the kind of practical support that almost any wife would give, nonetheless, they did not question the inevitability of this situation. Only a 'wife' – who is by definition female – could be relied upon to run the home and be there when she was needed. (Barron et al. 1991: 98)

In addition to the domestic implications, there is also a loss of earnings associated with being a councillor, for which the annual stipend does not provide full compensation. Scotland is not a high-wage economy. Women's earnings, whether from the grey shadow world of part-time cleaning and catering, or from the middle class professional occupations, are an essential component of the economy of their households. For many women the financial disincentives of being a councillor may well tip the balance in favour of not standing.

The second underlying issue in considering why so few women become councillors lies in their motivation. Few women become councillors simply because they have time on their hands. Most women councillors have previously been activists, either in their local political party, or in their community. Politics, especially at the local level, is not for shrinking violets.

> Where resources of any kind – educational attainment, voluntary group involvement, or work experience – build up in a cumulative manner, an individual will feel increasingly able to engage in political action of some kind. (This is not to say that they will do so.) Conversely, where class, gender, race or occupational experience limit resources (as they do particularly for women) those individuals are less likely to acquire that minimal level of self-confidence which is a necessary (if not sufficient) prerequisite for embarking on a political career. (Barron et al. 1991: 46)

Few women see the role of councillor as a stepping stone to that of MP. Most are motivated by the ideal of public service. Most are strong-minded and assertive. (Shy, retiring types don't make speeches or go out canvassing.) Most are unlikely to accept anyone's 'party-line' without question. Teamwork is second-nature to most, but women don't belong to the male privilege clubs of old school ties and masonic handshakes. They also share a tendency to be unamused by sexist jokes told at their expense.

All of this tends to put women councillors outside any cosy 'club' arrangement that may be operating within an authority. Women, in these circumstances, almost inevitably become questioners of established practices and, if they survive long enough, harbingers of change.

As long ago as 1913, the writer Rebecca West observed, 'People call me Feminist whenever I express sentiments that differentiate me from a doormat.'[1] On this basis, women councillors may find themselves typecast as feminist viragos. That is very far from the truth. In Scotland at least, it is very much a case of 'it ain't what you do, it's the way that you do it'. Most feminists would identify the role of women councillors as feminist, but the councillors themselves rarely identify openly as 'feminist' and often seem uncomfortable with the term. They do identify as being pro-equality, whether that be in access to council services or to employment within the council. In support of this, many will insist on effective consultation with local communities to improve services, and the introduction of measures, such as flexi-time and dependency leave, which enable more women to work within the council. In those councils with Women's or Equal Opportunities Committees there are also likely to be other progressive measures, such as job-sharing and provision for childcare.

In those councils where women have a strong voice, effective service delivery is likely to be high on the agenda. A stress on communication and consultation with local communities, alongside some form of decentralised working, will probably be a feature. (How effective these measures are in improving service delivery may well be open for debate, but there can be no quarrel with the intention.)

In my experience, councils lacking input from women deal with issues such as homelessness in a different way from those with a better gender balance. Where women have influence, much effort will be expended in finding effective ways to deal with this most complex of issues. This contrasts with certain Scottish councils that view homelessness primarily as an image problem for the authority, to be hidden or, better still, exported from the area.

Where women have been well-represented over a period of time, more diffuse issues for Council Services, such as the implications of violence against women and the need to have a childcare planning policy, will also figure prominently.

This configuration of issues and stress on effective consultation is common to all Scottish authorities where women have a strong voice, and where equal opportunities is more than just a slogan. The emphasis may vary, but the themes remain the same.

Another area where women are increasingly active is that of economic development. Women elected members as well as officers are pushing for better funding for training schemes and education programmes aimed at women, childcare provision in training for women returners and 'partnership' agreements for nursery provision, and insisting that grant-aided economic development agencies monitor their clients and take remedial action if women are under-represented. Until now, the LECs (Local Enterprise Companies) have been relatively insulated from these influences. At least in its initial stages, Scottish Enterprise seemed to have little awareness of, or interest in, the fact that the client group of the LECs is not an undifferentiated homogeneous mass. This now seems to be changing. Training 2000's recent report (Bamford 1991) for Scottish Enterprise was well received. At least some LECs are now aware that an unquestioning acceptance of youth training and employment training is not the answer. The LECs have local authority representatives on their boards. They also have to work closely with local authorities and programmes linked to economic regeneration. If authorities insist on equality of access, and the main Scottish Enterprise board is also pushing the issue, there is every chance of a change in approach from LECs. This would be in line with the approach south of the Border, where some Training and Enterprise Companies have equal opportunities officers, and others have advisory groups on issues of concern to women.

_ Compulsory competitive tendering and _ women's issues

One area of local authority activity where, until very recently, women appear to have had little success in influencing outcomes has been in those areas subject to CCT (Compulsory Competitive Tendering). There have been some undoubted beneficial effects of CCT, much as intended by central government. There is little doubt that in, for example, Sports and Leisure Services there has been a greatly increased awareness of the need to attract and retain a wide spectrum of the community as customers. Women have become a target market. Service managers have become aware, not only that women are themselves enthusiastic consumers of sports and leisure provision, provided they feel safe and comfortable, but also that women are the means to reach children and young people. If the younger age group has early pleasurable experience of participation in sports and leisure, the pattern will be set for future years.

Staff, previously trained in little more than health and safety issues and cash handling techniques, are now exposed to 'customer care' training. Previously neglected buildings have had some capital spent on them, and consumers benefit. Government, taking the Mandy Rice Davies approach – 'Well, they would, wouldn't they' – likes to emphasise this side of CCT. But there are other effects that cannot be said to have been beneficial, either for consumers or staff.

The areas of local authority work, aside from Sports and Leisure management, that have had most exposure to CCT so far are those where there is a high concentration of manual workers. Building-cleaning and catering (which covers everything from schoolmeals to lavish dinners for conference delegates right down to the tea-pot in the councillors' lounge) were first in the queue, shortly followed by grounds maintenance, street cleansing and refuse disposal.

The Government's expressed purpose in introducing CCT was to root out inefficiency in public services. It could well be argued that the history of CCT has also exposed the inadequacies of the private sector. A PSPRU publication (PSPRU 1992: 7), working from a database of more than 5000 contracts, came up with the following:

> Falling standards and a drop in the quality of service are given as the reason for problems in the vast majority of contracts. This is true across all services and sectors that have been subject to compulsory tendering.

It also had some interesting things to say about failure rates, where contractors have gone bust, or the authority has terminated the contract because of poor performance:

The failure rate of contracts held by private contractors is four and a half times higher than for contracts held by the in-house workforce in local government and eighteen times higher in the health service.

Especially in the very early days, something not unlike panic gripped both officers and elected members. No one knew what the private sector could deliver, nor at what cost. It took time to develop the cost management and quality assurance systems that are now familiar aspects of work within many local authorities.

In those first early days, many local authority manual staff were faced with a 'like it or lump it' approach. Cuts in hourly rates were generally avoided, but usually through cuts in actual hours worked – especially in the case of building cleaners – or a greatly increased productivity rate. The latter had a particularly adverse effect on older manual workers, many of whom were forced into premature retirement on medical grounds. Terms and conditions also suffered, with women manual staff particularly bearing the brunt. A common cost-cutting method was to remove the small retainer that school dinner ladies used to receive during the holidays. All of this had the effect of making local authorities less caring employers and of driving down employment standards towards those of the private sector, which, in these employment areas, cannot, by any stretch of the imagination, be called high or even reasonable.

In those early days, a straw poll of members of the National Association of Local Government Women's Committees (NALGWC) showed that neither staff nor elected members were having much success in accessing the CCT processes. In most authorities the accountants, lawyers and embryo Direct Service Organisation (DSO) directors were in the driving seat. To a man, cost-control was their mantra. Quality was not a word heard very often in the mid to late 1980s in many authorities. For a short time, it seemed that, in the name of cost-control, the word 'equality' was to be expunged from the local authority lexicon. 'Equality', which always equates with 'effort' (as in making the effort to examine and improve on established practices) became instead associated with 'expense' (as in 'this costs money, we can't do it'). The latter association is in fact, incorrect, but it provided a convenient peg on which to hang well-established prejudices.

– PUBLIC SERVICE AND E/QUALITY –

In Scotland, 'municipal socialism' has never gone out of style and, at least in the larger districts, there is a commitment to equalities work (championed by women, and supported by them, often in the face of less than overwhelming support from their male colleagues). This combination was to produce a new approach to council services, where cost was not to be the sole criterion.

Although it could never be less than dominant, given the requirement on all DSOs to produce a 5% return on capital, quality was to be the pass-key to more effective service delivery.

'Quality' equates with 'equality'. E/Quality means improved service delivery, tailored to meet the needs of local communities. This, in turn, means developing effective methods of consulting local communities, to ask their opinion both of service standards and of types of provision. E/Quality means investing in staff. This means training, both in skills development and in awareness of consumer needs. E/Quality means using non-discriminatory practices in recruitment and selection that will ensure the composition of a local authority's workforce matches that of the community it seeks to serve. E/Quality means having structures that maximise the potential for effective, efficient service delivery. The pursuit of E/Quality is what brings most women into local authorities, and is what keeps them there.

Commitment to public service is reflected not just in the attitudes of women who are elected members, but of women staff. This was demonstrated in a 1984 study of male and female managers and professionals in public and private organisations (Metcalfe 1984). The study showed that women in general were better qualified than men, with public sector workers far more likely to have first degrees and postgraduate qualifications. Women in the public sector, in common with their private sector counterparts, were also far more likely to be single than men (25 per cent women; 3 per cent men); parenthood was also restricted, with only 13 per cent of men in the public sector having no children, compared with 58 per cent of women. (The private sector women fared even worse, with 66 per cent having no children.) Family size too was smaller for women than for men.

In her analysis of this study, Beverly Metcalfe comments:

> Women, it would appear, have to make important life choices, apparently not faced by the majority of professional males, or they carry far greater domestic and career pressures to succeed at both. This would appear to contradict directly the widely held myths such as those identified by Rosen and Jerdee (1974) that male managers believe their female employees are not willing to take risks or make sacrifices for the sake of career development.
>
> Beliefs abound that women are less interested in advancement and in playing an active role in organisational affairs. The data presented here, however, dispute the assumptions of women's lesser career commitment and ambition. Women in this sample were as concerned as the men with opportunity for advancement and were in fact more concerned with challenge, development, and feedback than the men, irrespective of whether they worked in private or public sector organisations, whereas the men were more concerned with extrinsic factors to the job such as high earnings, fringe benefits and job security. Women were also significantly more concerned than men in this sample that their job made a contribution to society. This finding, together

with the fact that men regarded external reinforcements as far more important than women, may lead some readers to conclude that women represent a better organisational investment than do male managerial employees.

Given that the patterns for work preferences appear more similar with respect to an individual's gender than the sector of employment in which they work, what differences emerge when comparing females and males working in the two sectors? Women in the public sector, whilst they sought and achieved greater degrees of appreciation and perceived that their jobs gave them more opportunity than the men to make a contribution to society and were more satisfied with the location, did not perceive higher degrees of feedback, development opportunities, better outside job fit, and working with friendly people. All were rated fair to good as they were for females in the private sector. Males in the public sector, who it may be recalled regarded fringe benefits, high earnings and security significantly more important . . . may well be among the most frustrated in the sample. (Metcalfe 1984)

It would be heartening to report that Scottish local authorities have recognised the quality and commitment of their women managers and professional staff by awarding them promotion to directorate and chief executive posts. This is manifestly not the case. No Director of Education is a woman, despite the fact that numerically women dominate the teaching profession. Social Services, another area where women predominate in numbers, has only two women Directors, in Dumfries and Galloway and Grampian. There is only one woman Chief Executive in Scotland, in Badenoch and Strathspey, which even its greatest admirers could hardly call a powerhouse within the local authority structure. Housing fares little better, with only Cunninghame and Shetland having women as Directors.

Despite this dispiriting roll call, women are beginning, albeit slowly, to make the breakthrough at principal officer and assistant director level, especially in those authorities with a commitment to equal opportunities.

Ensuring that women have a more proportionate representation in higher level posts can only be beneficial to service delivery. This comment arises from simple realism, not from a romantic belief in the virtues of women. Scotland is a small country with a low-wage economy and a consequently high reliance on public services. Even now Scotland still has a far larger proportion of public sector housing than England. Those who administer the public sector in Scotland are, by and large, its product. They were brought up in council housing, and educated in local authority schools. They have first-hand experience of being on the receiving end of service delivery. Most public sector administrators still send their children to local authority schools. They may themselves no longer live in council housing, but many of their close relatives still do. The adequacy, or otherwise, of service provision sits very close to home. This effect is magnified for women, who still have the primary responsibility for domestic matters and caring for the family.

For women working as public service administrators, their personal struggles and sacrifices can be justified only by a commitment to quality in service delivery, a very real sense of making a contribution to society and to their local communities.

– WOMEN IN SCOTTISH LOCAL GOVERNMENT –

What then for the future role of women in Scottish local government? No one can seriously doubt that central government wants to restructure local government. In Scotland, we will not have the benefit of a public commission. The Scottish Office issued an initial consultation document, and received a wide-ranging variety of responses. Coopers and Lybrand are carrying out a preliminary study, though neither the principles of their brief, nor their method, has thus far been made public. Despite the present lack of clarity, Ian Lang and the Scottish Office will eventually have to come clean with their intentions.

Before serious preparation for the necessary legislation can get underway, the Scottish Office will have to issue a second document, stating how they see the future of local government in Scotland.

At that time there will be a two-fold opportunity for women in Scotland. As consumers, providers and elected members, women have a tremendous depth of knowledge about what makes a good local authority. From the day the Scottish Office paper is issued, to the hour the Act is drafted, women must make their views heard. They must do so at every level of the debate, from the local Women's Guild to committee rooms of Parliament. Then they must force recognition of the validity of their views. This is the only way to ensure that whatever framework for local authority services finally emerges will be capable of effective service delivery and answerable to local communities.

The restructuring process will also provide the opportunity greatly to increase women's representation in local politics. Before the last election, agreement, of a sort, was reached that would have guaranteed women at least 50 per cent representation in a future Scottish Assembly. At least for the moment, a Scottish governing body seems out of reach, but that is no reason to lose the principle of equal representation. Whatever the future structure of local government in Scotland, women must be guaranteed a full representation. For any such guarantee to be worthwhile, this has to be backed by realistic allowances for elected members, and provision for the care of children and dependent relatives.

It would not be easy to gain agreement for these proposals. Those who have most to lose would not be slow in bringing forward their defence. The recent sad saga of Kirkcaldy would no doubt be brought into play. The old chestnuts – lack of suitably experienced women, cost, feasibility and so on – would, no doubt, be trotted out. Despite all of this, women have too much to lose not to fight for equal representation on the new local authorities. Local communities need good-quality local authority services tailored to local needs. These can best be delivered by authorities where women are equally represented. Despite some recent commendable efforts, the history of local government in Scotland is littered with examples of male-dominated councils remote from the concerns of their communities. Had women had a stronger voice sooner, it is debatable whether central government would have been able to propose such wholesale changes less than twenty years after the last reorganisation.

– Acknowledgements –

Thanks to Morag Gillespie of the Scottish Low Pay Unit and to Marion Keogh and the staff of the Scottish Local Government Information Unit, who were very patient and helpful in answering my questions. Also to Councillor Margaret McGregor of CEDC.

– Note –

1. *The Clarion*, 14 November 1913, cited by Dale Spender (1983), *There's Always Been a Women's Movement this Century*, London: Pandora Press.

– References –

Barron, J., C. Crawley and T. Wood (1991), *Councillors In Crisis*, Basingstoke: Macmillan.

Bamford, C. (1991), *Local Enterprise Companies and Women: Realising the Potential*, Glasgow: Scottish Enterprise.

Metcalfe, B. A. (1984), Note on 'Current Career Concerns of female and male managers and professionals'. An analysis of free-response comments to a national survey in *Public Administration*.

Public Services Privatisation Research Unit (PSPRU) (1992), *Privatisation: A Disaster for Quality*, March, London: PSPRU.

Rosen, B. and T. H. Jerdee (1974), 'Sex Stereotyping in the Executive Suite', *Harvard Business Review*, 52.

CHAPTER 9

The Case of Zero Tolerance: Women's Politics in Action?

FIONA MACKAY

A longer version of this chapter appears as 'The Case of Zero Tolerance: Women's Politics in Action?' *New Waverley Papers*, Department of Politics, University of Edinburgh, 1995.

> Husband, Father, Stranger: Male Abuse of Power is a Crime.
> (Zero Tolerance Campaign (1994))

> Zero Tolerance came from actually asking women: 'What concerns you?' We never dreamt, of course, that it was going to take off as it did.
> (Councillor Margaret McGregor, Convener, Edinburgh District Council Women's Committee (1994))

The Zero Tolerance campaign is a ground-breaking public awareness initiative which challenges social attitudes and myths surrounding violence against women and children. It originated with Edinburgh District Council's Women's Committee in 1992 and was launched with broad political, civic and church backing. By March 1995 the campaign had been taken up by eleven other Scottish councils, by the Association of London Authorities and by seven other English councils and had also been launched in South Australia.[1] The campaign succeeded in generating high levels of public debate and pushed the issue of violence and sexual violence higher up the political agenda. It has been marked by success in terms of not only public response, but also uptake from other authorities and support from a wide range of agencies and women's groups. Additionally, the campaign has won acclaim for its design.

The Zero Tolerance campaign can be seen as distinctive and an exception to local authority politics for several reasons. It is a radical initiative in that it seeks to challenge existing power relations and effect far-reaching social change. The campaign challenges *all* men to acknowledge male violence, and individual men to take responsibility for their violence. In addition, it is an explicitly feminist campaign in a number of ways. Firstly, it shares a feminist perspective in its 'naming' of violence as a political issue. Secondly, it uses a feminist analysis of violence as a male abuse of power and it links sexual violence, domestic violence and child sexual abuse as part of what feminists have identified as the 'continuum of violence' (Kelly 1988). It also defines emotional and psychological abuse as forms of violence. Thirdly, it specifically uses empowering images of women – rather than 'victim' imagery. This builds upon the women's movement's philosophy of self-help and personal empowerment. The Zero Tolerance campaign – although it comes out of local government – can thus be positioned as an initiative based upon and informed by twenty years of groundwork by the women's movement.

This chapter is based upon initial findings from a larger research project carried out by the author into women in local government.[2] The study was developed to explore the link between the feminisation of politics and the process of promoting gender equality in terms of social policy outcome. It examines the processes by which this radical, but genuinely popular, campaign reached the agenda, how consensus and legitimisation were constructed, and other factors accounting for its success. It explores the importance of the presence of women in the local state as elected members and as officers and the significance of women's committees as proactive agents of feminist change. It considers the view that there has been a convergence between women's movement activists and the agenda of women working in local authorities as elected members and as officers. Furthermore, it suggests that the case study of Zero Tolerance provides evidence of an emerging 'women's politics'. (For an account of the campaign's development in Strathclyde see Cosgrove, Chapter 10 in this collection.)

Feminist theory suggests that the entry of women into decision-making channels may have an impact upon political elites leading to, for example, an increased focus upon gender issues and a change in the style of politics (Dahlerup 1988; Haavio-Mannila et al. 1985), although different models suggest different degrees of outcome in terms of success in implementing social change. Concepts of a 'women's politics' based upon notions of a shared 'women's culture' are both notoriously vague and fiercely contested. Some feminist academics (Hedlund 1988; Carroll 1992) suggest there is a core of shared interests, common values and patterns of interaction which arise out of women's specific position as a result of the sexual division of labour in society. Others find these constructs problematic and are critical of their reactionary and essentialist potential (Randall 1987; Barrett 1987). Empirical evidence is mixed although many feminist political scientists, including, for example, Ellen Boneparth and Emily Soper (1988) have argued that the presence of women elected office-holders, whether feminist or not, is one of the factors in the successful promotion of women's issues.

– The Zero Tolerance campaign –

It was a bit like I'd died and gone to heaven. There above all the shoppers in Edinburgh's Princes Street ran the bold message, 'There is never an excuse.' There on the grassy bank halfway up the Mound sat a white Z of flowers. There at Hibernian a huge 'Z' symbol was emblazoned across the nets. Men on the terracing were eating their pies out of cartons and boxes overprinted with Zero Tolerance statistics . . . In doctor's surgeries patients sat beside posters proclaiming, 'No Man has the Right'. In swimming pools, school galas splashed off beside the happy image of three young women, and the message, 'When They Say No, They Mean No' . . . The campaign for Zero Tolerance of violence against women is really HAPPENING all over Edinburgh . . . (Riddoch 1994)

Broadcaster and journalist Lesley Riddoch, writing in the Scottish feminist magazine *Harpies & Quines*, voiced the sense of empowerment and positive support felt by many women in Scotland since the launch of the Zero Tolerance campaign. The success of the campaign has been on a scale beyond the expectations and experience of local government women's committees in general. In addition, despite being a radical campaign on a classic 'feminist issue' it was received with broad political, civic and public support and there is evidence that it has galvanised local communities and women's groups in Scotland.

The initiative was informed by the long-term British anti drink-driving public awareness campaigns and was also based, in part, on a Canadian government national anti-violence programme which was launched in response to the death of fourteen young women in the 'Montreal Massacre'.[3]

The Edinburgh District Council (EDC) campaign sought to 'name' the problem of violence against women, to challenge men to take responsibility for their actions and to work towards the 'Zero Tolerance' of violence against women.[4] The campaign is built around the idea of The Three Ps: Prevention; Provision and Protection. Its stated long-term objectives were to generate public debate and focus on strategies to *prevent* crimes of violence against women; to highlight the need for the *provision* of adequate support services; to highlight the need for appropriate legal *protection* for women and children victims/survivors of violence.

In the shorter term, the campaign sought to highlight the prevalence of various crimes of violence against women and children, linking these crimes as part of a continuum of male abuse of power; to promote a criminalisation strategy and send out a clear message that these forms of violence should not be tolerated; and to debunk some of the myths around these crimes. In particular the campaign sought to challenge commonplace perceptions that violence is solely a working class problem, that women and children are most at risk from strangers, and that sexual violence or violence only happens to certain women because of their age, their appearance, dress or behaviour. These ideas and insights have been well-known for many years within the women's movement, but the messages were less familiar to the wider public, including many local government politicians and officers. Indeed, campaigners clearly acknowledged the pioneering work of the women's movement and have positioned the campaign within the feminist tradition.

– ORIGINS OF THE CAMPAIGN –

The campaign was developed in response to two pieces of research commissioned by Edinburgh District Council's Women's Committee. Local women interviewed in 1990, as part of EDC Women's Committee's regular three-yearly consultation exercise, identified violence against women/women's safety as one of their main issues of concern along with childcare and access to training and employment (Blake Stevenson 1990). In 1992, a survey of secondary school pupils was undertaken by Nancy Falchikov to examine adolescents' attitudes about violence against women. It revealed disturbingly high levels of acceptance of, and misconceptions about, domestic violence amongst adolescents. It found that boys, some as young as twelve, were more accepting of violence towards women than girls. Both girls and boys found violence more acceptable if the victim was married to the abuser. The majority of boys and girls reported that they expected violence to feature in their personal relationships in the future. One positive finding was that exposure to information about violence against women appeared to influence attitudes and make it less acceptable (Falchikov 1992).

In response to these findings, EDC Women's Committee agreed to fund a six-month public awareness campaign around issues of violence against women and children. The campaign was produced in-house by women's officers who brought in freelance feminist designer and photographer Franki Raffles. The campaign team argued that very little work had been done in terms of challenging social attitudes about violence or in challenging male perpetrators to take responsibility for their actions. The main focus of previous initiatives had been to provide personal safety strategies for women to avoid attacks by strangers, which reinforced the myths that women and children are most at risk from strangers and that women are themselves somehow responsible for preventing or avoiding violence. One of the team explained:

> There was stuff going out about violence from the Scottish Office and the [Lothian] Region but it was putting the responsibility on to women – to avoid places, to hide their femaleness, if you like. I can remember one set of guidelines which advised women if they broke down in their car to try not

to look like a woman! We didn't feel the way violence was being discussed was helpful. Zero Tolerance wanted to name the problem – which of course wasn't a new message in the women's movement – but we wanted to make it much more public – to reach a wider public.

The initial campaign, which ran from December 1992 to May 1993, consisted of posters challenging stereotypical views of different aspects of violence such as domestic violence, child sexual abuse and sexual assault. It was devised in consultation with local women's aid and rape crisis groups and MOSAC, a self-support group for mothers of sexually abused children. The campaign used powerful positive black and white photographic images of women of all ages in cosy domestic situations alongside information about the nature and prevalence of domestic and sexual violence. The purposes of this strategy were two-fold: firstly, a decision to portray women as 'survivors' rather than 'victims' and thus be a resource of support for women to draw upon; secondly, to underline the hidden nature of abuse by juxtaposing comfortable images with uncomfortable messages in the text. The use of middle class imagery was designed to challenge common myths that domestic violence and sexual abuse only happen in certain social classes or sections of the community and that it does not happen to women and children from 'normal' families.

The initial campaign consisted of four posters. The first dealt with child sex abuse: it portrayed two girls playing, with the text: 'By the time they reach eighteen, one of them will have been subjected to sexual abuse. From Flashing to Rape: Male Abuse of Power is a Crime.' The second poster dealt with domestic violence and portrayed a woman in tranquil domestic scene, with the text: 'She lives with a successful businessman, loving father and respected member of the community. Last week he hospitalised her. Emotional, Physical, Sexual: Male Abuse of Power is a Crime.' The third dealt with rape; the poster showed a small girl and her grandmother reading a bedtime story. The accompanying text was: 'From three to ninety-three, women are raped. Husband, Father, Stranger: Male Abuse of Power is a Crime.' The fourth poster was all text, and read: 'No Man has the right', with a large 'Z', which is the logo for Zero Tolerance.

The posters were displayed on billboards and Adshell display sites throughout the city as well as indoor sites such as public houses, libraries, police stations, community and recreation centres. Subsequently, posters were displayed on the large, prominent tripods which line Edinburgh's main shopping area, Princes Street, with statements such as 'No Man has the right' and 'Male Abuse of Power is a Crime' as well as statistics about the prevalence of violence against women. A fifth poster about date rape was launched in 1994 which showed three young women chatting, and the text: 'When They Say No, They Mean No. Some men don't listen. Whoever, Wherever, Whenever – Male Abuse of Power is a Crime.' In addition, a general campaign leaflet and Zero Tolerance bookmarks were distributed through libraries and other recreational outlets. Postcard packs describing the campaign were sent out to those requesting further information. People were encouraged to sign 'pledges' of their Zero Tolerance of violence against women and children and were urged to lobby local and national governments to tackle the issue.

– EVALUATION –

An evaluation of the first phase of the campaign was carried out by Jenny Kitzinger and Kate Hunt of the University of Glasgow Media Group in 1993. The exercise was designed to assess public response to the campaign, including public perceptions as to the need for, and acceptability of, advertising campaigns around issues of violence. A street survey was conducted with a representative sample of 228 people in Edinburgh in order to elicit the views of the general population. In addition, focus group discussions were conducted with a number of interest groups in order to explore a range of opinions.

Findings indicated that the Zero Tolerance campaign had been extremely successful in attracting attention and in gaining a positive reaction from the public. The campaign achieved its initial aim of generating public debate and highlighting the prevalence of male violence, sending out a clear message that it was not to be tolerated. Focus group data suggested that the campaign raised people's knowledge about the shortfall in provision of services for women subjected to violence and the shortcomings of the legal system in protecting women and children. Once people were aware of these shortfalls they expressed discontent at the *status quo*. People also recognised that the campaign was seeking to debunk some of the myths around violence against women, such as the myth that it is only a working class problem, or that most sexual assaults are perpetrated by strangers. The women in the images were seen as 'people with rights'. The evaluation suggested that the campaign provided people with new information and perspectives and had been thought-provoking (Kitzinger and Hunt 1993). A member of an incest survivors self-help group, who took part in the evaluation exercise, described her reaction to the campaign:

> You know that sort of prickly feeling, like when you see something and think . . . oooooh! It was when all the posters were up along the tripods along Princes Street . . . I couldn't believe it. I was going along in the bus and I thought: 'There's one over there. There's another one! They haven't got them all along Princes Street . . . YES! They have! It was very good. [I felt] Yes, this is what I want. I want people to see this. (reported by Kitzinger and Hunt 1993: 21)

– UPTAKE AND DEVELOPMENT OF THE CAMPAIGN –

The Edinburgh campaign sparked enormous interest from other local authorities and organisations in Britain, Europe and worldwide. For example, in 1995 the campaign was run in South Australia. Meanwhile, a co-ordinated and coherent campaign developed in Scotland in 1994–95 which involved several local authorities and other agencies. As a result, the campaign covered most of Scotland. One of the original Zero Tolerance team commented that they had achieved a Scottish national campaign 'by the back door'. In 1994, Zero Tolerance was launched by Tayside Regional Council with leading support from the City of Dundee District Council; by Strathclyde Regional Council with leading support from the City of Glasgow District Council; and by Central Regional Council. It was also taken up by the City of Aberdeen District Council, with some funding from Grampian Regional Council. Strathclyde Regional Council, the largest local authority in Britain until its abolition in 1996, and Central Regional Council both worked in partnership with their district councils, including Conservative-controlled local authorities, health boards, voluntary sector groups and other agencies. Although their campaigns have necessarily been more diffuse than Edinburgh's, they have made significant progress in inter-agency development work (see Cosgrove, Chapter 10 in this collection). For example, both Regions have developed educational materials and have worked with secondary schools.

The campaign developed a comprehensive and innovative publicity strategy amongst participating authorities in Scotland, including advertising on trains, subways and buses. There have been conferences, seminars, banners at festivals, training courses, theatre projects, local press and radio campaigns, school studies and a wide range of community events. Edinburgh continued to innovate, with a 'No Excuses' bus advertising and poster campaign in 1994. This challenged excuses commonly given for violence with the slogan: 'Blame the Weather, Blame the Drink, Blame the Woman . . . There is Never An Excuse.' It also launched a football initiative with star players from the city's two football clubs pledging their support for the campaign, and Zero Tolerance publicity prominently displayed at the club grounds. In parallel to the public face of Zero Tolerance, EDC also developed a 'within council' strategy, including a domestic violence policy for its own staff, drawn up with the help of the public sector union UNISON and believed to be the first of its kind in Britain.

Political and media support has also been high profile. A motion in support of the campaign was laid before the House of Commons and the campaign was raised in the European Parliament. Edinburgh District Council lobbied the Convention of Scottish Local Authorities (CoSLA) to call for a co-ordinated national, regional and local anti-violence campaign. It is widely accepted that the Scottish Office Crime Prevention Council's £300,000 advertising campaign against domestic violence which was launched in June 1994 was at least partly a result of the Zero Tolerance campaign and associated lobbying (Engender 1995).

In 1995, participating Scottish local authorities launched a joint football initiative which took the campaign to the grounds of most major football clubs. The second phase of the joint poster campaign, called 'What's Love Got to Do With It?', ran in the summer of 1995, backed up by a cinema advertisement aimed at 15 to 25 year olds. This phase tackled common myths about the causes of violence and built upon the earlier 'Excuses' phase in Edinburgh. The work of Scottish authorities, both jointly and individually, on Zero Tolerance has been cited as examples of best practice in an EOC (Scotland) report on equal opportunities initiatives in local government (Breitenbach 1995).

A national Zero Tolerance Trust was launched in 1995 in order to co-ordinate the development and promotion of the campaign and related issues on a Scottish and UK-wide basis in light of the growth in interest. Another key function of the Trust was to safeguard the campaign from fragmentation as a result of local government reorganisation post-1996.[5]

– Factors for success –

The Zero Tolerance campaign was high risk in its radical approach, it was provocative and delivered uncomfortable messages about the nature and prevalence of violence. Campaigners shared an understanding with feminist policy analysts and activists that policies which challenge existing power relations were likely to provoke resistance and counter-attack (Firestone 1972; Gelb and Palley 1987; Boneparth and Soper 1988; Kelly, Burton and Regan 1994; Young 1990). Thus, the EDC Women's Unit had expected political and public backlash, especially from men. Yet the campaign has been characterised by high levels of support and consensus. This is not to say that there has not been criticism. The messages of the campaign have undoubtedly offended certain politicians and other sections of the community. The main criticisms of the campaign have been that the messages are anti-men and that statistics used have been inaccurate. These claims have been vigorously refuted by the campaign team. The campaign has also provoked some extreme responses. The unit has had to deal with some abusive phonecalls and angry correspondence. There have been instances where posters have been defaced and other Zero Tolerance materials vandalised. However, in contrast to the reaction provoked by the work of women's committees in the 1980s, publicly expressed opposition to the campaign has not been sustained and there is little evidence to date of an organised political backlash.

– ENABLING CONTEXTS –

The fact that Zero Tolerance was a strong, innovative and well-planned campaign was no guarantee for success. However, there were several key factors which reduced the possibility of conflict and failure, and which facilitated the successful implementation and dissemination of the campaign. Firstly, a range of enabling political and structural contexts, some British, some more specifically Scottish, provided a 'window of opportunity' for a feminist campaign. These included the existence of women's and equal opportunities initiatives in British local government, together with the relative strength of the EDC Women's Committee in particular, and Scottish initiatives in general. In addition, the strength of women's networking, particularly within Scotland, was significant. Similarly, the campaign was able to tap the changed social and political context in which issues such as violence are discussed – a striking feature of which is the social, political and personal salience of the issue of violence to a wide variety of women.

At a specific level several factors can be identified which contributed towards the successful launch and development of the campaign in Edinburgh and elsewhere. These are: the initial political management of the campaign; the support of women in the local state (both councillors and officers); and wider public support.

– Women's committees –

The campaign originated in an environment where there were women's committees and equal opportunities structures in place. Halford (1988) has suggested that the existence of these structures signals that gender politics are at least formally accepted as part of the local authority agenda. The creation of local government women's committees, and their subsequent work, has been an interesting development in the pattern of feminist activity in the 1980s and 1990s (see, for example, Lovenduski and Randall 1993; Edwards 1995). Vicky Randall (1992) contrasts the 'gloomy picture' of complacency and indifference towards gender equality policy issues at national government level with this 'paradoxical and quite heartening development' at regional and local level. She suggests that women's committees 'have provided a real if precarious "window of opportunity" for feminism in these otherwise unpropitious years'(Randall 1992: 83).

The first Women's Committee in Scotland was set up by Stirling District Council in 1984. By 1995 there were eleven full women's or equal opportunities committees and four sub-committee/advisory group structures in Scotland. Eleven authorities had one or more specialist staff in post (Kelly 1995). In 1994, there were 32 full women's/equal opportunities committees which meant that Scotland, with around 9% of the UK population, had around a third of all women's/equal opportunities initiatives (Kelly 1995).

As elsewhere in Britain, women's/equal opportunities committees in Scotland have had a difficult history (Lieberman 1989; Coote and Patullo 1990). Few women's committees and units were adequately staffed or resourced, and most have had to struggle in marginalised positions both politically and organisationally. The media, particularly in the 1980s, has often been hostile and seldom sympathetic. Several women's committees have not survived, including Stirling's. In addition, women's and equal opportunities committees have had to operate within a deeply macho political and organisational culture (Kelly 1995). Many officers appointed to women's initiatives in the early days were 'outsiders' and found themselves floundering in the unfamiliar and unfriendly structures of local authority bureaucracy.

However, despite real tensions and difficulties, there has been a steady growth of women's and equal opportunities initiatives in Scotland, which may be contrasted with the position in England and Wales where development has been more uneven (Lovenduski and Randall 1993). Julia Edwards in her examination of local authority women's committees notes the 'cohesiveness' of Scottish local government women's committees in contrast to those in England (1995: 58). In Scotland there is cautious optimism. Women's committees in Scotland are seen as having had a limited but marked impact as agents of change and, in the case of Edinburgh, as succeeding in challenging and changing the ethos of the authority (Kelly 1992, 1995; Breitenbach 1995). (For further discussion of women's committees see the introduction to this collection.)

Edinburgh District Council had been led by a progressive Labour Left administration since 1984. Women were visible as both councillors and officers within the authority. Edinburgh District Council has had a women's committee, with specialist staff, in place since 1985, and the administration remained committed to an equality agenda. Key support for Zero Tolerance was maintained by the Labour leadership – Mark Lazarowicz when the campaign was first launched, and then Lesley Hinds from her election as council leader in 1993.

Edinburgh District Council's Women's Committee was set up in 1985. It is one of several proactive or radical model committees in Scotland, and is commonly recognised as one of the most innovative. Ellen Kelly, women's unit policy officer at Edinburgh since 1987, notes that EDC learned lessons from the GLC women's committee, in particular it has become skilled at producing alternative information and publicity about its work to counter media attacks.[6] In addition, it has established and maintained good communications with women's groups and community groups. Kelly argues that these lessons have both informed the committees' work and supported them in tackling political, organisational and media resistance to change. She suggests these links may also have contributed to the survival of the women's committee (Kelly 1995: 116).[7]

By the time EDC women's unit launched Zero Tolerance, it had developed strategies of popular consultation and had strong, well-rooted links with women in the community and with women's groups. In addition, unlike the experience of some other women's units, especially in the 1980s, it had become successfully established within the political and organisational structures of the authority, and it was staffed by officers experienced both in local government and in campaigning work.

– Women's networking –

The Zero Tolerance campaign also took place against a backdrop of extensive formal and informal networking and exchanges of information amongst women's groups in Scotland. Networking between women's groups is well established in Scotland, facilitated by both geographical size and also the marked mobilisation of a wide cross-section of women, partisan and non-partisan, feminist and non-feminist, around the issue of women's representation in the proposed Scottish Parliament (see Breitenbach and Brown in this volume). Generally good relationships exist between women's groups and women's and equalities structures in Scotland. Several key activists in the women's refuge and rape crisis movement are now Labour councillors. In other cases, existing councillors from all parties have subsequently become involved in anti-violence work or campaigning.

Therefore the campaign originated in an environment where there were structures in place; where there was extensive networking and exchanges of information between women's groups; and where there was experience of working in loose alliance around specific issues. Indeed, the existence of women's networks has been an important factor, not only as a supportive and enabling context, but also because of the key role they played in the dissemination and progress of the campaign throughout Scotland and Britain. For example, the campaign is supported and promoted in local authorities throughout Britain by the alliance of women's committees, the Women's Local Authority Network (WLAN).

– Public support –

The scale of public support for the campaign was far beyond the expectations of the campaign team and served to strengthen the women's committee's claim to speak for ordinary women's concerns. This support bolstered any 'wobbles' in the construction and maintenance of political consensus. It also indicated a changed political and social context in which violence is discussed, arguably as a result of the groundwork of the women's movement in raising the issues, and the possible diffusion of some feminist values into popular culture, including a greater willingness by women to 'break the silence'. The Zero Tolerance campaign tapped a wellspring of support and recognition from women in the community, and also women in local authorities: officers, workers and councillors. In the first few months of the Edinburgh campaign, the unit received hundreds of letters and phonecalls from women. Campaign workers in all participating authorities reported that they have been overwhelmed by the support of women.

The Edinburgh evaluation exercise found that although support for the campaign was generally high, it was gendered. Women were markedly more supportive of the campaign than men. In addition, women's support tended to be more active and they were knowledgeable about the issues.[8] Both Zero Tolerance campaigners and the Edinburgh evaluation exercise found that women were more accepting of the Zero Tolerance statistics about violence than were men, and that a major reason for accepting or rejecting the statistics lay in people's personal experience or their knowledge of friends or relatives with personal experience.

> Those who had friends they knew had been raped, battered or abused were more likely to accept the figures than those who believed that they did not know anyone who had been physically or sexually assaulted. (Kitzinger and Hunt 1993: 10)

Many women who had experienced violence and sexual abuse welcomed the campaign. Participants in the evaluation focus groups said Zero Tolerance posters made them feel less isolated and made them feel better able to deal with past experiences and instances of continuing violence. 'They complained it was *silence* which was the problem – not being confronted with unpleasant facts' (Kitzinger and Hunt 1993: 25).

To summarise, therefore, in the case of the Zero Tolerance campaign, a number of enabling factors existed at both Scottish and local level. These contexts worked to make space for feminists to create and implement initiatives; they also provided crucial support networks.

– INITIAL MANAGEMENT OF THE CAMPAIGN –

The success of Zero Tolerance can also be attributed to the initial management of the campaign by the Edinburgh team. There was an anticipation that there would be a backlash – based on both theory and practice. Therefore extensive steps were taken to minimise and manage the backlash – and conversely to work to build and maintain support and legitimacy for the campaign. In addition, the campaign team sought to prevent any dilution of the message by retaining control over the definition of the issue, and the development of materials. The campaign was legitimised by strategies of popular consultation and targeted research, as discussed earlier. The strength of the campaign came from EDC Women's Committee's authority to speak for 'ordinary women'. This is a feature and a strength of women's committees and equal opportunities committees who have, in many cases, pioneered and developed effective strategies of popular consultation.

The expertise and experience of specialist women's groups like Scottish Women's Aid (SWA), Edinburgh Rape Crisis Centre (ERC) and Mothers of Sexually Abused Children (MOSAC) was also recognised and they were consulted about the material. In addition, a relatively long period of time, some six months, was spent pre-launch in lobbying in order to build up a broad consensus of support for the issue from key political, civic, religious and community groups. The campaign secured advance support from various notable agencies and opinion-leaders, including Lothian and Borders Police and all the main churches and, crucially, the local media. The city's evening paper, the *Edinburgh Evening News*, adopted the issue and ran its own 'Free Us From Fear' campaign in parallel with Zero Tolerance, with feature and news articles on each of the issues addressed by the posters.

In addition, cross-party political support was secured within the authority, but again the detailed content of the campaign was not discussed. Apart from the convener of the Women's Committee, no other politicians saw the material prior to the launch. This was a conscious strategy by the officers, who were clear that they needed to keep the campaign under wraps until the launch to prevent the radical message being diluted. They argued from the experience of other women's groups and women's committee campaigns that issues tended to be modified or diluted.

– THE SUPPORT OF WOMEN COUNCILLORS –

Although women councillors in Scotland do not generally identify themselves as feminist, many are 'pro-equality' and do act as agents or supporters of change (Kelly 1992). For example, in the current study women councillors from different political parties showed high levels of awareness of women's groups and women's issues. Furthermore, some 83% had aims which they perceived as relevant to women, and 49% saw themselves as representing women.

Perhaps the most striking evidence of common interests and understanding around issues of violence has been in the crucial political support for Zero Tolerance from women councillors, both feminist and non-feminist, across all four authorities studied. Support for the campaign was also cross-party. For example, in Edinburgh one of the key supporters of the campaign has been a Conservative woman councillor and former Conservative group leader who commented that she has discovered that the quickest way to clear a space around oneself at a cocktail party is to raise Zero Tolerance.

It has caused quite a few ruffles among men and women in all political parties, because it is an uncomfortable thing to be faced with . . . . I think the campaign has done a very good job in raising public awareness and in causing debate and controversy . . . I have consistently opposed the sort of loony elements of women's committee spending and thinking in this council . . . but this is something that I wholeheartedly support, because unless you have the image-raising of the issues then you will not get action. (Con.)

The Zero Tolerance campaign was able to tap into parallel debates within women's circles in the Scottish Conservative party around violence against women, in particular erratic sentencing policies for convicted rapists and sex attackers. 'Judy', a prominent party activist, put violence against women firmly on the Scottish Conservative political agenda after a remarkable speech she made to the Scottish Conservative Party Conference in May 1993. She spoke of her ordeal after being attacked by a bogus priest in her Edinburgh home. She attacked the judiciary who reduced her attacker's life sentence to six years on appeal and called for sweeping reforms, including the recruitment of more women judges.[9] Several female Conservative councillors, including EDC councillors, were involved in the back-stage manoeuvrings which brought 'Judy's' story to the Scottish Conservative Party Conference. They used EDC women's unit briefings and Zero Tolerance statistics to prepare their cases.

More than half the women councillors interviewed rated Zero Tolerance and/or issues of violence as important on their personal political agendas. A further third saw the issue as quite important and only three viewed it as of little or no importance. There were high levels of support for the initiative from women councillors across party. Many critics of women's committees cited it as 'the best thing the women's committee has ever done'.

This is not to say, however, that there was unconditional support for the campaign. Not all women shared the feminist analysis of violence as a male abuse of power. Some, particularly Conservative women, favoured a stress upon protection and reform of sentencing policy for sex offenders. Others would have preferred an emphasis on providing women with information about rights and resources. However, the Zero Tolerance campaign was, in general, seen to be concerned with too important an issue to let women's reservations about its analysis or 'emphasis' prevent them from giving their support. Women who made criticisms of some aspects of the campaign also gave praise. Even the most vocal female critic of Zero Tolerance, a Conservative councillor at Edinburgh, made it clear that she supported the *principle* of the campaign, although she objected strongly to its 'radical feminist' emphasis in practice.

There was a striking determination shared by women across party and across generation that the issues of violence, sexual violence and sexual abuse should be 'out in the open'. In a clear parallel to the feminist approach of 'refusing to keep men's secrets', women councillors saw the Zero Tolerance campaign as part of an ongoing process of making violence and abuse visible. There was also widespread understanding of the scale and prevalence of violence against women.

> There's no doubt whatsoever that an awful lot of women have been subjected to appalling violence. I wasn't aware of the scale of it until I became a councillor. (Lab.)

> I think it is probably a lot larger and a lot deeper than the average person thinks. Perhaps people like myself . . . women that are involved – they probably realise it is on a fairly wide scale . . . and I think the most deadly aspect to me is the violence in the home. It needn't be somebody thumping somebody, it can be far more subtle than that: bullying and mental bullying and all sorts of more subtle things. (Con.)

> The under the carpet approach, when it was never talked about, is thankfully now being shed and people are becoming more able and willing to talk about the experience. I have a horrible feeling that we're still only at the surface and there's a heck of a lot more icebergs still under the water – and it worries me a bit that our society is in such a state. (SNP)

As noted earlier, the evaluation exercise showed that women were more likely than men to accept statistics indicating a high prevalence of violence and abuse, and that people in general were more likely to accept figures if they had experienced violence or had knowledge of others' experience. Many women interviewees had knowledge of the issues through their work as councillors. District councillors, in particular, saw themselves at 'the sharp end' through their responsibility for dealing with housing matters.

> It's the *normality* of it all. In my ward, there's a woman in her fifties who walks with a limp. I asked her, did she fall? 'Och no, it's him, he used to beat me up a lot – all my life. He's getting too aul' now so he disnae hit me ony more'. This goes on. (Lab.)

> I feel [domestic violence] is something women don't admit to. The few cases I have seen could be the tip of the iceberg. Also I'm sitting here in my cosy suburb, where it will be different to some inner city wards. I don't *think* it's widespread in my ward – having said that, the ones I have dealt with I've dealt with only because of housing queries – they've needed to be rehoused or whatever – so they've *had* to say something, otherwise I think they wouldn't. (Lib. Dem.)

As a result, women councillors argued that that violence against women was a massive problem which was hidden and under-reported. However, not all reaction was entirely sympathetic – a small number of women were impatient that women 'kept going back' into abusive situations.

> I'm sure this is controversial if I say to you that I have been appalled by the weakness of women – because we have helped people and gone out of our way and done everything physically possible and then the wife still goes back to the husband. Now, I cannot understand that. (Lib. Dem.)

Other councillors had experience of dealing with issues of violence through other work or counselling activities. One SNP councillor spoke about her work as a medical social worker counselling women survivors of child sexual abuse: 'I have spent hours trying to convince a woman that she was in no way guilty as a child.' A number of councillors spoke about their campaigning work within trade unions, writing and speaking to resolutions against violence against women.

> Working with so many women – you are always aware of the different violences that are projected on women. (Lab.)

Refuge and rape crisis groups have long recognised the potential of lobbying elected women members to support their work. A number of women had become involved in the field as a result of such approaches. A Liberal Democrat councillor discussed her response to a lobby by women's aid campaigners in her area.

> I became a member of Women's Aid and a full working member of that because I felt I needed the knowledge and I needed the experience and . . . if I was going to argue their case for funding – I had to know what I was talking about. And that probably was the one thing I felt that being a female – there's tremendous responsibility because I was a woman and I thought it's not me I'm letting down here, it's everybody else if I don't get this right. (Lib. Dem.)

A majority of women councillors had personal experience of violence, including sexual assault and sexual abuse, or knowledge of close friends and relatives who had been assaulted or abused, and as such felt a connection with other women. A number of women said they doubted that any woman could avoid the experience of violence or abuse of some description at some time of their lives.[10]

> I think every woman has had some experience of either sexual assault or whatever or [been] attacked or beaten up. I think if you speak to every woman – people always seem quite shocked by the statistics – but then, if you actually think about your own experiences and speak to other women, then you realise

the statistics are probably underestimated. People tend not to speak about it, tend to sort of say 'well, it was my fault 'or 'I'll take that down to experience and I'll move on' . . . and they don't ever report things and they don't ever speak about it. So I think one of the good things is [Zero Tolerance] actually brought people out to speak about the issue. (Anon)

As a result women politicians, in common with women in the Edinburgh evaluation exercise, felt that one of the most important roles for the Zero Tolerance campaign was to 'break the silence'.

There was sexual abuse when I was a kid . . . That's made Zero Tolerance so important to me. I blame that [the abuse] for a lot of things, maybe that's why my marriage didn't last. I have now got grand-daughters and that fear is still there . . . It really was a stigma before, now with this Zero Tolerance – it's really giving women the opportunity to get it off their chests because until such time as they do . . . I used to make myself ill when I was younger, I had nobody to talk to. (Anon)

Only one woman argued that the campaign should not be undertaken because it would increase councillors' workloads.

It's just going to give us more work – towards that sort of problem and we really cannot handle any more, we're not there as *counsellors* . . . I don't know about the rest of them, but I certainly don't like dealing with that sort of thing, I'm more interested in planning. (Lib. Dem.)

_ WOMEN COUNCILLORS' SUPPORT FOR ZERO TOLERANCE: _ 'A SORT OF SOLIDARITY'

Women understand. We may differ politically . . . one thing is we're all female; we all experience the same problems to a certain extent. Your financial position doesn't alter the fact that you're a woman . . . or how you're treated by men so I suppose that does lead to *a sort of solidarity*. (Lab.)

Being a woman colours everything. (Con.)

Women councillors gave their support in a number of ways. They worked with women officers and with activists within their own parties to push the campaign in their areas. Several women councillors in participating authorities have publicly spoken about their own experience of violence and there is some evidence that male politicians who were generally sceptical about the prevalence of violence, or were uncertain about the campaign, have changed their minds as a result of these disclosures.

In the case of one of the authorities in the current study, resistance to the proposed campaign within the Labour group evaporated when a woman councillor disclosed her experience of sexual abuse as a child. The woman, who had never spoken about her experience in a large mixed group before, made an on-the-spot decision to speak out after male colleagues began talking over the Zero Tolerance presentations being made to a crucial Labour group meeting and the safe passage of the initiative as Labour group policy looked uncertain. After her disclosure the campaign was adopted as policy with no objections.

Personal testimony has been a characteristic feature of feminist politics and feminist strategy, especially in issues of the body, for instance abortion campaigning. However, there is evidence that this process has taken place on a large scale in areas where Zero Tolerance has been adopted; from straw polls in offices and pubs, to difficult personal disclosures by public figures. The validity of personal experience has, it appears, been taken on board by women, who would not call themselves feminists, in a variety of social, organisational and political settings. There is also evidence that public disclosures have encouraged other women to speak out, sometimes for the first time.

Another major way in which women councillors progressed the Zero Tolerance campaign was in lobbying their male colleagues. They did this in the initial stages to secure support and, as an ongoing process, they maintained the momentum by discussing and defending the campaign from criticisms, especially the charge that the campaign was 'anti-male' and that it's message was that 'all men are rapists'. This work has been important in defusing potential resistance and backlash as well as in demonstrating the 'sort of solidarity' that women felt about the issue.

> It is a continuous process of re-education. This message is a positive one. It is not doing men down. If you like, it is trying to bring out the best in men: the feminine qualities in men; the caring qualities in men; and letting them see that rape isn't funny in any circumstances. But you don't get these lessons across in one session – you have to sustain them and reinforce them, and you have to keep going. You know, it is not a one-off. (Con.)

> I've heard the attitudes of one or two of them [male councillors] saying: 'That's normal – you give them a belt around the ear.' They don't think there's anything wrong – but I see a change in them. They're becoming more aware – I think Zero Tolerance is working to educate male councillors. (Lab.)

Although there was no direct confirmation from Conservative women themselves, a number of Labour women and specialist officers interviewed believed that Conservative women in participating authorities had 'kept the men in line' in their party groups.

The picture formed from the interviews is that women have worked hard at defusing opposition from male colleagues – but that they have also challenged the 'blandness' of men's attitudes on a political and social level.

The fact that it has caused some people to get really angry has been useful . . . people saying, 'This is ridiculous you're labelling all men as this and that'. It has caused a degree of discussion which is actually quite important because there is a lot of *blandness* around – a lot of, 'Oh, yes violence against women is a dreadful thing', because nobody would actually say it was a good thing! . . . The tendency politically is that, you may have had a resolution passed saying how dreadful it was and nobody opposes it, so it never gets discussed. And that's not necessarily a good thing – the crucial things aren't actually being addressed. (Lab.)

Some of the guys here are really miffed because they think the Zero Tolerance campaign adverts are – they're upset at them and I said: 'Well, what you have to do is to start thinking about your own attitudes – OK you're not involved in that but we cannae apologise because you're not involved in it. It's *happening*, other guys are doing this – it's happening to women and what you have to say when your pals or your brothers or your cousins or whatever or you're in the pub and people come away with something particularly offensive involving violence in a joke – or they say, "What she needs is a right smack in the mouth", that sort of thing – challenge them on it. That's all we're saying you should be doing. Don't get mad at us, get mad at them, they're the ones who have made us have to do the campaign in the first place.' (Lab.)

The degree and form of women's support has varied widely. A small number of women have been proactive agents of change, closely involved with the campaign. They pushed it on to agendas, have spoken at meetings and have worked closely with women's officers. Others, whilst not involved at the agenda-setting stage of the campaign, have been active in keeping the campaign on track; they have had input into policy development, have encouraged and worked in local groups; they have also intervened in promoting the campaign in departments where officers have resisted. Others have been supportive in smaller ways, displaying Zero Tolerance car stickers and badges. Another important way that women politicians have supported the campaign has been in their almost unanimous refusal to be drawn into public criticism of the campaign or to join in any attempted backlash.

This analysis of the importance and pattern of support is tentative and is based upon women politicians' perceptions which were sometimes at variance with other key actors. Not all women councillors were even minimally proactive; a few were complacent. However, in general, what these local politicians did *not* do was to trivialise, minimise or deny the problem of violence against women and children. It may be this display of a minimal level of solidarity which may have prevented a build-up of backlash. This support indicates not only the personal and political salience of the issue for the women councillors themselves but also a recognition of its significance to women in the community. In addition, it also illustrates the marked change in the social context in which issues of violence are discussed and a possible diffusion of feminist values into the cultural mainstream.

Initial findings indicate that high levels of legitimacy were given to the campaign by women councillors across parties. About three-quarters of the interviewees in the current study discussed whether they thought Zero Tolerance and similar campaigns were a legitimate function of local government. The question had been designed to allow women to express opposition to the campaign without being identified as 'pro-violence'. However, all but a few argued that this issue was indeed a legitimate part of local politics.

> We're representing a huge amount of people so therefore we have to represent their rights – and anything that is going to enhance their lives, we have to look at and that sort of issue has to be raised, and that sort of issue has to be looked at it can't stay hidden under the carpet or behind doors – and that's where it was. (SNP)

> Over half the electorate in the City of Edinburgh are women and at the moment it is not safe for women to go out, dressed however they wish, whatever time of day or night in all parts of our city without being in danger of sexual attack. And I think it is perfectly legitimate for civic leaders to be trying to create an environment in which they can do all these things . . . There is still, in this city, a view among some men that a girl walking across The Meadows at 2 o'clock in the morning, wearing a mini-skirt, is quotes 'asking for it' close-quotes. That is very wrong and that actually creates an atmosphere which tolerates attacks on women and I think it is part of our job to change that. (Con.)

Furthermore, women councillors, both feminist and non-feminist, appeared to be becoming increasingly convinced that their presence makes a difference in terms of the promotion of women's interests. In the current study, 93% of the women councillors interviewed believed that the campaign would definitely not or was unlikely to have happened without the existence of an equalities structure; 89% believed it would not or it was unlikely to have happened without the presence of elected women members.

> I doubt it – I can't see any man grasping that particular nettle. (Con.)

> It would be light years away because lots of men wouldn't accept that there *is* violence. (Lab.)

This would seem to indicate a greater sense of the acceptance of gender and equalities issues as legitimate across parties within local government than has generally been argued. It also supports the view that the presence of women councillors in sufficient numbers is significant in terms of both the promotion of women's interests and the definition of politics as broader than traditional conceptions.

_ CONCLUSIONS: TOWARDS CONVERGENCE – A WOMEN'S _ AGENDA?

The Zero Tolerance campaign reflected the shared values of feminists within the state and the women's movement. There was a shared definition of violence as an abuse of the power that men are accorded in present social structures. In evaluations and other research this naming of men and the analysis of violence as an abuse of power have proved the most challenging and controversial aspects of the campaign. There was a shared understanding of the links between all forms of violence and sexual coercion, for example, domestic violence, child sex abuse and rape. There was also concern to 'name' emotional and psychological abuse as forms of violence and to place them along a continuum of violence.

Although Women's Aid, Rape Crisis and other women's support groups did not 'own' the campaign, their definition of the issue was shared by the women with power – the femocrats – within the policy community. Uniquely, the issue was not given to politicians or senior managers for definition or negotiation. The existence of a full-time campaigns officer in the Women's Unit meant that, in this instance, the policy community was the women's unit and women's movement groups were 'insiders'. This was in marked contrast to the experience of women's groups in the run-up to the Scottish Office campaign where, although they were included in the policy process, they were unable to shape the agenda. Furthermore, the Scottish Office was able to flag their involvement in the working party as evidence of consultation and co-operation, despite their substantive reservations about the campaign.

Support for the Zero Tolerance campaign by Women's Aid, Rape Crisis and other women's support groups has remained largely firm, despite increased pressure on their services. They have been active and proactive in developing Zero Tolerance and have taken the lead in developing materials and organising seminars and conferences. This is in contrast to received wisdom that the women's movement's relationship with the state and women's initiatives within the state are likely to be characterised by ambivalence, suspicion and disappointment. Despite increased workloads and as yet little pay-off in the shape of increased resources, women's groups have taken a long-term view that the Zero Tolerance campaign will provide them with leverage to press for adequate funding, and has shifted the focus of public perception about the issue from one of social welfare to one of political concern. As such, the case study would suggest a convergence between the agendas of feminist activists and 'municipal' feminists.

Evidence from the study suggests that feminists may be gaining some leverage from their intervention in the state, through women's committees and women's units, to control and define certain issues. This underlines the importance of the creation and maintenance of reasonably strong and integrated women's or equal opportunities structures in order to provide both the space and the initiatives for promoting change, and suggests that women's committees can act as proactive agents of feminist change. The women's committee at Edinburgh was mature in terms of its structure, staffing, support and resources. It had learned lessons from the early history of women's initiatives, particularly skills of political manage-ment and the construction of legitimacy via consultation with women in the community and autonomous women's groups. Indeed, all the participating authorities running Zero Tolerance have women's or equalities structures in place (although in one case, Strathclyde, it has only the status of an advisory group). In addition, all the participating authorities have had at least one specialist officer in post who has liaised through a Zero Tolerance officers' network, part of the established Scottish Women's and Equal Opportunities Officers' Forum (SWEOF).

Alliances of women specialist officers, other women officers, women coun-cillors, activists in the women's movement, the trade union movement, political parties and voluntary and public service sectors have been instrumental in getting Zero Tolerance over any overt 'wobbles' and covert resistance. They have ensured the continued high profile of the campaign in Edinburgh and have, in different configurations, ensured that the campaign has been adopted and progressed by other authorities throughout Scotland (and Britain).

The massive support which characterised the Zero Tolerance campaign illustrates the salience of the issue of gender violence for women in general, and a possible diffusion of feminist values which has changed the social and political context in which violence against women is discussed. It would appear that feminism has been successful in revealing the political nature of so-called women's issues such as violence, and that many women politicians now share these newer definitions of what constitutes 'proper' politics. This is underlined by the findings of the study, where there was consensus amongst female politicians across party, generation and degree of gender consciousness that tackling such issues and taking a moral lead were a legitimate part of local government. It also underlines the significance of the presence of women in politics, both feminist and non-feminist, for the articulation and promotion of women's concerns. The case study suggests violence is an issue around which women, political and non-political, feminist and non-feminist, can work together. Finally, the evidence tentatively suggests the existence of an emerging 'women's politics', a broad-based woman's politics which crosses traditional boundaries and where women as women are successfully intervening in the local state and making a difference.

– NOTES –

1. Source: Edinburgh District Council's Women's Unit, March 1995.
2. A study of four Scottish local authorities participating in the Zero Tolerance initiative was conducted between March 1994 and February 1995. Evidence is drawn from three sets of data: in-depth semi-structured interviews with 53 women councillors; briefings with specialist staff, conveners of women's and/or equal opportunities committees and other key informants in political parties and women's advocacy groups; and a documentary review, including council minutes and policy documents, Zero Tolerance campaign literature, and reports of the campaign in assorted media. Material used in this chapter focuses upon women councillors' involvement with, and attitudes towards, the Zero Tolerance campaign.
3. On 6 December 1989, 14 young female engineering students were murdered in Montreal, Canada, by a young man who wanted to kill 'those damned feminists'. The 'Montreal Massacre' was the catalyst which spurred the Canadian Federal Government into taking action to end violence against women. On 10 February 1991, the Government announced a four-year Family Violence Initiative with funding of 136 million dollars, which was implemented from January 1993. It builds upon provincial, municipal and grassroots initiatives, notably in Ontario, where work has been carried out since 1983. (Zero Tolerance Briefing paper, 'Canadian Initiatives on Violence Against Women', 'Making Z-Way': Ayrshire Zero Tolerance Conference, 6 March 1995). Since 1992, Ontario has run a public awareness campaign as part of their Sexual Assault Prevention campaign, involving TV, radio and press advertisements, posters, badges and other promotional materials. They have also run a public education campaign aimed at 'wife assault prevention' (Westmount Research Consultants Inc, 1992, cited by Kitzinger and Hunt 1993).
4. The phrase 'Zero Tolerance' was drawn out of the Canadian literature and headlined by the Edinburgh team. The 'Z' logo was designed by freelance designer Franki Raffles.
5. The campaign received a major blow with the death of the creator and designer of Zero Tolerance, photographer Franki Raffles, who died suddenly on 6 December 1994 shortly after giving birth to twin girls.
6. It is not immune to hostile media coverage. For example, the so-called 'Condomgate' incident in March 1992, when a Conservative woman councillor caused a political and media storm by producing what she alleged were used condoms found after a party in the City Chambers to celebrate International Women's Day. The media responded with headlines such as 'Sin City Chambers: Orgy Outrage over Used Condoms' (Daily Record, 9 March 1992). The Chief Executive launched an inquiry and the 'evidence' was sent off to the public analyst where they were duly found to contain nothing but carpet dust ('Orgy Claim Missed Target', Edinburgh Evening News, 27 March 1992). See extensive coverage between 9 March and 27 March 1992 in the Edinburgh Evening News, Herald, The Scotsman, Scottish Sun and Daily Record.

7. Post-reorganisation, the City of Edinburgh Council's Women's Committee remained the only stand-alone women's committee in Scotland.
8. In the street survey, 86% of women felt 'positive' or 'very positive' about the campaign compared with 68% of men (Kitzinger and Hunt, 1993: Table 4a).
9. *The Scotsman*, 15 May 1993.
10. Twenty-five women (out of 53) said they had experienced violence, sexual violence or sexual abuse; three others specified that they had experienced sexual harassment. Two women did not answer the question. Of those who said they had no personal experience: four had family members or friends who had experienced violence; 13 had experience of dealing with victims of violence through their work or as councillors. In total 42 out of 53 councillors had direct or indirect experience of violence, sexual violence or sexual abuse. Quotations concerning women councillors' personal experiences of violence are anonymous.

– REFERENCES –

Barrett, Michèle (1987), 'The Concept of "Difference", *Feminist Review*, 26.

Blake Stevenson (1990), *Women's Consultation Exercise*, Edinburgh: Edinburgh District Council Women's Committee.

Boneparth, E. and E. Soper (eds) (1988), *Women, Policy and Power: Toward the Year 2000*, Oxford: Pergamon Press.

Breitenbach, Esther (1990) '"Sisters are doing it for themselves": The Women's Movement in Scotland', in Alice Brown and Richard Parry (eds) *The Scottish Government Yearbook 1990*, Edinburgh: Unit for the Study of Government in Scotland, University of Edinburgh.

Breitenbach, Esther (1995), *Quality through Equality: Good Practice in Equal Opportunities in Scottish Local Authorities*, Glasgow: Equal Opportunities Commission.

Breitenbach, Esther (1996), 'The Women's Movement in Scotland in the 1990s', *New Waverley Papers*, Edinburgh: Department of Politics, University of Edinburgh.

Brown, Alice (1995a), 'Plans for a Scottish Parliament: Did Women Make a Difference?', in *Waverley Papers*, Edinburgh: Department of Politics, University of Edinburgh.

Brown, Alice (1995b), *In the Name of Democracy: The Fight for Equal Representation in Scotland*, paper presented to Political Studies Association Conference, York, April.

Brown, Alice (1995c), 'The Scotswoman's Parliament', *Parliamentary Brief*, April.

Brown, Alice (1996), 'Women and Scottish Politics', in Alice Brown, David McCrone and Lindsay Paterson, *Politics and Society in Scotland*, Basingstoke: Macmillan.

Burness, Catriona (1995), 'Will Scotland lead the way for Women?' in *Parliamentary Brief*, March.

Carroll, Susan (1992), 'Women State Legislators, Women's Organizations, and the Representation of Women's Culture in the United States' in Jill Bystydzienski (ed.) *Women Transforming Politics*, Bloomington, IN: Indiana University Press.

Coote, A. and P. Patullo (1990), *Power And Prejudice: Women And Politics*, London: Weidenfeld and Nicolson.

Dahlerup, D. (1988), 'From a small to a large minority: Women in Scandinavian Politics', *Scandinavian Political Studies*, 11, (4).

Edwards, J. (1995), *Local Government Women's Committees*, Aldershot: Avebury.

Engender (1995), *Gender Audit 1995*, Edinburgh: Engender.

Falchikov, N. (1992), *Adolescents' knowledge about, and attitudes to Domestic Violence, summary findings*, report to the Women's Committee Unit, Edinburgh District Council.

Firestone, Shulamith (1972), *Dialectics of Sex: The Case For Feminist Revolution*, London: Paladin.

Gelb, J and M. L. Palley (1987), *Women and Public Policies*, Princeton, NJ: Princeton University Press.

Haavio-Mannila, E. et al. (eds) (1985), *Unfinished Democracy: Women in Nordic Politics*, Oxford: Pergammon Press.

Halford, Susan (1988), 'Women's initiatives in Local Government: Where do they come from and where are they going?', *Policy and Politics*, 16 (4).

Hedlund, Gun (1988), 'Women's Interests in Local Politics' in K. Jones and A. Jonasdottir (eds) *The Political Interests of Gender*, London: Sage.

Kelly, Ellen (1992), 'The Future of Women in Scottish Local Government', *Scottish Affairs*, 1, Autumn.

Kelly, Ellen (1995, unpublished), 'Sweeties from the Boys' Poke?': An Examination of Women's Committees in Scottish Local Government, MSc dissertation, Glasgow: University of Strathclyde.

Kelly, Liz (1988), *Surviving Sexual Violence*, Cambridge: Polity Press.

Kelly, Liz, Sheila Burton and Linda Regan (1994), *Beyond Victim or Survivor: Sexual Violence, Identity and Feminist Theory and Practice*, paper presented to the British Sociological Association Conference, Preston, April.

Kitzinger, J. and K. Hunt (1993), *Evaluation of Edinburgh District Council's Zero Tolerance Campaign: Full Report*, Edinburgh: Glasgow University Media Group/Edinburgh District Council's Women's Committee.

Lieberman, Sue (1989), 'Women's Committees in Scotland', in Alice Brown and David McCrone (eds) *The Scottish Government Yearbook 1989*, Edinburgh: Unit for the Study of Government in Scotland, University of Edinburgh.

Lovenduski, J. and V. Randall (1993), *Contemporary Feminist Politics: Women and Power in Britain*, Oxford: Oxford University Press.

Randall, V. (1987), *Women and Politics* (2nd Edition), Basingstoke: Macmillan.

Randall, V. (1992), 'Great Britain and Dilemmas for Feminist Strategy in the 1980's' in Jill Bystydzienski (ed.) *Women Transforming Politics*, Bloomington, IN: Indiana University Press.

Riddoch, Lesley (1994), 'Zero Tolerance: the Second Wave', *Harpies & Quines*, No. 12, March.

Young, K. (1990), 'Approaches to Policy Development in the Field of Equal Opportunities' in W. Ball and J. Solomos (eds) *Race and Local Politics*, Basingstoke: Macmillan.

Zero Tolerance (1995), Briefing papers, 'Canadian Initiatives on Violence Against Women', 'Making Z-Way': Ayrshire Zero Tolerance Conference, 6 March.

Chapter 10

No Man has the Right

Katie Cosgrove

'No Man has the Right', in Chris Corrin (ed.) (1996) *Women in a Violent World*, Edinburgh: Edinburgh University Press.

> Has woman a right to herself? It is very little to me to have the right to vote, to own property, etc. if I may not keep my body and its uses in my absolute right.
> (Lucy Stone in a letter to Antoinette Brown, 11 July 1885)[1]

Feminists have long since been aware of the extent of male violence against women, and understood its significance in our continuing subordination. Locating this abuse within the context of structural inequality, we have identified its role as a key mechanism in the exercise of male power and control over women.

In recent years there has been an increasing awareness of the scale of the problem. The UK Government in its response to the Home Affairs Committee stated that:

> Domestic violence is pervasive. Throughout society, many people, predominantly women, are at risk of attack in their homes from their spouses and partners, both current and former. The Government is entirely convinced that domestic violence must be tackled vigorously and that it must be treated as a crime. (Government Reply to the Third Report from the Home Affairs Select Committee, June 1993)

Research on the prevalence of this violence has shown consistently high levels of abuse. The National Working Party Report on Domestic Violence observed that this is more common than violence in the street, pub, or workplace (National Inter-Agency Working Party Report on Domestic Violence, July 1992). Accompanying this is the recognition that violence against women is a grossly under-reported crime. A local survey in Glasgow in 1989 by the Women's Support Project and the local newspaper found that 52% of the 1503 respondents had experienced some form of male abuse, and that relatively few had reported this officially.[2]

As the body of empirical evidence on this violence grows, there is a parallel acknowledgement of the inter-relationship between the different ways in which men abuse, and the realisation that this can only make sense if we understand the continuum of male violence it represents and why it occurs.

Accepting this, however, means accepting its concomitant: that women are more likely to be abused by men known to them than by strangers. Against all the received wisdom on the risks we face in relation to our personal safety, we have to confront the reality that the home is the least safe place for women, not the streets. This is more difficult to address, for it means that our safety is not dependent on obeying exhortations to restrict our freedom of movement, lifestyle, dress code. It also means that we have to look more searchingly at the relationships we have built with men, and the specious notion of protection which these have afforded us.

Whilst there is undoubtedly more information, it persists in being a largely hidden problem. Thousands of women continue to experience abuse in silence. Against a backdrop of political indifference, cultural acceptance, and social legitimacy it is still marginalised and dismissed. In recent years the Zero Tolerance campaign has made a major contribution to the process of changing this in Scotland. Its high profile and unswerving commitment to highlighting this issue has created a forum for discussion and debate, and a focus around which initiatives to tackle the problem can coalesce. It has been, and still is, a catalyst for action. Born from consultation with women's groups and organisations, it has established the parameters for the debate on male violence within a feminist ideological and philosophical framework, yet has done so also from within the framework of local authority structures and priorities.

The success of the Zero Tolerance campaign is the focus for this chapter. In the space of three years it has been launched by thirteen councils/local authorities. It has achieved international acclaim, and has recently been adopted by the Health Authority in South East Australia. In looking at its content and implementation in Strathclyde, I hope to explore the context within which this has occurred, and how this success can be understood as a paradigm for future campaigns and initiatives on male violence.

– BACKGROUND TO THE CAMPAIGN –

The Zero Tolerance campaign is essentially a crime prevention initiative which tackles the issue of male violence against women. It was first launched in November 1992 by Edinburgh District Council's Women's Committee. Initially designed to highlight the nature and extent of this abuse, it used a series of four posters to focus on its most common forms – domestic violence, rape/sexual assault and child sexual abuse – and to link these with the unifying theme that no man, irrespective of his relationship with a woman or child, has the right to abuse them. It sent out a clear and unequivocal message that there is no acceptable level of male violence.

The campaign was created by two women: Evelyn Gillan, then Women's Officer at Edinburgh District Council, and Franki Raffles[3], a freelance photographer and designer. The impetus for the campaign came from the results of a consultation exercise carried out with women in the city during which they identified the threat of male violence as an issue of concern. Coupled with this were the findings of research conducted in Edinburgh schools which sought to clarify the perceptions and views of adolescent students towards this problem in society, and which showed that:

- boys, some as young as twelve years old, were more accepting of violence against women than girls;
- boys and girls found violence more acceptable if the perpetrator was married to the victim; and
- the majority of young people interviewed expressed some likelihood of using violence in future relationships.

– AIMS AND OBJECTIVES –

The primary objectives of the first stage of the campaign were identified as:

1. Informing people of the scale of the problem.
2. Dispelling many of the myths surrounding this issue.
3. Emphasising the criminality and unacceptability of this violence.

From the outset the designers were clear about the way in which the campaign should proceed. They wanted to change societal attitudes towards male violence by making it socially unacceptable, and by challenging the norms, beliefs and values which give rise to, and sustain it. They were equally clear, however, that a public awareness campaign could not, in itself, eradicate male violence. They did not present a simplistic espousal of public education as the sole means for political and social transformation, but stressed that this could be only one component of an overall strategy for change.

They derived some inspiration from the approach of the Canadian Government which had implemented a $136 million programme to tackle this issue. The catalyst for their 'Call to Action' had been the so-called 'Montreal Massacre' – the slaying of fourteen women engineering students at a university in 1989 by a man who objected to their presence in what he considered to be a male domain, and who loudly proclaimed his virulent anti-feminism as he gunned them down.

In response, the Canadian Government devised a strategy for tackling violence against women which incorporated public education, service provision, and reforming the judicial service.

The three-pronged approach of the Zero Tolerance campaign reflects this influence, and calls for the reduction and elimination of violence towards women by:

Prevention – active prevention of crimes of violence against women and children.

Provision – adequate provision of support services for abused women and children.

Protection – appropriate legal protection for women and children suffering abuse.

– MALE ABUSE OF POWER IS A CRIME –

The campaign is explicitly informed by a feminist analysis of male violence, and articulates the irrefutable links with male domination and power in society which create, sustain and perpetuate this abuse. In drawing on the understanding of male violence as a result of structural inequality and cultural acceptance, it insists that the root causes of such violence have to be addressed if the problem is to be tackled in any meaningful way. It is clear that seeking recourse to individual and pathological explanations serves only to obscure, mislead and deny the reality of male violence, which ultimately merely assures its continuation.

Essential to the process of designing the campaign was the consultation with women's organisations, particularly Women's Aid and Rape Crisis; not only because of their role in tackling male violence, but because it was reasonable to assume that a campaign of this nature would inevitably increase the demands on their services. Given the degree to which they are presently over-stretched, this was not a minor consideration, a fact that has been borne out by the responses to Zero Tolerance. Their support and advice were crucial in developing the campaign, the centrality of which remains one of the most important features in initiatives that have such an explicitly feminist base.

The political clarity of its creators determined the fundamental precepts upon which Zero Tolerance is based, and which are indivisible from its overall aims, which are as follows.

– To illustrate the continuum of male violence –

Demonstrating the links between the different forms of male violence is pivotal to the attempts of Zero Tolerance to encourage people to view the issue in a wider context, and to see it as an abuse of power accorded men in society. In using the series of posters, and linking them together under the statement 'No Man has the Right', the campaign challenges perceptions of these as discrete problems. In the inclusion of psychological, emotional and sexual violence in the definition of abuse, it covers some of the range of abusive behaviours experienced by women. This is a crucial element in explaining the analysis underpinning the campaign, and in ensuring that it does not get subverted into a narrowly restricted debate on the issue of physical brutality. In Strathclyde[4] this has been very important, since the first stage of our campaign coincided with the launch of a campaign by the Scottish Office which dealt only with the physical aspects of domestic violence. It is essential that this definition of abuse does not prevail. For whilst people may not be comfortable discussing domestic violence or its repercussions, they do seem able to mention it without visibly flinching. Replete with difficulties though this phrase is – for example, in its gender-neutral terms, and narrow definition of abuse – it has at least been acknowledged as a growing problem. With sexual violence and child sexual abuse, however, this is less apparent.

Identifying the continuum of violence permits us to focus on why men abuse, why this violence exists on such a scale, and why the judicial sanctions which are in place to deal with it are so seldom invoked, and so seldom protect women and children.

– To empower women and challenge men –

The use of victim imagery was rejected at the outset by the designers who had no wish to provide a voyeuristic spectacle of suffering, or a vision of powerless, abused women. In contradiction to the usual portrayal of 'victims', the posters show women in their everyday lives. No bruises, no dishevelled clothing, no piteous gaze for the camera. In using indoor locations, they challenge the belief that women are most at risk from abuse by strangers in the street.

Using predominantly white, middle class images and settings, the posters depict comfort, security, warmth and 'normality'. An elegant woman perusing a magazine in her graciously appointed lounge. An elderly woman reading to a child. Nice, gentle images into which the text shockingly intrudes.

> She lives with a successful businessman, loving father and respected member of the community. Last week he hospitalised her.

> From three to ninety-three, women are raped.

Can they really have asked for it? Are they the archetypal victims? How are we to understand the abuse of these women? That is the point. There are no archetypal victims. They could be anyone. From any social class, ethnic background, age group. Logically, therefore, so too are their abusers.

The effectiveness of this iconography was noted in the evaluations of the Edinburgh and Strathclyde campaigns, as the examples from Jenny Kitzinger and Kate Hunt from Glasgow University Media Group (1993, 1995) illustrate:

It's not always a drunken bricklayer who comes home on a Friday night and beats up his wife. (Kitzinger and Hunt 1993)

Middle class men think that what they do in the house nobody knows about, and that poster displays that that's not the case. (Kitzinger 1995)

Tellingly, they portrayed women as 'people with rights'.

Even where there is opposition to the campaign it has encouraged people to reconsider their assumptions of male violence, although not always convincingly so! One man within the Regional Council, for example, protested that while it may be commendable to highlight this problem, it was 'a bit over the top' sending it to his department because he worked alongside 'educated, intelligent men'. His female colleagues did not merit a mention. Clearly we should not be bothering this irreproachable group, but should focus on their proper target – the Great Unwashed. The rejoinder that men such as those he worked with also abuse was received in silence. Middle class men are clearly unaccustomed to being included in this debate, far less identified as possible perpetrators of these crimes. Some seem to take it as a personal affront. In shattering the illusion of this as a working class problem, Zero Tolerance removes the comforting distance of higher social class and status.

There has been some criticism of the under-representation of black and ethnic minority women in the campaign. Whilst this was a conscious decision by the creators of Zero Tolerance to avoid reinforcing racist stereotypes, and was discussed with black women's organisations, it is problematic. The fifth poster, designed in January 1994, does redress this a little, but there is concern that the relative absence of black women will serve only to silence their experience. It is noteworthy, however, to consider the responses of the focus groups during the Edinburgh evaluation: when looking at the child sexual abuse poster showing two little girls, they were predisposed to believe that it was the black child who had been abused. Defining the problem in terms of male power is of paramount importance in the campaign. As such it is clear that when attempting to challenge the prevailing ideology within society, the onus must fall on the dominant group to respond to the charge, and that responsibility must not be deflected by making this an issue of race or class.

There has also been some contrast of the campaign with the format adopted in London. The latter focused solely on domestic violence, particularly on physical abuse: 'He gave her flowers, chocolates and multiple bruising'. It used images of men, rather than women, although these too did not portray stereotypical notions of abusers. One perceived consequence, however, is that whilst challenging men, women have been rendered invisible.

— Naming the problem —

The boldness and innovation of the Zero Tolerance campaign lies partly in its unflinching insistence that this is not a gender-free issue. Beginning with the premise that it is usually men who commit these crimes, and usually women and children who are the targets of their aggression, it identifies male violence as the primary issue. Some people have difficulty with this. They want the campaign to remove the word 'male' and simply conflate male and female violence. The women's movement recognised a long time ago the importance of naming. If we cannot name a problem, how can we solve it? 'One must speak truth to power' writes Andrea Dworkin (1988). Zero Tolerance recognises this. It has taken what is commonly defined as a women's issue – and therefore for many not particularly worthy of male gaze or attention – and insisted that it is a men's issue. It says that male violence is the responsibility of *all* men, as a social class, to accept and act upon. Revolutionary. It dismisses the bad, mad or sad theories of male violence. It simply calls on all men – abusive and non-abusive – to end the violence.

— Strathclyde campaign —

The campaign has been tremendously successful in Strathclyde, and in other areas where it has run. This is a remarkable achievement for any movement advocating social change, but particularly for one which is avowedly feminist. It is all the more significant given the political context in which it has operated. There has been a Conservative, neoliberal government in power in the UK for the last sixteen years which has systematically been dismantling the welfare gains of the post-war period. Under the pretext of 'rolling back the state' it has peddled its ideology of rampant individualism and reaction. The backlash against the inroads made by women has accompanied this period of hostile government. Inimical to the interests of women, it has sought to debate the issue of equality within an arena dominated by discussions on the need to get 'back to family values' (the definition of 'family' being a two-parent, heterosexual, nuclear unit). The growth in lone parent families has been heralded as the most insidious social evil responsible for moral degeneracy, social breakdown, and economic decline. Women are getting out of control. Of men, that is. Clearly a situation that cannot be allowed to continue.

The ongoing struggle to protect the limited access women have to abortion in Britain is paradigmatic of the way in which our attempts to create a radical agenda are stymied. In having to deploy our energies and resources in preserving our few gains, it is difficult to shift the focus on to our rights to control over our own bodies.

Scottish politics have traditionally been more left wing than in the UK as a whole. Electorally we have consistently rejected the Tories, although the iniquity of our electoral system has meant this has been of little importance in a national context. We therefore operate within a system which is an anathema to most Scots, with a tradition of protest and a sense of our own distinctive identity and culture. Perhaps this explains to some degree the way in which the campaign has developed, unfettered by the constraints of the New Right.

The Strathclyde campaign has differed in structure and implementation from other areas, primarily because of its size and geographical diversity. The largest local authority in Europe, it has a population of approximately 2.5 million. It encompasses a major city, towns, villages, rural areas, and island communities. Planning and executing a public awareness campaign to cover such a vast area is thus a major task. The Regional Council opted to approach this as a partnership venture, but one in which it would provide the management and co-ordination. The support for the campaign across the region has consequently been of immense importance in ensuring its success. Of the nineteen district councils covering this area, only two refused financial support. They cover the political spectrum in Strathclyde, thus underlining the fact that this is not a party political matter. The four Health Boards in Strathclyde are also key funders of the campaign. The significance of this collaborative approach lies not simply in the material provision, but in the acceptance of these organisations of their role in tackling the issue, and, crucially, in the tacit recognition of the scale of the problem and its causation. In supporting Zero Tolerance they acknowledge both the legitimacy of their role as service providers to abused women, and their remit in working to eradicate this violence.

The weight and authority ascribed to the campaign because it is a local government initiative is considerable. It has enhanced its delivery and scope, and has ensured that the central message of Zero Tolerance – that this is a major social and political problem requiring social and political solutions – is disseminated. Within Strathclyde it has been incorporated into the Council's keynote policy for tackling poverty, disadvantage and discrimination – The Social Strategy. The Social Strategy is the jewel in the Region's crown. As an integral part of this, the legitimacy of the campaign is unassailable, a fact which has not been lost on those for whom it is an abomination: 'Fear and loathing on the rates' observed one incensed commentator (Warner 1994). In practical terms it has meant we have been able to distribute campaign material throughout all twenty-seven Regional Council departments, and insist that they are displayed as a part of the Council's policy. This has been of considerable importance particularly when those who oppose it seek to undermine it, or question its presence.

As in Edinburgh, the endorsement of the campaign by prominent men within the region has been obtained. For example, the Chief Constable and Chief

Executive launched our bus campaign challenging the excuses used by men to minimise or deny their violence. Their public support has been useful in silencing the claims of some men that this is an anti-men campaign which only women could support. The inclusion of men in the campaign has been a shrewd, strategic part of this initiative. Men have not been asked to validate what we are saying, nor to co-opt this issue or take credit for the achievements of the women's movement, but to accept the centrality of their role in ending male violence.

– Structure of the campaign –

The Strathclyde campaign was launched on International Women's Day, 8 March 1994, at the Royal Concert Hall in Glasgow. Over 400 women and children from all age ranges and backgrounds attended. In an atmosphere charged with hope and excitement there was a very early signal to us that the campaign had meaning for women. They felt ownership of it and identified with it. The advertising campaign throughout the next twelve months comprised of bus, train, subway and billboard advertising, supplemented by the distribution and display of over 150,000 posters, 400,000 leaflets, and thousands of information packs, car stickers, and badges. A distribution company was employed to display posters in pubs, clubs, shops, cafes, laundrettes etc. across the Region. It is difficult to verbalise the emotional response to seeing a billboard saying simply 'No Man has the Right'. One woman, on seeing the Edinburgh campaign, said she stood there and simply said 'Yes'. How can you convey the sense of power – the power to name, the power to object, the power to reject male violence, the power to be? 'Yes' encapsulates the fist raised in defiance, the spirit raised in hope and the voice raised in accord with women. I have lost count of the number of times women have expressed their elation on seeing the campaign, and the value it places on their experience. For many it is a very visible and audible declaration of their rights to themselves. One woman, describing herself as middle class and a typical 'victim', called us up to say that she had been abused by her husband for years. Driving behind a bus carrying a Zero Tolerance poster she decided that she would leave him. Zero Tolerance cannot assume credit for her decision. This was obviously an ongoing process. But what it seemed to do was provide the additional fillip to her decision to go – it re-affirmed her right to do so.

Whilst the campaign has succeeded in attracting funding which financed the outdoor advertising, the budget is still fairly inconsequential in comparison with other campaigns. It has been the degree of local community involvement in Zero Tolerance which ensured its success. To create and sustain a local profile for the campaign, twelve Implementation Groups were established across Strathclyde. The composition of these differed according to the needs of different areas, but generally included representatives from Strathclyde Regional Council, the local District Council, Health Board, Women's Aid and Rape Crisis Groups and other local women's organisations. The commitment and hard work of the women and men who made up the groups have been of immeasurable importance to the campaign. They have helped transform Zero Tolerance from being simply a public awareness initiative, to a process in which people, especially women, have investment and ownership.

In tandem with this has been the burgeoning involvement of all kinds of community groups who have responded to the focus it provides. Throughout the region, there have been theatre productions, safety days, writing workshops and discussion groups raising the issue of male violence. Stalls bearing Zero Tolerance leaflets, car stickers and badges have had a presence at every community venue imaginable. The material has been used with women who are experiencing abuse, with young people in schools and community centres and with offenders. One youth project, assisted by the local police and Procurator Fiscal, staged a mock trial of a young man accused of beating and raping his girlfriend. In Ayr, the four local Implementation Groups organised a major conference aimed at taking the initiative forward to tackle the issue of service provision, which included international speakers, and which attracted a tremendous degree of local interest. Since its launch there have been dozens of invitations for an input on the issue it raises at a huge variety of events held by different organisations, including Trade Unions, women's groups, church groups, and the Worker's Educational Association.

These represent just a few examples of the responses to Zero Tolerance. It has enthused, excited and prompted people to take action. It has provided the space for the issue of male violence to be raised and debated. Accounts of arguments, conversations and discussions held about male abuse, simply because of the display of a poster, are often quoted to us. Whether or not these are supportive of the campaign, they signal the success of a central objective: to get people talking about the problem, and acknowledging its scale. People who hitherto would be embarrassed or uncomfortable with the subject have engaged vigorously in discussing it; whilst others who may have considered it too esoteric have propounded their views on why and how it happens. In the evaluation of the Strathclyde Campaign this was reiterated:

The community health volunteers in Glasgow picked up on it. There was a lot of quite heated discussion – it was really very positive. It certainly helped some men who said they didn't realise the extent [of violence against women] and one of the men was quite disturbed by it because he had been violent to a partner in the past . . .

A fellow that I used to work with approached me and said . . . 'My next door neighbour is beating his girlfriend, I hear it every night, I cannae listen to it any more . . .' He knew about Zero Tolerance and had seen the advert on the telly and that made him think about [doing something] rather than doing nothing . . .

There have been young people who have raised the issue with me – not violence direct to them but within the family unit. Just through asking questions round what the badge means. (Kitzinger 1995)

Whilst the advertising campaign and corresponding work in communities have been successful, there have been shortcomings in the campaign we are still seeking to address.

As mentioned earlier, the under-representation of black and minority ethnic women, whilst deliberate to avoid racist stereotyping of male violence, provoked concern that its corollary had been the silencing of their experience. To address this, the Black and Ethnic Minority Women's Zero Tolerance Forum was established in Strathclyde in February 1994. It is composed of representatives from a variety of statutory and voluntary organisations. Within the Forum, there has been much discussion on the most effective way of ensuring the visibility and accessibility of the campaign within different communities. The paucity of existing local data concerning violence relating to black and minority ethnic women has been raised consistently at the Forum as well as at a seminar held in October 1994 looking at the particular needs of black and minority ethnic women vis-a-vis the campaign. A preliminary research proposal was accordingly drawn up in response which identified ways of addressing this issue. The research focuses on ascertaining the nature and extent of service provision for black and minority ethnic women experiencing abuse; how, if at all, this is monitored to ensure it is responsive to their needs, and whether any gaps have been identified by agencies working in this field. It is also envisaged that it will provide an opportunity to recognise and highlight areas of good practice which currently exist. A consultant, Rosina McCrae, was commissioned to undertake this work, scheduled for completion in October 1995, which forms the basis for further consultation within agencies and minority ethnic communities. It is also hoped that it will contribute to the ongoing development of the Zero Tolerance campaign at a local and national level. [See McCrae and Brown 1995.]

Another feature of the campaign, as it is presently constructed, is the invisibility of disabled women. To generate discussion on the needs and experience of disabled women in relation to male violence, Jan Macleod of the Women's Support Project in Glasgow was commissioned to consult with disabled women in Strathclyde and outline the salient issues in a report. Entitled *We Are No Exception*, this report has formed the basis for the establishment of a group within Glasgow to act upon its recommendations. We are presently at the stage of organising further consultations with disabled women to explore the most effective way of addressing these. Disability Awareness training is planned for women in voluntary organisations which work in the field of male violence and we are also hoping to work with disabled women to devise a proposal for more in-depth research in this much neglected area. A similar approach has been adopted in relation to the issues facing rural women. Janette Forman, also of the Women's Support Project, compiled a report – *Making Us Visible* – following consultation with women from around Strathclyde. Again the recommendations of this are currently being explored. Training initiatives, and development of curricular materials for use in schools constitute further examples of development work within the Region.

– Impact of the campaign –

The success of Zero Tolerance throughout Scotland, and in parts of England where it has run, is undoubted. Whilst the evaluations which have been carried out attest to this, and to the support it has amongst the general public, it has also stimulated a great deal of debate and controversy. Some critics seem to have reserved their most bilious attempts at polemic in assessing the campaign. 'This Goebbels style exercise in hate propaganda is a disgrace to a mature and democratic society,' was the tentative view opined by Gerald Warner. He bemoaned the impact of these 'grisly placards' which he considered will subliminally assault the senses of young women. 'Like water dripping on a stone, the insistent message is: men are evil . . .' (Warner 1994). Whatever could have triggered such an attack of apoplexy? Warner identified the instigation behind such malevolence: the Feminist Conspiracy, 'an attempt to create an abyss of distrust and fear between two halves of humanity' (Warner 1994). His splenetic tirade reflects some of the more extreme responses to the campaign, yet paradoxically highlights the very 'core' of the campaign's success: its feminism. Zero Tolerance challenges the existing order; it challenges the prevailing ethos in society on the causation, extent, and remedy for male violence. In eschewing notions of the typical abuser, the campaign's challenge goes right to the heart of the problem – if it is not the result of alcohol abuse, poverty, race, intergenerational transmissions of behaviour, then why does it happen?

The cleverness of the campaign lies in its radicalism, presented in a straightforward, common-sense way. For example, 'No Man has the Right' evokes an intense reaction for some. Yet it leaves the argument of its critics wanting. How can they object to the directness and simplicity of the message? Do men have the right to abuse? Most would retreat from affirming this right publicly even whilst assuming it privately. Even cloaked in the obfuscation of female provocation, enjoyment and collusion, they might balk at being so explicit. Similarly, the strapline – 'Husband, father, stranger – male abuse of power is a crime!' How can this be refuted, unless by seeking recourse to the 'rantings' of the redoubtable Mr Warner who warns 'Fathers – the ultimate symbols of patriarchy . . . are not to be trusted' (Warner 1994). Yet, it is incontrovertible that it is predominantly men who abuse, and women and children who are the targets of their aggression. Nevertheless, we are presented with the clichéd, apocryphal epidemic of female abusers whose pervasive maltreatment of men is hidden by the latter's shame and humiliation. Messrs' Lyndon and Ashton find no difficulty in believing the extremely tenuous and discredited evidence for this hypothesis, and instead direct their visceral attacks on the overwhelming evidence of male violence. Claiming to 'expose' the true extent of this abuse they decry the 'ludicrous and baseless exaggerations . . . [which] . . . reflect a general pattern of grotesque misrepresentations of the domestic violence phenomena'. Instead they lambast the 'professional parasites on the domestic violence racket . . . [who] will be dismayed at the prospect of their easy money drying up' (Lyndon and Ashton 1995). No more world cruises for Women's Aid Workers then! Commenting on the exponents of the feminist conspiracy 'theory', Usha Brown wonderfully captures their loathing of the 'Hoods' (The Sisterhood that is)!

> In covens all over the country we crouch over our cauldrons – double double toil and trouble, fire burn and cauldron bubble – here we are, destroying the family as we know it, society as we know it, and for all I know, the world as we know it . . . Perhaps someone should tell them we're only making the dinner – not boiling patriarchs' parts or hatching the Gunpowder plot. (Brown 1993)

It makes you wonder if they see the atrophy of male power before their eyes, or perhaps have a more physical sense of this? But what they have identified, and so patently abhor, is our success in defining the parameters of the debate. Perhaps the singular most important aspect of Zero Tolerance is that it has changed the terms of reference in relation to male violence. It has created the agenda to which others must respond. Bold. Innovative. Trenchant and uncompromising in its analysis and integrity, Zero Tolerance has shaped the political discourse and deflected attention from those who would minimise and deny the experience and voice of women.

In some ways the plaudits accorded the campaign since its inception have overshadowed the radicalism of its approach, which is perhaps more obviously displayed in the outpourings of feminism's erstwhile opponents. The 'slogan' Zero Tolerance (helped by the pervasive use of the Z logo) has now become almost idiomatic; it requires little in the way of preamble or explanation – for the campaign has been received less hysterically by people in general than the accounts quoted above would suggest. This has been accomplished in part by its ability to engage people in the debate who have different perspectives. It operates at a variety of different levels. Those who consider they take a 'logical' approach to issues like this recognise the economic imperative of dealing with the costs of male violence. Others see it as a moral issue, one of 'right and wrong'. For others it is political. But whatever the angle from which it is viewed, the clarity of the theoretical understanding which infuses the campaign is unmistakable.

The evaluations of the campaign in Edinburgh, Strathclyde and Central Region vouch for the correctness of this approach. In Edinburgh, 79% of people had positive feelings about the campaign, whilst only 9% agreed with the statement that 'Violence against women is not the sort of issue that should be publicly discussed.' Even amongst men there was broad support for the campaign; only 12% were negative about it overall. The gender specific nature of the campaign has been received well, although some are discomfited by it. For example, one man commented:

. . . taking the men out and saying you're at fault, predominantly, so we're going to have a campaign aimed at you. I don't think it's right. (Lyndon and Ashton 1995)

Other men, however, have recognised the legitimacy of this:

There are undoubtedly other forms of violence within relationships, but the predominant one is male violence . . . so let's not cloud the issue. (Lyndon and Ashton 1995)

– CONCLUSION –

Zero Tolerance is probably the most successful local authority campaign ever undertaken in the UK. Radical and pioneering, it has framed the issue of male violence in terms of looking at men's behaviour – not women's. It insists that men take responsibility for their violence. Yet it also insists that the political, social and cultural context in which it occurs and is allowed to continue, must be changed. It has sought refuge in neither justification of its feminism nor in pandering to the injured feelings of men who feel personally indicted.

Whilst there is still a great deal of work to do, it is important that we recognise the importance of the women's movement, both in creating the conditions in which such a campaign could exist, and in providing the intellectual and political framework for its development. Zero Tolerance did not emerge from a vacuum. Its genesis is in the women's movement. Its integrity and future development depend symbiotically on its continuing identification with this. What Zero Tolerance has been able to do is incorporate these principles, values and beliefs into a campaign which is endorsed by local authorities, health boards and trade unions. It presents an intrinsically feminist view of power relations in society, and the way in which these continue the subordination and oppression of women.

Andrea Dworkin, in writing about her work, said she writes because she believes 'that women must wage a war against silence: against socially coerced silence; against politically preordained silence; against economically choreographed silence; against the silence created by the pain and despair of sexual abuse and second class status' (Dworkin 1988). The Zero Tolerance campaign aims to be part of that process; to challenge and change the legitimacy of women's oppression, and to contribute to the struggles of women in Scotland and beyond for equality and justice.

– Notes –

1. Cited by Leslie Wheeler (1983) 'Lucy Stone: Radical Beginnings, in Dale Spender (ed.) *Feminist Theories*, London: The Women's Press.
2. The Women's Support Project/*Evening Times* Report was based on responses from 1503 women to the survey on Violence Against Women, March 1990. The Women's Support Project is a voluntary organisation, based in Glasgow, which aims to raise awareness about rape, sexual abuse and domestic violence. It provides a development and education service on issues relating to male violence, and works to promote an improved and positive service for women and children who have suffered violence.
3. Franki Raffles, one of the creators of Zero Tolerance, died in childbirth in December 1994, aged 39. Her work as a feminist photographer and designer, for which she was renowned, reflected her commitment to women, and her belief in their ability to bring about change. Her warmth, humour, vision and creativity suffuses her work, attests to the uniqueness of the contribution she made to women's lives, and stands as a poignant reminder of the extent of our loss.
4. Dates for release of posters in Strathclyde:
   March/April 1994 – 'She lives with a successful businessman . . .'
   May/June 1994 – 'From three to ninety-three . . .'
   July/August 1994 – 'By the time they reach eighteen . . .'
   September/October 1994 – 'When they say no, they mean no . . .'
   November/December 1994 – 'No Man has the Right'.

– References –

Brown, Usha (1993), 'Women and Power' speech to the Scottish Labour Women's Caucus Conference.

Cosgrove, K. and Forman, J. (1995), *Making Us Visible: Male Violence Against Women in Rural Areas*, report to Strathclyde Regional Council, February.

Cosgrove, K. and Macleod J. (1995), *We Are No Exception: Male Violence against Women with Disability*, report to Strathclyde Regional Council, January.

Dworkin, Andrea (1988), *Letters From A War Zone, Selected Writings 1976–1987*, New York: Secker & Warburg.

Government Reply to the Third Report from the Home Affairs Select Committee (1993), Session 1992–93, London: HMSO.

Kitzinger, Jenny (1995), *Interim Evaluation of Strathclyde Regional Council's Zero Tolerance Campaign*, Glasgow: Glasgow University Media Group.

Kitzinger, Jenny and Hunt, Kate (1993), *Evaluation of Edinburgh District Council's Zero Tolerance Campaign*, Glasgow: Glasgow University Media Group.

Lyndon, N. and Ashton, P. (1995), 'Knocked for six: the myth of a nation of wife-batterers', *Sunday Times*, 29 January, London.

McCrae, R. and Brown, U. (1995) *No Voice–No Choice: A Report on Domestic Violence within Black and Ethnic Minority Communities*, report to Strathclyde Regional Council.

National Inter-Agency Working Party (1992), 'National Inter-Agency Working Party Report on Domestic Violence', *Victim Support*, July.

Warner, G. (1994), 'Time to give Zero Tolerance to the Sex Warriors', *Sunday Times Scotland*, 9 October.

Women's Support Project/*Evening Times* (1990), *Report on Responses from 1503 Women to the Survey on Violence Against Women*, March, Glasgow: Women's Support Project/ *Evening Times*.

CHAPTER 11

Keeping Gender on the Agenda: Local Government in Scotland

ESTHER BREITENBACH AND FIONA MACKAY

This chapter looks at the role of women's and equal opportunities initiatives in local government in Scotland. It draws on recent research into equal opportunities in local government which has provided an overview of the situation following the reorganisation of local government which took place in 1996.[1] We examine some of the key findings that emerged from the research, and discuss the role that local government may play in continuing to promote equal opportunities in the changing political context in Scotland. We argue that local government has played an important role in keeping gender issues on the political agenda in Scotland at a time when central government showed little interest or was actively hostile to gender and other equality issues. A continuing process of development of equal opportunities policies and practice has meant an accumulation of experience and knowledge that can usefully be transferred across to devolved government and to other areas of public, voluntary and private sector work, where there is a renewed interest in equal opportunities. However, none of this has been achieved without struggle, or without difficulty, and while there are strengths and successes, there are also weaknesses and failures.

As researchers, our interest in this area was prompted by a number of factors. Academic writing on women's and equal opportunities committees in various parts of Britain tended to give a very pessimistic assessment of their capacity to remain a radical force in local government, and often predicted that gender issues would be pushed off the agenda or be diluted by attention given to other equality issues such as race or disability. This did not tally with our experience in Scotland, where there appeared to be evidence of a steady, if slow, development of women's and equal opportunities initiatives in local government. There was thus an incentive to explore and to record the distinctive experience of women's and equal opportunities committees in Scotland.

_ ASSESSMENTS OF WOMEN'S AND EQUAL _
OPPORTUNITIES INITIATIVES

Women's committees as a part of the structures of local government in Britain began with the creation of the Greater London Council's Women's Committee in 1982. The subsequent growth of these in a number of London boroughs, and later in other parts of England, and in Scotland and Wales, produced a flurry of academic interest (see Edwards 1989, 1995; Halford 1988, 1992; Bruegel and Kean 1995; Lovenduski and Randall 1993). However, with the abolition of the GLC and the defeat of the left in London, and with the relative decline of women's and other equality initiatives, academic interest also tended to die down. Characteristically, these writers concluded that the success of women's committees had been short-lived, and their remit, if they continued, would be more restricted. Reservations were expressed about the more generic approach to equal opportunities that was emerging, as it was perceived to mean that gender issues had lost ground. For example, Lovenduski and Randall comment that under pressure of the Thatcherite challenge, 'some authorities abolished their women's committees or subsumed them into small units within equal opportunities committees' (Lovenduski and Randall 1993: 154).

An even more pessimistic view of the potential of local government for feminists is taken by Bruegel and Kean, who argue that the 'moment' of municipal feminism took place between 1983 and 1987. They offer a quite specific definition of 'municipal feminism' which they see as part of a 'distinct socialist feminist project'. Their definition is as follows:

> The new municipal feminism took from the early 20th century experience of municipal welfarism a concern with the local and day-to-day conditions of 'ordinary' working-class women, but broke with welfarism, in emphasising the need to control the processes and personnel of the local state, as much as to get policies formally adopted. It contained within it as great a critique of bureaucracies as of markets and can be seen to have brought the process, network thinking of the second-wave women's movement . . . into the arena of the local state for the first time. It also broke with the old municipal feminism in wanting to challenge male power within the labour movement. (Bruegel and Kean 1995: 150)

Key features of this municipal feminism were its mobilisation of women, the funding of local initiatives, and a concern to foster changes in the market sector by a variety of forms of intervention, such as 'contract compliance'.[2] They argue that there has been a 'pragmatic and cosmetic adoption of municipal feminism's equal opportunities agenda within the urban left'. This has resulted in a more market-oriented equal opportunities agenda being adopted in local government, a depoliticisation of equal opportunities and a limitation to 'the shortest of all possible agendas: getting some women up the hierarchy, but leaving the majority hanging'. (Bruegel and Kean 1995: 162)

In a similar vein, Angela Coyle has written critically of equal opportunities policies in local government, assessing them as 'bureaucratic and inflexible', and equality structures as 'often divorced from line management'. She concludes that 'since the late 1980s equal opportunity initiatives in local government have been in decline due in part to a reluctance to be associated with high profile, radical policies, and more significantly, to a lack of resources to support them' (Coyle 1996: 3).

Part of the reason for the pessimism of these assessments was the decline of women's committees in London. 'By 1994 only two women's committees remained in London boroughs, their functions either lost or subsumed in a much diluted form into the terms of reference of equal opportunities committees with responsibility for race, disability, class, etc.' (Lovenduski, Margetts and Abrar 1996: 13). However, as the same authors note, London boroughs tend to have higher proportions of women in senior management positions, and as councillors, than local authorities elsewhere in the UK.

Some commentators have noted that the situation in Scotland has differed from England and Wales. For example, Julia Edwards writes that 'in Scotland women's political representation (in the broadest sense) is developing more cohesively through networking on a regional basis than the more fragmented picture in England and Wales' (Edwards 1995: 125). Lovenduski and Randall also identify the situation in Scotland as different. 'There is no doubt that the visible national feminist movement has declined. As we travelled to collect the material for this book, everywhere we went, except Scotland, we encountered a sense that numbers of activists were fewer, that old networks had broken down' (Lovenduski and Randall 1993: 359). They also note that a number of new committees appeared in Scotland at the end of the 1980s, 'perhaps reflecting the success of Scotland's strong oppositional political culture'. However, they conclude, 'despite their Scottish revival, there are many signs that the immediate potential of women's committees has been exhausted, and their routinized future will be in straightforward equal opportunities work for local councils and in servicing local women's groups' (Lovenduski and Randall 1993: 154).

The judgement that women's and equal opportunities initiatives are in decline in London and other parts of England may be correct. It is difficult to judge this in the absence of any overview of the situation, but clearly policies continue to be developed in particular authorities, and there is evidence of slow progress in the numbers of women in Chief Executive and senior management posts, though the position of women manual workers has probably deteriorated.[3] There are variations in the patterns of development in Scotland, Wales, and England, and within regions within these countries. The development and growth of women's and equal opportunities initiatives started later in Scotland than in England (though it must be remembered that this refers largely to London and other large urban authorities, and that many authorities in England have not developed such initiatives), and even later in Wales. This difference in patterns of development is recognised by Lovenduski and Randall, who comment:

> Women's committees in the south proliferated in the heyday of radical town hall politics. In the north their origins involve rather more of a political struggle, and their politics have been adjusted accordingly. Born under more difficult conditions, these may prove long-lived. (1993: 208)

Indeed, up until the mid 1990s the pattern of development of women's and equal opportunities initiatives in local government in Scotland had been one of slow growth overall, with occasional reversals in particular local authorities due to changes in administration, such as Stirling and West Lothian District Councils. However, with local government reorganisation about to take place it was not clear what the outcome might be for equal opportunities staff and structures, and concern was expressed by equality activists that reorganisation might be used as an opportunity to marginalise both staff and structures. The reasons for suspecting this might be the case were that both political and bureaucratic resistance to women's and equal opportunities initiatives had typically been encountered in the process of setting these initiatives up, and also had continued to be a factor as equal opportunities work developed. Thus, though progress had been made, there was reason to believe that the position of women's and equal opportunities initiatives was by no means secure. Indeed, equality practitioners and activists took steps to ensure that the issue of equal opportunities in local government was kept on the agenda during the process of reorganisation. In particular, the EOC in Scotland commissioned a report, based on a survey conducted by the Convention of Scottish Local Authorities (CoSLA), which put the case for the continuing need for equal opportunities structures and policies in local government, and which provided case studies of good practice (Breitenbach 1995).

– BUREAUCRATIC RESISTANCE –

From a research perspective, local government reorganisation provided an opportunity to test feminist theories about the nature of bureaucracies and organisational change, and because reorganisation was taking place simultaneously in Scotland and Wales, it also provided an opportunity to make a comparative study of the impact on equal opportunities structures in both countries (though our focus here is on the situation in Scotland). Assessments of the gendered nature of bureaucracies and of the capacity of feminists and other equality activists and practitioners to promote change within bureaucracies, whether at central, devolved or local government level, range from the wholly pessimistic to the cautiously or guardedly positive. Feminist debates in Britain about the nature of the state have in the past tended to objectify it, theorising it as an agent of capital and inherently patriarchal. However, a post-structuralist feminist model gives more emphasis to processes internal to and surrounding the state, treating it as less monolithic, and as perpetually changing. While male power may have been institutionalised historically, this more fluid conception of the state implies that there is scope for reshaping of the state through feminist intervention. Feminist empirical studies of the local state in Britain have focused on the operation of equal opportunities policies and resistance met by these, thus illustrating the gendered nature of power within both political and bureaucratic local authority structures (Stone 1988; Edwards 1989, 1995; Lieberman 1989; Halford 1988, 1992; Cockburn 1991). Halford has suggested that the widespread existence of equal opportunity policies, albeit varying enormously in content and commitment, signals a recognition of the gendered nature of local authority policy and practice and an implicit commitment on the part of these councils to positive change for women.

There has been little empirical research in Scotland that has addressed these themes. Sue Lieberman has noted that location of equalities staff within the local government hierarchy, their status and skills, are important to their potential influence, as are the ways in which staff attempt to work (Lieberman 1989). For example, attempts by the staff of women's units to work collectively were in conflict with the hierarchical nature of local government and undermined their effectiveness. However, as Kelly has argued,[4] lessons were learned from the London experience of the failure of attempts to work collectively, and in Scotland equality practitioners have found ways of working with rather than against the grain, though Kelly also points out that under-representation of women in senior management positions has inhibited progress. Mackay and Cosgrove, in their respective discussions of development of Zero Tolerance campaigns in Strathclyde and Edinburgh (see chapters 8 and 9), illustrate how it has been possible for women's and equality officers to work within the bureaucracy of local government to secure support for a radical policy, as well as securing political support.

In contrast, Marchbank (1994) offers a much more negative account of bureaucratic resistance to feminist politics. In her discussion of a strategy for under-fives in Strathclyde, she claims that 'patriarchy' used various tactics to marginalise women's issues, a process she describes as 'nondecision making'. In her case study example she cites a number of factors as responsible for the failure of a feminist childcare strategy to find support. These include suppression of the issue through ignoring the interests of particular groups of women – in this instance, working mothers; the isolation of the officer responsible for the strategy as the only woman in the senior management team; branding of this officer as 'feminist' as a way of delegitimising her position; and delaying tactics. In general she concludes that the bureaucratic culture of the organisation in question was unsympathetic to feminist demands. While there is no doubt much truth in this conclusion, Marchbank's claim that these tactics are a sign of a specifically 'patriarchal' practice are hard to sustain. Bureaucratic resistance to change and to radical policies of many kinds is not an uncommon experience within local government.

In her later study *Going Dutch or Scotch Mist* (1996), while Marchbank reiterates the position that bureaucratic systems respond to maintain the status quo, and therefore patriarchal power relations, she does acknowledge that Scottish experience indicates that certain achievements have occurred through women's initiatives and that marginalised voices have been heard to some extent. She makes a number of salient points relevant to the capacity of women's initiatives to continue to make progress. The structural position of staff and departmental divisions are important factors if initiatives are to be effective. The lack of a career structure for equality staff and the vulnerability of staff and units to political change can act as a block to development. The influence of the women's movement via local political activists has been the major thrust behind women's initiatives, rather than councillors themselves leading the way. Women's initiatives within local government have focused more on providing new services or on improving service delivery than on involving more women in decision making. All of these points are echoed in other writings and indicate the need to address both issues of the position of women within bureaucracies, and within the political system.

In general, the fact that the judgements made about the success of feminist interventions in the local state are so varied tends in itself to support the contention that state bureaucracies are not monolithic and that there is scope for reshaping the state through feminist intervention. The evidence from our research project on local government reorganisation confirms the view that the changing nature of the local state has provided opportunities for further development of structures and policies aimed at enhancing women's position as employees and as users of local government services. This is not to imply that these gains are necessarily secure, nor that they are uncontested.

_ THE CONTEXT AND PROCESS OF LOCAL _
GOVERNMENT REORGANISATION

It can be argued that the local government reorganisation which took place in 1996 was politically driven and that its primary purpose was to reduce the power of Labour-controlled local authorities, particularly large and powerful urban or urban-dominated authorities. In this connection, it is worth recalling John

Major's description of Strathclyde Region as a 'monster'. Over the period of Conservative administration, local government was subject to a number of significant changes, entailing approximately 200 pieces of legislation, which were designed to promote a change in local government's role from service provider to enabling authority. These changes included Compulsory Competitive Tendering,[5] devolved management of schools, removal of Further Education from local authority control, the introduction of community care, the poll tax/ community charge, 'right to buy' legislation in respect of council housing accompanied by prohibitions on the use of capital receipts to build more council housing, the creation of quasi-markets with respect to certain local government functions, and continuing tight fiscal discipline. Not surprisingly, therefore, local government reorganisation appeared as yet another onslaught on the power of local government, and it encountered considerable resistance. In Scotland there was widespread opposition to local government reorganisation, particularly in the absence of the creation of a Scottish parliament, which in any case would necessitate a re-examination of the role of local government (McCrone, Paterson and Brown 1993; Boyne, Jordan and McVicar 1995).

The two-tier system of local government was replaced by a system of unitary authorities in Scotland and Wales in 1996. This process took place within a comparatively short period of time. The Government White Paper proposing reorganisation was published in 1993; 'shadow' authorities were elected in 1995; the new unitary authorities came into operation on 1 April 1996. The position in England has been somewhat different. Changes have been more piecemeal, and unitary authorities have been introduced in some parts of the country but not throughout as has they were in Scotland and Wales.[6]

In Scotland there was a concern that the process of local government reorganisation might result in opposition to women's and equal opportunities initiatives becoming more evident, and in their marginalisation or abolition within new authorities. A more positive view was to see it as an opportunity, though this was difficult in the general climate of resistance to the reorganisation. Interviews and discussions conducted in the period immediately after reorganisation[7] discovered that there was a widespread view that equal opportunities procedures had been abandoned in the interviewing that had taken place in the upper echelons of local authority jobs, and that lower in the jobs hierarchy, where a process of transfer took place, women workers' interests were sometimes ignored, and the length of time taken for the process to be completed put them in a prolonged situation of considerable stress. Women activists in local government were angry and demoralised, and felt that the position of women had worsened. In some authorities women's and equal opportunities initiatives were thought to have been marginalised; in others, where committees and units had been created, officers and councillors were cautious in expressing their predictions for the future. Following reorganisation a climate of low morale persisted.

However, it has subsequently become more evident that the considerable experience and expertise that existed in equal opportunities policy making at the level of local government generally survived the transition to unitary authorities, and the development of this work has begun to gather pace once more.

As part of the research project, a postal survey of all the new unitary authorities was conducted in mid 1997.[8] This was at a relatively early stage after reorganisation, and clearly further changes have occurred since then. Nonetheless, the findings from the survey give an indication of the place of equal opportunities structures and policies within local government in Scotland. The majority of councils had structures (committees, sub-committees, advisory groups, member/officer groups, and so on) in place for dealing with equal opportunities issues both in personnel and within service provision, though only around a third had specialist committees or sub-committees. Those that did have specialist committees or sub-committees covered the majority of the Scottish population and the major urban conurbations. A minority of councils had specialist equal opportunities staff, though many others assigned the equal opportunities function to personnel staff, or occasionally to staff in Chief Executives' departments.

The vast majority of councils had equal opportunities policies covering a range of employment issues, such as recruitment, selection and promotion procedures; anti-harassment policies; flexible working hours and carers' leave. However, training provision on these policies varied, and in particular training for elected members appeared relatively uncommon. Data on the position of women employees was limited and patchy, despite the fact that women are the majority of the local authority workforce. They remain concentrated in lower grades and under-represented in senior management. The limited data available suggested that women were approximately 16% of senior management within Scottish local authorities. Immediately following reorganisation no Scottish local authority had a woman Chief Executive. At the time of writing, three of the 32 Chief Executives are women. The fact that data on women, minority ethnic and disabled employees is not routinely or systematically collected means that it is impossible to monitor change or to make comparisons.

The survey also confirmed the trend towards extending the scope of equal opportunities policies into areas of service provision, consistent with the emphasis that equality practitioners themselves have placed on this. The majority of councils had an equal opportunities policy in at least one service provision area, and over a third had equal opportunities policies in six or more areas of service provision. Areas most likely to have equal opportunities policies were Housing, Education, Social Work, Leisure and Recreation. There was, however, a pattern of uneven development both between and within authorities. Thus, the extent to which an equal opportunities ethos informs service provision throughout services generally remains limited, and in some cases equal opportunities approaches are still confined to special services or projects. Nor were policies consistently developed in relation to all groups experiencing inequality and disadvantage, with minority ethnic people and people with disabilities appearing to have a higher profile at the time of the survey. Though policies for women were less frequently mentioned, it was notable that combatting domestic violence was a significant area of policy development. The majority of councils supported Women's Aid; almost half had or were developing a policy on domestic violence; and several had developed multi-agency strategies involving the police, women's groups, voluntary organisations, and bodies such as health boards.

Only a relatively small number of councils appeared to have specific mechanisms for consulting women, such as women's forums, although many councils indicated that their decentralisation plans would take equal opportunities into account. Area based approaches, rather than interest groups, were, however, the most common form of consultation within decentralisation schemes. The majority of Scottish councils were giving support to some type of equality group organisations, including women's organisations. However, considerable anxiety had been expressed that women's projects have suffered disproportionately from budget cuts and their impact on funding of voluntary organisations, and also from the changing emphasis in the administration of urban programme funds. Data that would either support or disprove this thesis are not available, though reorganisation would appear to have had some negative impacts. For example, as Aileen Christianson and Lily Greenan note in their discussion of the Rape Crisis movement (see Chapter 7 in this collection), the disappearance of Strathclyde Region has completely changed the funding basis for the organisation, thereby creating serious problems for its continuing existence. A related point is that the disappearance of the regions has also led to the loss in some areas of specialist posts which advised on equality matters.

Finally, the survey found that there were serious weaknesses in evaluation and monitoring. With regard to employment, data was partial, patchy, not systematically reported, and little used in setting targets. Monitoring of equal opportunities in service provision was even less developed than monitoring of employment. Given that the survey was carried out at a relatively early stage in the new unitary authorities' existence, it can be anticipated that some improvements will have occurred in the development of monitoring and evaluation systems. In addition, the development of Best Value regimes in local government is also likely to have had an impact on the elaboration of Performance Indicators and other measures which will improve the collection of data relevant to the promotion of equal opportunities, as well as in other areas. Nevertheless, it seems surprising that this should be so under-developed in a sector which has made a significant contribution to the development of equal opportunities policies and practice over a period of more than 15 years.

Overall, the findings from the research project indicated the relative robust-ness of equal opportunities in local government. The general picture which emerged was that equal opportunities structures and staff survived the transition to unitary authorities, and in some cases moved to a more central policy making role. However, there were also examples of local authorities where women's and equal opportunities issues became more marginalised, through their being relocated in community development or social exclusion units, for example. While gender issues clearly remain relevant to these areas, in practice this seems to amount to a downplaying of women's issues.

Though equal opportunities initiatives survived the transition, in the process they changed somewhat in character. In particular there was evidence of a move towards the creation of generic equal opportunities committees and posts, rather than the retention of specialist sub-committees and staff dealing separately with women's, race equality, and disability issues. As noted above, this is a devel-opment that had already taken place elsewhere, for example in the London boroughs, and has been regarded as a setback for sex equality strategies (Loven-duski, Margetts and Abrar 1996). Equalities practitioners themselves have different views as to the significance of this change, and it is hard to judge whether it does represent a general downplaying of women's issues, though this can be seen to be happening within some authorities. The language of 'equal opportunities' may also serve to conceal women's and gender issues, as issues concerning equality for minority ethnic groups and people with disabilities come more to the fore.

Immediately following reorganisation, the main model for equal opportunities initiatives remained that of specialist solutions, but interest in 'mainstreaming' was growing. According to the European Union, mainstreaming is a strategy which aims at 'integrating a gender perspective in all mainstream development policies, programmes and projects' but, importantly, it 'does not exclude the need for positive action measures, programmes and projects' oriented towards women (European Commission 1996: 19). At the time that the research project was being conducted, the mainstreaming approach had also been adopted by the EOC and CRE in Britain. However, not all equalities practitioners in local government reacted positively to the idea of mainstreaming. In some cases it was seen as a way of getting rid of specialist staff, and of Chief Officers taking back control of equal opportunities from specialist staff (Mackay et al. 1995). In practice, local authorities are carrying out mainstreaming in different ways, some with specialist staff and some without. 'Mainstreaming' is the strategy that has been adopted both by the Labour government at UK level and by the Scottish Executive in their approach to equal opportunities, and as the political context in Scotland has been changing, the mainstreaming approach has also come more to the fore in local government, and has been endorsed by CoSLA (1999), who have published guidelines for local authorities in Scotland.

An important point to make, and one related to for mainstreaming's potential for success, is that the equalities 'policy community' remains very small, though it is growing. Although more local authorities are seeking to incorporate equal opportunities into their culture and practices, senior officers who endorse this approach may have a very limited understanding of equalities issues or analyses of the causes of inequality. This is one reason why mainstreaming provokes anxiety in specialist staff. It also means that the sustaining of equal opportunities practices is vulnerable to individual career moves, particularly in the context of budget constraints. To illustrate this we note that at least one authority has in fact preferred to focus on Social Exclusion rather than Equal Opportunities and has deleted its Equal Opportunities post.

In general there is a shift towards the inclusion of service provision within an equal opportunities framework, but many councils continue to view equal opportunities as a personnel function. The first women's committees in Scotland were concerned right from the beginning with service provision issues such as childcare, health, and violence against women, as well as the position of women employees. However, where councils have more recently begun to develop equal opportunities policies the pattern of development appears to be that employment issues are addressed first, followed by service provision. Characteristically, where authorities are developing equal opportunities policies for the first time they do so in employment-related matters and, locating responsibility in Personnel or Human Resources departments. Authorities with a longer track record of equal opportunities work are likely to have specialist staff both in Personnel and in central policy making departments, and may also have specialists within service departments.

Although there is evidence of a move towards more a comprehensive approach to the inclusion of service provision, the general picture is one of unevenness, and of pockets of good practice, rather than a systematic approach to 'structural transformation' (Turner et al. 1995) concerned with equality of outcome. The most comprehensive approach exists in authorities where there are specialist equal opportunities structures in place, though the development of equal opportunities practice is not attributable to equalities specialists alone, but also depends on practitioners across departments committed to equal opportunities, whether in an official or unofficial capacity. There also appears to be an association between the existence of equalities specialists and political commitment to equal opportunities, and the desire for greater democratisation, which may be seen in the creation of consultative mechanisms for a range of groups.

Many of the developments observable in equal opportunities policies and practices are in line with overall trends in public service management. For example, key trends outlined by Howard Elcock (1996: 196) are: a greater concentration on measuring and evaluating outputs; transfer of power closer to users; more responsiveness to the community with the aim of providing differentiated services relevant to diverse needs; production of 'mission statements' and plans with emphasis on quality assurance; and the change in the role of local government requiring new skills, new structures and new attitudes. The development of equal opportunities policies in service provision may fit well with these trends, though management approaches are not homogenous and range from a business-like customer orientation to a view of users as citizens with democratic rights, and these differences in approach also imply differences in understandings of 'equal opportunities'.

While an explicit commitment to equal opportunities is widespread both in terms of written policies and in terms of statements made by officials and politicians – both publicly and in interviews – the definitions and language used imply a range of meanings and degrees of commitment. The all-inclusive approach, for example, can turn out to be tokenistic and empty of content, indicating that little thought has been given to the specific needs of specific groups. The varying emphases in definitions and examples also imply that the definition of equal opportunities is a contested one, and that control of these definitions can represent shifts in the balance of power. The framework elaborated by Turner et al. (1995) usefully illustrates the different approaches that may be encompassed by the term 'equal opportunities'. They range from *laissez faire* to 'structural transformation', the former representing minimal compliance with legislation, and the latter being concerned with equality of outcome, collectivist approaches and social justice.

It is also worth commenting that some of the confusions and looseness in the usages of equal opportunities terminology imply very different levels of understanding and analysis. Indeed, our interviews suggest that – specialists and some personnel staff apart – understanding of equalities issues was at a very low level. This confirms the importance of specialist expertise in informing policy development and getting issues on the agenda. The research carried out by Lovenduski, Margetts and Abrar on feminist interventions in the local state in London also highlights the significance of such expertise in shaping the agenda (Lovenduski et al. 1996).

The extension of the scope of equal opportunities policies in local authorities is being driven by a range of forces – by legislation, by the current popularity or prominence of certain issues or groups, by political commitment, by specialist officers, and by lobbyists and advocates outside local government. The role of bodies such as the Commission for Racial Equality (CRE) and the EOC appears to be increasingly important, both in terms of developing codes of practice and in terms of providing networks and fora such as the EOC's Equality Exchanges. In various parts of Britain local government bodies, such as the Local Government Management Board, CoSLA, and the Welsh Local Government Association, also play an important role in co-ordinating activities, issuing guidelines, and publicising good practice.

– Conclusion –

The evidence from our research study leads to the conclusion that equal opportunities structures and policies have continued to develop within local government in Scotland, and have survived the transition to unitary authorities. While this development has been uneven, and while there have been reversals as well as advances, in general the pattern is of slow growth, in contrast to the experience in parts of England, especially London, where rapid advance, in the glare of frequently hostile publicity, was followed by decline. Through this process of development, local authorities have played an important role in keeping gender on the political agenda. At the same time, race equality and disability issues have gained a higher profile than previously. This was particularly significant prior to 1997 in a context where central government demonstrated little interest in equality issues or, at best, limited responses such as the Disability Discrimination Act. Local government has also provided support to many women's and equality organisations and thereby played a role building the capacity of the women's and other social movements. It has demonstrated concern with issues of consultation, participation, democracy, and citizenship, and has been open to the adoption of radical policies such as the Zero Tolerance campaign against violence against women. Yet beside these successes there remain problems and weaknesses.

Firstly, the pattern of development is very uneven, and many councils have not moved far beyond a tokenistic approach to equal opportunities policies. Political support for equal opportunities and women's issues is muted and less forthcoming than in the earlier phase of creation of women's committees, and women's representation as councillors has not increased. The high profile campaign for equal representation of women and men in the Scottish Parliament had no apparent influence on selection of women candidates for the 1999 local government elections.

The unevenness of development of equal opportunities policies within and between councils; the superficial understanding of concepts and issues that appears widespread; the lack of monitoring and evaluation, of targets and of clear outcomes; the continuing under-representation of women in senior management; tokenistic paper policies that are not implemented: are all the signs of resistance of male-dominated bureaucracies to a change in the gender balance of power.

Evidence of all the weaknesses and failures that are catalogued in earlier feminist writings on women's committees can be found. Instances of adherence to the short agenda of increasing the number of women managers; of equal opportunities initiatives being divorced from line management; of under-resourcing of staff and women's organisations; of shifting agendas away from gender; of lack of understanding of the issues; of the vulnerability of equal opportunities work to career changes of individuals and to political changes; and of loss of radicalism can all be found. To counterbalance this, however, there is also evidence of a much longer agenda of the promotion of active citizenship and social justice; of mainstreaming approaches drawing in line managers; of a growing policy community; of a commitment to the development of equality strategies that attempt to integrate gender and other equality issues; and of radical approaches such as the work on domestic violence. In a continuing climate of financial constraint, lack of resources remains a problem, and this makes all the more necessary the development of a collaborative approach amongst equality groups, in order to avoid potentially divisive competition over scarce resources.

Overall, our evaluation of women's and equal opportunities initiatives in local government in Scotland is more sanguine than the pessimistic studies based on English experience that we have cited above. Despite the problems, weaknesses, and setbacks, we would argue that the role of local government has been crucial in providing a growing space for feminist and other equality agendas to have an influence on shaping public services and attitudes. In the changed political context of devolved government, this role is likely to become more significant, as local authorities work in partnership with the Scottish Executive, public bodies, voluntary and other organisations to promote equal opportunities across Scotland and, in the ways in which local government itself will be reformed by the Scottish Parliament, it is likely to provide opportunities for increasing women's representation.

– NOTES –

1. ESRC-funded (Grant No R000236546) project on Gender and Transitions in the Local State, carried out by Esther Breitenbach, Alice Brown, Fiona Mackay, Janette Webb, University of Edinburgh.
2. Contract compliance was a mechanism through which local authorities could impose conditions, such as adherence to equal opportunities policies, on companies to which they were awarding contracts.
3. This information was given by Mandy Wright, of the Local Government Management Board, in a presentation at a seminar held in Edinburgh on 4 July 1997. The seminar was the first in a series on 'Gender Relations and the Local State', funded by the ESRC.
4. This view was expressed by Ellen Kelly at the seminar on 'Gender Relations and the Local State' held on 4 July 1997. (See above note.)
5. Compulsory Competitive Tendering (CCT): Conservative Government legislation compelled local authorities to put out certain of their services to competitive bidding from the private sector, though local authority Direct Service Organisations were also able to bid.
6. Local government reorganisation took place simultaneously in Scotland and Wales, with new unitary authorities coming into operation in April 1996. In Scotland the previous system of nine Regional Councils, 53 District Councils and three Islands

authorities was replaced by 32 unitary authorities; in Wales eight County Councils and 37 District Councils were replaced by 22 unitary authorities. The major functional divisions between the Regions/Districts and Counties/Districts were between strategic planning, education, social services, and transport; and housing, cleansing and leisure and recreation. In England the process of local government reorganisation has been both more prolonged and more piecemeal, from the abolition of the Greater London Council and the Metropolitan County Councils in 1986 to the creation of new unitaries in 1998. The final tally by 1998 was 34 County Councils, 238 District Councils, 46 new unitary authorities, 33 London Boroughs, and 36 Metropolitan Boroughs. The Labour government enacted further changes to the system of local government with the creation of a new Greater London Authority in 2000 and an elected mayor.

7. These were carried out as part of a pilot research project carried out by a research team from The University of Edinburgh (Fiona Mackay, Esther Breitenbach, Alice Brown and Janette Webb) from March to July 1996, funded by the EOC, whose support is gratefully acknowledged.

8. A detailed presentation of the survey findings from Scotland and Wales is contained in Breitenbach et al. (1999), *Equal Opportunities in Local Government in Scotland and Wales*, Unit for the Study of Government in Scotland, University of Edinburgh.

– REFERENCES –

Boyne, G., G. Jordan and M. McVicar (1995), *Local Government Reform: A Review of the Process in Scotland and Wales*, London: Joseph Rowntree Foundation.

Breitenbach, E. (1995), *Quality through Equality: Good Practice in Equal Opportunities in Scottish Local Authorities*, Glasgow: Equal Opportunities Commission.

Breitenbach, E., A. Brown, F. Mackay and J. Webb (1999), *Equal Opportunities in Local Government in Scotland and Wales*, Edinburgh: Unit for the Study of Government in Scotland, The University of Edinburgh.

Bruegel, I. and H. Kean (1995), 'The moment of municipal feminism: gender and class in 1980s local government', *Critical Social Policy*, 44/45, Autumn.

Cockburn, C. (1991), *In the Way of Women*, Basingstoke: Macmillan.

CoSLA/EOC (1999), *Mainstreaming: Integrating Equality into all Council Activities*, Edinburgh: CoSLA, October.

Coyle, A. (1996), *Women and Organisational Change*, Manchester: EOC.

Edwards, J. (1989), 'Local Government's Women's Committees', *Critical Social Policy*, 24, Winter.

Edwards, J. (1995), *Local Government Women's Committees*, Aldershot: Avebury.

Elcock, H. (1996), 'Local Government', in D. Farnham and S. Horton (eds) *Managing the New Public Services*, Basingstoke: Macmillan.

European Commission (1996), *Equal Opportunities for Women and Men in the European Union*, Brussels: EC.

Halford, S. (1988), 'Women's initiatives in Local Government: Where do they come from and where are they going?', *Policy and Politics*, 16 (4).

Halford, S. (1992), 'Feminist change in a patriarchal organisation: the experience of women's initiatives in local government and implications for feminist perspectives on state institutions', in A. Witz and M. Savage (eds) *Gender and Bureaucracy*, Oxford: Blackwell.

Lieberman, S. (1989), 'Women's Committees in Scotland', in A. Brown and D. McCrone (eds) *The Scottish Government Yearbook 1989*, Edinburgh: Unit for the Study of Government in Scotland, University of Edinburgh.

Lovenduski, J. and V. Randall (1993), *Contemporary Feminist Politics: Women and Power in Britain*, Oxford: Oxford University Press.

Lovenduski, J., H. Margetts and S. Abrar (1996), *Sexing London: the Gender Mix of Policy Actors*, paper to American Political Science Association 92nd Annual Meeting, San Francisco.

Mackay, F., et al. (1995), *Early Days: Local Government Reorganisation and Equal Opportunities Practice, New Waverley Papers, Edinburgh*: Department of Politics, University of Edinburgh.

Marchbank, J. (1994), 'Nondecision-making . . . A Management Guide to Keeping Women's Interest Issues off the Political Agenda', in G. Griffen et al. (eds) *Stirring It: Challenges For Feminism*, Abingdon: Taylor and Francis.

Marchbank, J. (1996), *Going Dutch or Scotch Mist? Making Marginalised Voices Heard in Local Bureaucracies*, Bradford and Ilkley: Centre for Research in Applied Community Studies, Bradford and Ilkley Community College Corporation.

McCrone, D., et al. (1993), 'Reforming local government in Scotland' in *Local Government Studies*, 19 (1).

Stone, I. (1988), *Equal Opportunities in Local Authorities*, London: HMSO.

Turner, E., S. Riddell and S. Brown (1995), *Gender Equality in Scottish Schools: The Impact of Recent Educational Reforms*, Glasgow: EOC.

Women and the Campaign for the Scottish Parliament

CHAPTER 12

A Woman's Claim of Right in Scotland

KATHY GALLOWAY AND JUDITH ROBERTSON

'Introduction' in Woman's Claim of Right Group (eds) (1991) A Woman's Claim of Right in Scotland, Edinburgh: Polygon

Although women make up about 52% of the population in Scotland, only four women, that is 5.5%, of Scotland's MPs are female: Ray Michie for the Liberal Democrats (Argyll and Bute), Margaret Ewing for the SNP (Moray and Nairn), Maria Fyfe for the Labour Party (Glasgow Maryhill) and Irene Adams, also Labour (Paisley North). This staggering statistic of gender inequality, well over half a century after women won the right to full political equality, was the starting point for A Woman's Claim of Right in Scotland. At the time the campaign began, the situation was even worse. Irene Adams was elected to replace her husband only after his sudden death in office in November 1990.

The context for the campaign, which includes women from different political parties and women who had no political affiliation, was the setting up of the Scottish Constitutional Convention with a task of producing proposals for an anticipated Scottish parliament.

The Convention included members of the Scottish Labour Party, the Liberal Democrats, the Scottish Green Party and the Communist Party, as well as representatives of the trade unions, churches, local authorities and various other community groups. We discovered that the number of women nominated for membership of the Convention, from all these sectors of Scottish public life, would number only around 10%. Once again, major proposals and decisions affecting the life and well-being of the Scottish people would be made with women being significantly under-represented.

It was therefore out of a kind of desperation at the failure of the Scottish political institutions to take the opinions and aspirations of women seriously that A Woman's Claim of Right (AWCR) evolved. We wanted to understand more fully the factors preventing Scottish women from becoming more engaged, and reaching responsible positions in representative politics.

From its inception, AWCR has believed it is crucial not only to challenge the forces which stand in the way of higher levels of involvement, but also to ask questions about the style of politics in Scotland today, and to ask how much that style has been hostile to women.

Although our first task was to monitor closely the work of the Scottish Constitutional Convention as it affected women, and to make submissions concerning women in a Scottish Parliament, we have also attempted to research the history and background of women's political activity in Scotland, and to talk to as many women as possible. We have drawn in both those politically engaged and those with no official involvement with a view to discovering what it is that stops women playing a greater part in the decision-making processes of Scottish political life.

We should lay to rest a myth that prevails in Scotland which may have caused damaging assumptions to be made about the shape of women's participation in Scottish politics. That is the myth that women are somehow 'non-political', that they are less interested, less informed or even less able to take an active role in politics. The truth is very different. It is the case that women are less numerically strong in party politics and it is certainly the case that women are greatly under-represented in holding office in political parties and local and national government. But when we look at women's participation in what is referred to as 'campaign politics' a very different picture emerges. In community and tenant groups, in campaigns on housing, transport, social services and child welfare, in groups concerned with sexual politics and the rights of women, and in a bewildering range of single-issue campaigns, women have played an energetic and often leading role.

This 'alternative' or complementary form of political activity has been increasingly important in Scotland in the context of a hostile political climate in Westminster and has been more accessible to women than the party-political process. It has valued their contribution more, and has drawn on their insights, experience and energy to good effect. So much so that a Zairean agriculturalist involved in the leadership of grassroots community projects in his own country said, after spending some time living in Easterhouse and visiting community projects there, 'I see that when I get home, we must spend much more time and resources on educating and training women for leadership, because I recognise now that social change comes about through women.' Would that this insight were more recognised here – the importance of campaigning politics (indeed, its recognition as a valid form of political engagement) is consistently undervalued, and so the competence of women to gain representative office is denied.

Thus, we are faced with two crucial questions. Firstly, given that women *do* have strong political opinions, passion for change and the ability to organise in campaigning politics, why do these not find greater expression in party politics? And secondly, why is it that campaigning politics are still seen as a secondary, even second-rate form of democratic expression, and those who engage in them find themselves patronised or ignored by party politicians?

The answers to the first question are complex, and that complexity should not be denied. They are touched upon in this book. Nevertheless, patterns emerge which suggest possible directions for action. A first, and strong, strand is simply the extent of practical difficulty women experience in party politics. This arises mainly, though not exclusively, from the fact that women are still the primary carers for children, for elderly relatives, for the sick and disabled, and, dare we say it, for men. The demands of cooking, cleaning, washing and shopping still fall mainly on women, most of whom are also in part- or full-time employment, some of whom are the sole breadwinner. To find time and energy for political involvement at the end of a hard day of work, domestic enablement and organising family activities is not easy. As the title for one of our conferences stated, 'I'd love to change the world, but I have to cook the tea!'

Other practical difficulties abound – the timing and location of meetings, sessions, sittings, which take place during school holidays, late at night, in places ill-served by public transport, or in ill-lit city areas. The lack of facilities, particularly crèche facilities, and the cost of political involvement, became a real disincentive to women who often have very little disposable income and no easy childcare alternatives.

These and others constitute very real hurdles for women in a way that they mostly do not for men, hurdles which are not so evident in campaigning politics where practical arrangements are designed to accommodate the participants' needs much more. It is a source of encouragement to A Woman's Claim of Right that submissions from a number of women's groups, as well as the greater awareness growing in society at large that these issues must be addressed, has led to a commitment from the Convention to the kind of practical support that would enable many more women to contemplate Scottish parliamentary involvement.

Other strands in the patterns of disadvantage to women in party politics are more subtle. They are social, cultural and ideological. The expectations that women should be more passive, should adopt a servant role or should be enablers, are hard to counter in a context where 'servant' really means 'subservient', and where service itself is devalued. Educational norms, conditioning and training make it harder for women to be assertive, and if they succeed in spite of these in finding a voice and in making it heard, they are likely to find themselves accused of being aggressive or domineering.

Our cultural contradictions catch women in a double bind again and again. The enabling role of women is essential and should not be underestimated, but the opportunity for women to assert themselves and share in, or lead, responsible decision-making can no longer be sacrificed to undervalued, unpaid servitude. We must be careful not to set these roles in opposition but ultimately to seek to ensure that both become a comfortable domain for both women and men.

The style of party political activity is another strand in the pattern. Women have repeatedly expressed to us deep dissatisfaction and unease at a style which they perceive as adversarial, competitive and careerist. The 'macho tendency' is still alive and kicking in Scottish politics. Women's experience of campaigning politics, on the other hand, is that they are more co-operative and more likely to work by consensus. Campaigns are also more concerned with the issue at hand than with the carving-out of personal power bases.

These are generalities rather than universal rules, as anyone who has been caught in the crossfire of a community group or tenants' association where battle lines are fiercely drawn and all the guns are blazing will testify. Nevertheless, it is a widely shared experience among women that campaigning groups are less rigidly controlled by an invisible bureaucratic structure than the parties they often seek to influence. Our alternative campaigns are less prone to sterile doctrinaire position-taking, more creative and more enjoyable. Parties which are serious about encouraging women need to address these perceptions and experiences seriously.

And of course, there is the sheer discrimination factor. There is much evidence that the biggest difficulty women face is not in being elected, but in being selected. None of the parties has a good record in this respect – and this not simply on the basis of enough available women.

More than seventy years after women have won the right to vote, the new struggle is on for all the electorate to have the right to vote for women. 'Votes for Women' is still an unattained goal. A Woman's Claim of Right is sceptical (to say the least) of the view that this can be achieved voluntarily – history does not give us much cause for optimism on this count. While we appreciate the issues raised by constitutional guarantees, we note that the equality of opportunity that presently exists does not include the equality to take advantage of that opportunity – for whole sections of society including women.

Which brings us to the second crucial question, of the undervalued nature of campaigning politics. While women are seriously under-represented in representative democracy, they are enormously engaged in participative democracy.

A healthy democracy is one which allows and encourages many forms of political engagement, in campaigns, in community groups, in local associations and networks, in media and the arts, in local and national institutions, as well as in representative politics. A healthy democracy encourages and safeguards such political plurality as essential to the freedom and well-being of its people and its structures. A healthy democracy works to ensure the free flow of ideas and people from one form of political engagement to another. A healthy democracy recognises that people's involvement should go much deeper than simply casting a vote every five years. A healthy democracy recognises the sovereignty of the people rather than the sovereignty of government.

By these criteria British democracy is not at all well. We have witnessed in recent years increasing centralisation, the blockage of the free flow of information and the undermining of local government.

In Scotland, the increasing frustration of a people which has seen its elected representatives rendered powerless to represent it, has been paralleled by disillusionment with representative politics, creeping apathy and the political marginalisation of significant sectors of society. There are areas of Glasgow where the sitting local Councillors have been elected with between 12 and 15% of the potential popular vote!

This malaise is well documented and increasingly recognised. It is in response to it that Charter 88 came into being, that A Claim of Right for Scotland appeared, that the Scottish Constitutional Convention was set up, and that A Woman's Claim of Right emerged. All of these have recognised that representative democracy is not enough, and that participative democracy is essential in a society where only a very small minority are actually members of political parties. And further, that representative democracy only allows people to feel truly represented when they are also participants in their democracy, whether in party politics or in any of the many other forms of political engagement available.

A Woman's Claim of Right has attempted to encourage the involvement of women in Scotland both in representative democracy and participative democracy. We think it is vital for party politics that more women be encouraged, enabled and, if necessary, constitutionally guaranteed increased representation.

We have gathered clear evidence that women have the desire, the experience and the ability to be involved in decision-making to the highest level. And, further, that the consistent determination of women to participate in their democracy, often against great odds, is a quality that we can ill-afford to lose from the political arena in Scotland.

In the current debate about electoral reform, it is well to remember that if proportionality is a desirable thing in party representation, then it is also desirable across the whole spectrum of democratic involvement, where concerns, causes and alliances may not necessarily always be represented within party lines. At present, groups which are proportionately under-represented in party politics find some creative participative expression in campaigning politics. We need to find better ways of drawing on that creativity. We need to find better ways of ensuring that 52% of the Scottish population produce more than 5.5% of its MPs – a lot more!

CHAPTER 13

Constitutional Change and the Gender Deficit

ISOBEL LINDSAY

'Constitutional Change and the Gender Deficit', in Woman's Claim of Right Group (eds) (1991) A Woman's Claim of Right in Scotland, Edinburgh: Polygon

The most striking feature of the position of women in Scottish politics is the lack of significant progress in the past fifty years. The evolutionary approach, based on the assumption that change would take place gradually and inevitably, was a plausible position in the early period after gaining formal electoral equality in 1928. By the 1980s, this belief in automatic progress bore no relationship to reality. Despite the extensive involvement of women in highly responsible positions during the war, there was no great post-war surge of women into elected office. Even the growth of interest in feminist issues in the 1960s and 1970s which produced legislation promoting measures of economic and social equality did not bring with it any increase in political representation. That very low representation of women continued to be the norm through the 1980s. It may have been possible to explain away the overwhelming dominance of men in positions of political power in 1931 or 1945 or 1959 as the first stage of a slow evolutionary process, but by the end of the 1980s this sounded increasingly implausible. There was no evidence of change and little reason to expect it to take place spontaneously. The supposed 'march of progress' had been left somewhere near the starting-line.

For many feminists this was not an issue high on their agenda. The extent of women's participation in formal political institutions was seen at best as an irrelevance and at worst as the propping-up of institutions which were in themselves repressive.

The failure to engage with formal political power arose largely because women's liberation came out of the anarcho-libertarian ethos of the late sixties. That movement rejected established societies which were seen as repressive and also rejected all the associated institutions and values. (Stacey and Price 1981)

During the course of the 1980s there appeared to be a modest increase in interest in women's capacity to succeed in formal organisations, particularly in employment but also in politics:

> For many feminists who had learned their politics from the women's movement it gradually became clear nothing was going to change unless power was challenged – only those who sat at the table would get a slice of the cake. (Coote and Patullo 1990)

In the Scottish context it was the prospect of a new and open debate on constitutional change which became the catalyst for a more radical and assertive response to the issue of women's representation in public life. The ensuing debate threw into sharp focus the clash between voluntarism and interventionism and exposed the continued existence of complacent evolutionary assumptions.

The Scottish Constitutional Convention was established as a means of achieving a consensus scheme for a future Scottish parliament. It was made up of representatives of Scottish Labour, Liberal Democrats, Greens, Communists, the Scottish Churches, local authorities, trade unions, and sections of the business community. The women's movement was represented through the Scottish Convention of Women, a co-ordinating organisation. A decision was taken in the initial stages of the [Constitutional] Convention to establish a committee, chaired by Maria Fyfe MP, whose principal remit was to produce proposals to increase the representation of women in a Scottish parliament. This marked a significant shift from the lack of interest in the issue which had prevailed a decade earlier.

During the intensive debate on constitutional change in Scotland in the 1970s and in most of the subsequent debates in the 1980s, the women's dimension was not an issue. At most there was an assumption that if there was a parliament based in Scotland, it would attract more women candidates because it would be easier to combine elected office with domestic responsibilities and would stimulate new interest in Scottish politics. In effect this was a Scottish version of 'the march of progress'. Constitutional change would automatically bring with it solutions to the problem of low levels of women's participation because it would reduce the practical problems and stimulate new interest in Scottish politics. A parliament in Scotland would be less geographically disadvantageous and would be expected to have better working hours and conditions. The assumption that these improvements on their own would produce a radical difference is questionable. Local government does not present geographical problems and to some extent the payment system presents fewer problems for many women than for men since it is similar to part-time employment which is common in women's work. Despite this, in the 1989 Regional Council elections only 16% of successful candidates were women. Practical difficulties undoubtedly discouraged women from political participation at higher levels but they are only part of a much more difficult problem. Women are grossly under-represented in the higher reaches of decision-making in society, and greatly over-represented in the social positions with little power, status and low economic reward. Political power is not in this respect different from other areas of social life. Domestically, economically and politically, women act predominantly in a service capacity to men. How do we change the role of women to one which offers a fairer distribution of the positions of command and control in society?

This is a radical agenda, since it challenges deeply ingrained attitudes and vested interests. It was to be expected that radical solutions would produce strongly antagonistic reactions.

One of the earliest submissions to the Constitutional Convention came from the Woman's Claim of Right group. This was a multi-party and non-party group with an active contribution from Green Party women. It had been established to make an effective response to the work of the Convention and ensure that the issue of women's representation was kept high on the agenda. They suggested a range of proposals – equality audits of political parties, a Scottish parliament women's committee, practical and educational measures to encourage women's involvement, and a strengthened Scottish Equal Opportunities Commission. They also supported the principle of positive action through the electoral system but did not specify the method.

The group which then took the most radical initiative, an initiative which dominated the subsequent debate, was the Women's Committee of the Scottish Trades Union Congress, who proposed that there should be a 50:50 gender balance in the new Scottish Parliament. The preferred system to achieve this was 'parallelism', i.e. that each constituency should return two members (or an equivalent multiple in a multi-member system), one of whom would be elected from a female list of candidates and one from a male list. All electors would vote for both. This would ensure full gender equality and in principle could be used in any electoral system. The strength of the proposal lies in its simplicity, its certainty in delivering equality of representation, and its ability to deliver such radical change with the first Scottish parliament. There are certain practical problems in combining such a system with party proportionality, primarily those of avoiding a parliament which is too large or constituencies which are too large.

Following the STUC initiative, a range of schemes was produced seeking to combine 50:50 with proportionality. Most used various versions of the Additional Member System used in West Germany. In this system, party disproportionality arising from first-past-the-post constituency votes is balanced by top-up seats from party lists. Permutations of this system can give gender balance, party proportionality, a reasonable size of parliament and constituencies which are not too large. Another proposal emerged which also required constitutional guarantees but did not specify parallelism. This suggested a legal requirement on parties to put forward an equal gender balance of candidates without specifying how parties should do this. Penalties for failing to do this could involve substantial financial loss, [for example,] through a new deposit system.

The STUC's Women's Committee proposal quickly gained the support of most of the major unions in Scotland. It was also passed overwhelmingly by the Scottish Labour party's 1990 conference. Some of this support in the Labour party was motivated by a hidden agenda, but this was not the case on the trade union side. The hidden agenda was the debate on proportional representation. Neither side in that debate wanted to offend the women's lobby, and those opposed to PR also saw the 50:50 proposal as one which would be easiest to combine with first-past-the-post or their preferred option, the alternative vote. It was the suspicion that the 50:50 proposal was a stalking-horse for opposition to proportionality which produced some of the early negative responses to the scheme, both within the Labour Party and among some of the Greens. This was a misinterpretation of the situation, since the strongest support for 50:50 was from the STUC and it was the STUC which provided the principal support in the Labour party for PR.

However, by no means all the opposition to 50:50 came from those suspicious of hidden motives. There was strong opposition from the leadership in the Liberal Democrats, from individuals in the Labour party and from some of the Greens. Some of the objections were pragmatic and some philosophical. The pragmatic objections were concerned primarily with how best to achieve a genuine long-term shift in the role of women in political life. The philosophical objections related both to issues of voters' choice and to the concept of gender differentiation in politics. Before looking at these rational arguments, it would be failing to reflect the debate adequately if we ignored the irrational. Issues related to gender are influenced by deeply entrenched processes of socialisation and it would be surprising if they did not produce emotional reactions. No matter what lip-service is paid on the surface, significant traces of chauvinism have not disappeared from Scottish public life. The 50:50 proposal has provoked its share of snide comments and humorous derision from some men. More sadly it has also produced strong antagonism from some women active in politics rather akin to the 'self-made man' philosophy – 'I have made it to senior positions so what prevents other women?' These responses are not new; they echo those with which the suffragettes had to contend from men and women in daring to suggest that there should be equality in voting rights.

By no means all objections were based on prejudice. There were objections of principle. For some the primacy of the voters' right to choose individual candidates was regarded as such a fundamental aspect of democracy that any interference was unacceptable. Therefore any attempt to determine the gender balance in parliament by constitutional requirement was seen as undermining that basic right. Another objection on principle was concerned with the notion that gender should be a distinguishing factor in politics. This was interpreted as denying the essential equality of males and females to be judged on the same criteria. It also raised the question of why gender and not other factors such as social class and ethnic origin should merit special treatment.

The more pragmatic objections were concerned with specific problems of building an undesirable rigidity into the system, of lack of availability of experienced women politicians, and of how to achieve genuine change. A legal guarantee was seen by some as a superficial change affecting a small number of women in senior positions – a version of tokenism, more substantial but still tokenist in nature. It would produce gender equality in the parliament but would not guarantee change for the majority of women or even a higher level of political participation for women at grassroots level. The solutions to the problem were seen to be educational and structural. Educational change would involve encouraging different perceptions of male and female roles and through this altering patterns of participation. Much of this educational work should involve campaigning activity by women themselves, so that the changes were female-generated. Structural change would involve creating conditions which facilitated women's participation, from changing the nature and timing of local branch meetings to changes in the organisation of the national legislature. The underlying assumption was that such changes would produce some form of 'organic' change which would secure the development of women's political role without formally enforcing change from the top down. These pragmatic objections typified the response of some of the Green women. The objections on principle to any legal interventionism was the official response of the Liberal Democrats.

The case for legally guaranteed gender ratios was also supported by a combination of principle and pragmatism. The principle underlying the proposal was that gender matters and that the claim for equality cannot simply be satisfied by theoretical equality of opportunity which has never succeeded in producing other than great inequality in representation:

> Equality has very little abstract meaning in a society based on inequality of resources and access to power. Having one equal vote is not equality. Women have to struggle against material inequality, social organisation which makes participation in the labour market and politics difficult, and the downgrading of issues which affect us. (Ross 1990)

Does gender truly matter as a political category? The case is not based on the assumption that women will be concentrated in one ideological section of the political spectrum. It is accepted that this will not be so. Nor is the case based on the assumption that women will prove superior to men in political understanding and political behaviour. When represented in larger numbers, that may or may not prove to be so. Political power is not in this respect different from other areas of social life but the prospect of constitutional reform in Scotland presents an opportunity to confront this problem in the political context. To argue that there are other forms of under-representation is not a justification for failing to take action on gender. Is it preferable not to progress on any front if you cannot progress simultaneously on all fronts? Gender happens to be easy to define and easy to legislate for.

To protest at the use of legal requirements to determine the gender make-up of a parliament ignores the fact that the law already intervenes in certain areas, [for example] on age limits. We have accepted the need for legal intervention in equal pay and equal opportunities legislation. There is hardly any great restriction in voters' choice in requiring that half of the parliament should be selected from over half the population. For those who believe there is some genuine difference in the experience of males and females, the justification of balanced representation is self-evident. For those who do not consider that there are differences of substance, the proposal should present no real problems since the gender make-up of the parliament should make no difference for better or worse. The only reason for objection would be on the pragmatic grounds that there were insufficient talented candidates among the 52% of the population which is female. There may be a short-term problem in the availability of women with experience, but this would last no longer than the first couple of years of the new parliament. Indeed, one of the strongest arguments for a gender balance requirement is that the parties could no longer neglect their female talent but would have to encourage and develop it. Women would no longer be seen as merely candidates for fund-raising and routine secretarial work rather than for the more highly politicised roles. The level of attainment to be reached before women politicians in Scotland reach the standards of the typical Member of Parliament or local councillor does not seem dauntingly high. The problem is how to channel the many able women who are active in voluntary associations, campaigning and community groups into senior levels of political decision-making. The very fact that these women are often uncomfortable with the confrontational style and the personal ambition of much party politics is a very strong argument for trying to have them as members of a national legislature.

To suggest that a legal requirement for gender balance would not produce real change but would be another form of tokenism, seems to have an almost puritanical basis. It is almost as if an achievement which is not the product of blood, sweat and tears must as a result be ineffective. No one is suggesting that a constitutional requirement for equal representation would on its own solve the problems of women's participation in political activity. It has to be part of a range of measures which include educational and structural changes, but in itself it would be a great catalyst for such changes. Men and women would come to see it as normal to have women equally represented in the higher reaches of politics. It would help to develop women's self-image and to change men's perceptions of women. Senior political women would not be categorised as exceptional but would become so familiar as to be regarded as ordinary. A Scottish parliament from its inception would not have the atmosphere of a male club. It would develop from the start as a legislature where men and women had equal status. There is nothing wrong with taking short-cuts if they help to get you where you want to go. If we have to wait until hearts and minds have been changed and power structures radically reformed before women are equally represented in political decision-making, we may find we are well into the next century and can still count the number of Scottish women MPs on one hand. The evolutionary approach has not been successful. *Laissez-faire* has reinforced the status-quo. Those who oppose interventionism have failed to produce evidence that there are other routes to effective change. Unless that change is achieved in the first Scottish parliament, there will be powerful vested interests which will make it difficult to introduce change thereafter. If the case for constitutionally led change is won, we may see in three or four years a Scottish parliament which is the most radical in the world in its representation of women.

– REFERENCES –

Coote, A. and P. Patullo (1990), *Power and Prejudice: Women and Politics*, London: Weidenfeld and Nicolson.

Ross, Jennifer (1990), *Equal Voice*, Glasgow: STUC.

Stacey, M. and M. Price (1981), *Women, Power and Politics*, London: Tavistock.

CHAPTER 14

A Woman's Place? The Future Scottish Parliament

CATRIONA LEVY

'A Woman's Place? the Future Scottish Parliament', in Lindsay Paterson and David McCrone (eds) (1992), *Scottish Government Year Book 1992*, Unit for the Study of Government in Scotland, University of Edinburgh

This chapter examines the current debate on women's representation in Scotland and the role played by the Scottish Constitutional Convention in raising the issue. It identifies arguments around women's representation within the Convention, and underlines the opportunities for improving Scottish women's representation presented by the creation of a Scottish Parliament or Assembly. It is revealing, however, to set the current interest in women's representation in context; some discussion of the lessons that might be drawn from the historical experience of women's representation at Westminster precedes the section on the Convention. It is hoped that this chapter will provide encouragement to aspiring women politicians, and the conclusion attempts to offer a constructive but realistic assessment of the prospects of making a Scottish Parliament a woman's place.

– WOMEN AND PARTY POLITICS IN SCOTLAND SINCE 1918 –

In 1918 most women over 30 got the vote and women over 21 won the right to stand as parliamentary candidates. The vote on equal terms with men was won in 1928 when the vote was extended to women over 21. Yet, as Table 14.1 shows, from 1918 to the present day, only 21 women – eleven Labour, six Conservative, three SNP and one Liberal Democrat – have represented Scottish constituencies at Westminster.[1] The UK's under-representation of women has been mirrored in Scotland. However, low levels of women's representation have gone hand in hand with low levels of interest in improving women's representation.

Women were certainly the political novelty of the 1920s, and there was great uncertainty as to how the new female electors would vote. As the suffragette historian Ray Strachey noted, the emergence of a Women's Party was dreaded, and men did not know how best to win women's votes (Strachey 1979: 366). The welcome discovery in 1918 that 'there was no appearance of anything like a tendency to a block vote' (*Scotsman* 1918) and that women voted on the same party lines as men, ensured that the novelty faded. In addition, as Deirdre Beddoe has commented, 'larger events, including the economic crisis at home, the rise of Fascism in Europe and the growing threat of war . . . crowded women off the stage of history' (Beddoe 1989: 132). Only five women were returned for Scottish seats in the inter-war period, but the lack of women MPs does not seem to have been a burning issue. The preoccupation of the parties was winning women's votes, not in providing the electors with women to vote for (Levy 1992). The few people urging measures to increase women's representation were swimming against the tide (Levy 1992; Lee 1981: 168; Mann 1962: 42). The assumption of the inter-war years seemed to be that a gradual and natural increase in women's parliamentary representation might be expected.

Women's representation at Westminster, however, has remained low. With 44 women MPs currently in the House of Commons, UK women's representation has reached its highest-ever level of 6.8%. The highest levels of Scottish women's representation occurred in 1959 and 1964 with the return of five Scottish women MPs, or 7%. The proportion of women MPs out of the total of Scottish MPs returned has been marginally higher than the UK average at 14 of the 20 general elections since 1918.[2] Since 1979, however, Scotland has returned a lesser proportion of women to Westminster than the UK average. Most of the present campaigners for better women's representation have underlined the poor return of only three Scottish women MPs at the 1987 election.

It seems likely that there is a connection between the raising of the issue and increasing awareness of far higher levels of women's representation outside the UK. In most European countries there has been a continuing upward trend since 1945, particularly in the Scandinavian countries.[3] The upward trend in Norway and Sweden has been most marked since the beginning of the 1970s, when major parties in those countries adopted quota systems to make sure that a certain proportion of parliamentary candidates was female. In Scotland and the UK instead of a gradual upward trend there has been a rise and fall within a low level. Table 14.2 compares the percentage of women MPs returned in Norway, Sweden, Scotland and the UK at general elections since the 1960s.[4]

Over the 1980s the Social-Democratic, Liberal, Green and Labour parties began to explore options for improving women's representation. Formed in 1981, the SDP adopted candidate selection rules seeking a minimum of **two** women on every shortlist where possible. In 1987 the Alliance put up the highest number of women candidates of all the parties – 105 in the UK and one in Scotland

Table 14.1
Scotland: Women MPs, 1918–91

1923–38	Katherine, Duchess of Atholl (Con)	Perth & Kinross (West)
1919–31	Miss Jennie Lee (Lab)	North Lanark[a]
1931–45	Rt Hon Miss Florence Horsburgh (Con)	Dundee
1931–35	Mrs Helen Shaw (Con)	Bothwell
1937–45	Mrs Agnes Hardie (Lab)	Springburn[a]
1945–70	Rt Hon Margaret (Peggy) Herbison (Lab)	North Lanark
1945–59	Mrs Jean Mann (Lab)	Coatbridge
1945–46	Mrs Clarice Shaw (Lab)	Kilmarnock
1946–66	Lady Grant of Monymusk (Con)	Aberdeen South[a]
	(as Lady Tweedsmuir after 1948)	
1948–69	Mrs Alice Cullen (Lab)	Gorbals[a]
1958–59	Mrs Mary McAlistair (Lab)	Kelvingrove[a]
1959–79	Rt Hon Betty Harvie Anderson (Con)	Renfrewshire East
1959–87	Rt Hon Dame Judith Hart (Lab)	Lanark (Clydesdale 1983–)
1967–70	Mrs Winifred (Winnie) Ewing (SNP)	Hamilton[a]
1974–79	Mrs Winifred (Winnie) Ewing (SNP)	Moray & Nairn
1973–74	Mrs Margo MacDonald (SNP)	Govan[a]
1974–79	Mrs Margaret Bain (SNP)	Dunbartonshire East
1987	(as Mrs Ewing)	Moray
1982–83	Mrs Helen McElhone (Lab)	Queen's Park[a]
1983–87	Mrs Anna McCurley (Con)	Renfrew West & Inverclyde
1987	Mrs Maria Fyfe (Lab)	Maryhill
1987	Mrs Ray Michie (SLD)	Argyll & Bute
1990	Mrs Irene Adams (Lab)	Paisley North[a]

[a] indicates first elected in a by-election.

Source: House of Commons *Women in the House of Commons*, Factsheet No 5, undated.

Table 14.2
Women MPs returned as a % of the total number of MPs at general
elections over 1961–89 in Norway, Sweden, Scotland and the UK

Norway	1965	1969	1973	1977	1981	1985	1989		
	8.0	9.3	15.5	23.9	25.8	34.4	35.6		
Sweden	1961	1965	1969	1971	1974	1977	1980	1984	1988
	11.2	11.5	13.8	14.0	21.1	22.9	27.8	28.9	38.1
Scotland	1964	1966	1970	1974[a]	1974[b]	1979	1983	1987	
	7.0	5.6	2.8	4.2	5.6	1.4	2.8	4.2	
UK	1964	1966	1970	1974[a]	1974[b]	1979	1983	1987	
	4.6	4.1	4.1	3.6	4.3	3.0	3.5	6.3	

[a] February
[b] October

(Vallance 1988: 88). Following the Liberal-SDP merger, the Liberal Democrats have adopted a variation of the SDP women and shortlists rule: the obligation to have at least one woman on a shortlist if a woman is nominated. Over the 1980s the Green Party has explored a number of options for increasing their proportion of women candidates including adopting quotas and targets. Since 1987 the Labour party has adopted measures to raise the profile of women in the party. In 1988 Labour adopted 'one woman on a shortlist where a woman is nominated for selection' and since 1989 the Parliamentary Labour Party has been obliged to vote for at least three women for the 18-strong Shadow Cabinet. At the 1990 Labour Party Conference the NEC was instructed to establish a programme which will within ten years phase in 50% women's representation within the PLP. These developments mark a radical shift. Clare Short, Labour MP for Birmingham Ladywood, recently commented, 'It's unbelievable . . . I keep waiting for the resistance but it doesn't happen' (*Tribune* 1991).

Despite the steps taken by some of the parties, however, a recent *Labour Research* report indicated that women's representation at Westminster is unlikely to improve dramatically at the next election (*Labour Research* 1991: 9–11). In the context of the record of low women's representation at Westminster, the implications of the discussion on women's representation in a Scottish Parliament can be viewed as dramatic and far-reaching.

_ THE SCOTTISH CONSTITUTIONAL _ CONVENTION AND WOMEN

The current debate on women's representation in Scotland has taken place in the context of the premiership of Britain's first woman Prime Minister, who dominated British politics in the 1980s. How much Mrs Thatcher achieved for other women during her period in office is a matter of controversy. In a recent assessment of Thatcher's legacy for women in Scotland, Alice Brown commented that 'an unintended consequence of Thatcherism can be argued to be . . . the debate within the Scottish Constitutional Convention about the equal representation of women in a Scottish Parliament'. Brown suggested that this might be interpreted as part of the general response to Thatcherism in Scotland, linked to declining Scottish Conservative fortunes, the arrival of the 'doomsday scenario' in 1987 and the setting up of a Scottish Constitutional Convention to arrive via consensus at proposals for Scottish constitutional reform (Brown 1991a).

Before the 1987 General Election, the unpopularity of Mrs Thatcher and her policies in Scotland led to speculation about the political and constitutional implications of the return of a third Thatcher government combined with declining Tory fortunes in Scotland. This was the so-called 'doomsday scenario', and in 1987 it arrived in no uncertain terms. Mrs Thatcher was returned to office with a parliamentary majority of 102, but in Scotland her party suffered its worst election defeat since 1910, being reduced from 21 seats to ten.

Against this background, the cross-party Campaign for a Scottish Assembly (CSA) revived the idea of holding a Constitutional Convention. The CSA invited a committee of prominent Scots (but not including any prominent politicians) to draw up a report on the state of the current government of Scotland, and to make recommendations as to what should be done. This committee met from January to June 1988. Its main recommendation was the setting up of a Constitutional Convention to press for a Scottish Assembly. In the months following the launch, there was a series of consultation meetings with the political parties and other Scottish institutions to test the support for the Convention proposal. While it was no surprise that the Conservative party refused to take part, by late autumn of 1988 all the opposition parties seemed likely to participate in the Convention and strong support had come from the trade union movement, the churches, and local authorities. The SNP, however, withdrew in early 1989. The Green Party withdrew in early 1991 but may yet rejoin – as indeed may the SNP. Yet in its methods of working via cross-party consensus and in the emerging proposals for the status, powers and financing of a Scottish parliament, the Convention has now moved far beyond the 1978 Scotland Act. A symptom of this movement is the increasing use of the term 'Parliament' rather than 'Assembly'.

An important and fresh dimension in the devolution debate has been the raising of how best to ensure women's greater involvement in a Scottish parliament. As will be seen, the activities of the Woman's Claim of Right Group publicised low levels of Scottish women's representation while the setting up of a Women's Issues Group along with other Convention working groups provided a focus for submissions on how to improve women's representation. This provides a contrast with the campaign in the run-up to the referendum on devolution in March 1979. While the contribution of individual women on either side of the devolution debate is noted in Bochel, Denver and Macartney's account of the referendum campaign (Bochel et al. 1980), there was little focus on involving women in a Scottish Assembly. The Scottish Convention of Women (SCOW) was one of the few groups which attempted to raise the question of attitudes to women's representation in an Assembly. Formed in 1977 out of work initiated in the UN International Women's Year (1975), SCOW had a membership based on representatives from trade unions, local groups including the Women's Guild, and individuals, with the aim of promoting the quality of life for all women and men. SCOW circulated a questionnaire to the political parties in an attempt to discover what they were thinking of in terms of women's representation. Maidie Hart of SCOW has since described this exercise as 'not very productive . . . and then the whole (devolution) debate fell apart anyway'.[5]

The Women's Legal and Financial Independence Campaign also made a contribution to the devolution debate by preparing a Charter for legal reforms in the areas in which an Assembly would have powers. The Scottish Women's Charter covered areas such as divorce, financial provision, and custody; housing, abortion, contraception and maternity services; childcare and violence against women. It drew on the concerns of the women's movement which was raising issues it saw as crucial in the shaping of women's lives, but outwith the formal structures of the political parties. But as Esther Breitenbach has pointed out, the Legal and Financial Independence Group did not take up a position for or against devolution (Breitenbach 1990: 216). In 1979, the feminist *Msprint* actually went so far as to comment, 'On the whole the women's movement ignored the referendum or saw it as irrelevant' (quoted in Breitenbach 1990: 216).

Kate Phillips, Esther Breitenbach and Alice Brown have recently argued convincingly that the perceived impact of Thatcherism on women in Scotland has had the effect over the 1980s of diverting the energies of women, who had previously involved themselves exclusively within the women's movement, into party political activity, principally although not exclusively within the Labour and Green parties (Breitenbach 1989; Breitenbach 1990; Brown 1991; Phillips 1989). This development can be argued to have played a part in sharpening the focus on women's representation in the revived devolution debates over 1988–91. In response to the Claim of Right and the setting up of the Constitutional Convention, A Woman's Claim of Right was launched in April 1989, 'because 52% of this country's population provide just 4% of its MPs' (Woman's Claim of Right 1989). While Green Party women were prominent in its launch, it was a cross-party and non-party group of women committed to drawing attention to women's low representation in government and to campaigning on four points set out in an April manifesto:

- An Assembly which deals urgently with obstacles to women in housing, education, employment, childcare, health and personal safety.
- A move away from the battleground style of present day politics and a move towards greater co-operation in the cause of social justice, recognising the value of women's experience and wisdom.
- Positive support, training and encouragement to enable women from any sector of society to take an active part in public life.
- Constitutional reform *guaranteeing* equal representation for women in the political arena!

(A Woman's Claim of Right 1989)

The campaign mounted conferences in 1989, won a certain amount of publicity, and promised to set up working groups and a data and monitoring unit on women's representation, and to form local groups. A submission was made to the Scottish Constitutional Convention and individual members such as

Jackie Roddick have contributed articles on women's representation to Radical Scotland (Roddick 1989–90). Although the book, A Woman's Claim of Right in Scotland, was published in the summer of 1991, at the time of writing the organisation appears to have faded (Woman's Claim of Right Group 1991). This is perhaps because A Woman's Claim of Right found itself pushing at an open door in the spring of 1989.

It was not, however, immediately clear that this was so. The first meeting of the Constitutional Convention on 30 March 1989 has been dubbed 'mainly manly' by Emma Simpson, as only 23 women attended the first meeting of around 140 delegates from political parties, local authorities, trade unions, churches, business and industry, ethnic minorities and the Campaign for a Scottish Assembly (Simpson 1990: 21). The Convention unanimously adopted a Declaration acknowledging the sovereign right of the Scottish people to determine its own form of government and pledging the Convention to work towards the preparation of a scheme for an Assembly or Parliament for Scotland which would be put to the Scottish people for endorsement. Detailed work was to be carried out in working groups to examine areas including constitutional issues and the structure of government, powers and responsibilities, financing Scottish expenditure, and 'making the Scottish Parliament truly representative'. Criticism of the low numbers of women involved in the Convention's proceedings (albeit a much larger showing than at Westminster) prompted Labour members of the Convention Executive to propose the setting up of a Women's Issues Working Group to consider how to make a Scottish parliament truly representative. The Group was chaired by Maria Fyfe, Labour MP for Glasgow Maryhill and then Labour deputy shadow spokesperson for women's affairs. Other members were Yvonne Strachan of the TGWU, the Rev. Norman Shanks, Labour MP John McAllion, and Bruce Black, CoSLA Deputy Secretary and Secretary of the Constitutional Convention.

– THE WOMEN'S ISSUES GROUP –

The Women's Issues Group set about its task with constructive optimism. As Maidie Hart of SCOW put it, 'Women had got in at the ground floor for once' (Simpson 1990: 40). In May 1989 the Group wrote to a wide range of Scottish organisations seeking their views on how it could be ensured that a Scottish parliament involved women. Views were sought on six areas identified as crucial in the shaping of the Parliament. These areas were: working patterns; remuneration; provision of allowances and facilities; the Parliament's format; reflecting women's views; and electoral arrangements. In September 1989 an interim report was drawn up for the Women's Issues Group by the present author (Scottish Constitutional Convention 1989: 85–103). Further submissions were received later but did not significantly depart from the initial findings and recommendations. The Interim Report had set the agenda for discussion within the Convention of women's involvement in a Scottish parliament.

Submissions received by the Women's Issues Group were unanimous on the need to ensure that the low level of women's representation in Scottish politics was not continued into a Scottish parliament. Several barriers to women taking an equal part were identified. The STUC Women's Committee summed up the major barrier to women's participation:

> The present political system is constructed in such a way as to virtually exclude women from participation. In a society where the main domestic responsibility for child and dependent care lies with women, it is not surprising that there are so few women MPs or local government elected representatives. This responsibility or assumption that the responsibility is a woman's is unlikely to disappear in the next few years, if even within this century. A Scottish Assembly should, from the outset, therefore, make itself accessible to women. (Scottish Constitutional Convention 1989: 93)

Domestic responsibility and the range of practical limitations it poses on what kind of work women do and where they are able to do it was seen as the major barrier. Other areas identified included women's lack of confidence and experience in operating in formal power structures, the Westminster timetable, and women's discomfort in the formalised slanging match epitomised by Westminster. The submission from A Woman's Claim of Right noted that 'because a Scottish Assembly would be more local and accessible, we would expect some natural improvement in female representation to follow its introduction in any case'. Yet Lothian Regional Council commented that 'within the present structures and processes of central and local government women's representation is substantially less than would be expected on the basis of both population qualifications and experience'. Discrimination against women in party selection procedures was not emphasised as a barrier, however; the underlying assumption was that women were ruled out of consideration a long way short of the selection meetings (Scottish Constitutional Convention 1989: 93).

The interim report listed proposals intended to boost women's representation. Throughout, Westminster served as a powerful negative model. On the working pattern of a Scottish parliament, submissions were unanimous in favouring parliament's sitting during office hours and taking recesses in line with school holidays. There were various options for the parliamentary week, such as three days in the chamber and two days in the constituency. There was a consensus that members of a Scottish parliament should hold their seat as a full-time salaried post paid in line with Westminster MPs. Submissions were unanimous too on the need for a flexible system of child and carer allowances and crèche facilities. Travel, research and secretarial expenses were also considered necessary. There was considerable support for fixed-term parliaments and for the development of a committee structure to deal with the main business of a Scottish parliament. The creation of a Scottish Equal Opportunities Commission and a Ministry for Women within the parliament found support, as did the idea of requiring each political party to publish an equality audit at elections (Scottish Constitutional Convention 1989: 92, 99–100). The report made by the Convention on 30 November 1990, *Towards Scotland's Parliament*, confirmed that the working structures and patterns of a Scottish parliament should positively encourage the involvement of women, and ethnic and other minority groups (Scottish Constitutional Convention 1990: 17).

_ Making a Scottish parliament _
TRULY REPRESENTATIVE

The area of least consensus in the submissions was and remains that of electoral arrangements; that is, the arrangements by which the increased representation of women is to be achieved. The options which have emerged within the Convention have included electoral reform, quota systems and the 50:50 option. The parties involved in the Convention have each expressed a preference among these options without yet arriving at a final position.

The most radical proposal, in the sense of its certain impact on women's representation, is the 50:50 option. Originally proposed in a submission to the Women's Issues Group by the STUC Women's Committee, 50:50 is based on the requirement that 50% of elected representatives should be men and 50% should be women. Despite the similarity between 50:50 and Bernard Shaw's earlier proposal of the 'Coupled Vote', the STUC Women's Committee drew their proposal from the recommendations of the Kilbrandon Commission that a Scottish parliament should have two-member constituencies.[6] The STUC submission proposed:

> We would suggest that each constituency should be entitled to return two representatives to the Assembly; one woman; one man . . . If current parliamentary constituencies were changed this principle could still apply; and indeed, it would work if PR was introduced. If constituencies were changed to area groups, two categories of voting would still be applicable. (Scottish Constitutional Convention 1989: 102)

The 50:50 option, if compulsory, would bring about an instantaneous transformation in Scottish women's representation at least at the level of a Scottish parliament. The option moved to the centre of the political argument on representation when it became Labour Party policy. At its 1990 Scottish Conference the Labour Party ruled out 'first-past-the-post' for elections to a

Scottish parliament; decided that men and women should be equally represented in the chamber; and began a process of consultation on electoral systems.

Although Labour committed itself to moving away from first-past-the-post for a Scottish parliament, as it adopted the goal of equal representation of men and women Labour's commitment to 50:50 has been viewed with suspicion by the Liberal Democrat and Green parties in particular, lest Labour use 50:50 to scupper PR. Those opposed to 50:50 inside and outside the Labour party have argued that it is not feasible to combine 50:50 with proportional representation. The Chair of the Women's Issues Group, Maria Fyfe, has been a firm defender of the 50:50 proposal, seeing it as 'the opportunity to create an equal say for women for the first time in the history of Scottish politics' and arguing that:

> As a matter of fact, it would be perfectly possible to ensure equal numbers of women and men under any electoral system . . . Under the Alternative Vote, the voter would list male candidates in order of preference, and female candidates likewise. Under the Single Transferable Vote in multi-member constituencies the number of members in each constituency would need to be divisible by two, and odd numbers would need to be avoided. If, say, six members were required, then three men and three women would be elected. In the Additional Member System, a male and female MSP would be elected in each constituency, and each political party entitled to additional members would top up with equal numbers of men and women. (Fyfe 1989–90)

In 1989 the Green Party offered electoral reform as the solution to improving women's representation. Any form of proportional representation was regarded as likely 'almost certainly in and of itself (to) raise the number of female members of any future Scottish parliament, though it might not do so immediately in the parties which the majority of voters choose' (Scottish Constitutional Convention 1989: 101). The Green Party initially recommended the use of a 30% quota of female candidates and the adoption of the Additional Member System (AMS) on the former West German model. The quota policy has now been replaced by a 'trigger mechanism' whereby party members will be alerted if it seems as though fewer than 30% of candidates will be women in any round of selections. To an extent the trigger seems to be connected to an unloaded pistol in that it will not guarantee that a certain proportion of women candidates will always be selected. However, if a selection round fails to select over 30% women candidates then there would be an inquiry into why women were not selected or did not come forward.[7] The Green Party was also closely associated with the idea of requiring each political party to publish an equality audit before elections.

The Liberal Democrats have adopted a similar approach to that of the Greens – supporting the idea of an equality audit, attempting to devise internal party structures that will prove appealing and supportive to women, support for would-be women candidates, training and encouragement, and the setting of targets as distinct from quotas. In an internal consultation, Scottish Liberal Democrat women were asked how best to ensure the involvement of women in a Scottish parliament. The outcome of the consultation given in the recent *Report of the Scottish Liberal Democrat Women's Commission* showed that 50:50 was overwhelmingly rejected by the members (Scottish Liberal Democrat Women's Commission 1990: 4). Its radicalism was acknowledged but many objections were raised. It was feared that 50:50 would marginalise women; that the men's election would be treated more seriously than the women's election; 'that if, for example, the man who came second in the male ballot got more votes than the woman who won the woman's ballot, it would seriously undermine the woman'; that it might be unpopular with the voters and so make a Convention package more difficult to sell; that it might in some areas as in Gordon lead to a decrease in women's representation. (Liberal Democrat women's representation on Gordon District Council is uniquely high, around 60% of the party group.) Quotas were also rejected by the Commission (Scottish Liberal Democrat Women's Commission 1990: 4–5). In the Convention, Liberal Democrat Sheila Ritchie vigorously insisted that she wanted to beat men as well as women.[8] While the Liberal Democrats have now modified their strong preference for the STV form of PR, the party retains its commitment to the introduction of PR, and echoes the Greens in maintaining:

> If the Constitutional Convention leads to a Scottish Parliament elected by a sensible system of PR there will be opportunities for women. If there is a sufficient number of women candidates they will get elected. (Scottish Liberal Democrat Women's Commission 1990: 6)

So what kind of electoral system is likely to emerge?

It is still difficult to say, although some signposts are now in place. Emma Simpson's survey of Convention members in 1990 found that 70% supported special measures to increase the numbers of women in a Scottish parliament. Thirty per cent wanted proportional representation, 20% a quota system and 18% the 50:50 option. It is perhaps relevant that the survey was carried out before Labour formally adopted the 50:50 option in March. Support for 50:50 may have increased after the March conference. From her survey, however, Simpson concluded that women were on the march in Scottish politics and that there were prospects of a breakthrough in women's representation (Simpson 1990). The Labour party at its 1991 Scottish Conference reaffirmed a shift away from 'first-past-the-post' for a Scottish parliament adopting the following position:

> The Labour Party in Scotland therefore reaffirms its view that 'first-past-the-post' is not an appropriate system for a Scottish Parliament; that both the

Alternative Vote and the Additional Members System or some form of it justify further consideration; that whatever system is used it must take account of the Party's declared support for equal representation for men and women in the Scottish Parliament and that the Party should seek agreement on one of these systems.[9]

All of the parties involved in the Convention's negotiations on electoral arrangements have shown flexibility, reflected in the report made by the Convention on 30 November 1990, *Towards Scotland's Parliament*:

1. The present 'first-past-the-post' electoral system is not acceptable for Scotland's Parliament and does not produce a truly representative assembly.
2. The Convention seeks for Scotland's Parliament an electoral system which should be assessed in terms of the following principles:
   (a) that it produces results in which the number of seats for various parties is broadly related to the number of votes cast for them;
   (b) that it ensures, or at least takes effective positive action to bring about, equal representation of men and women, and encourages fair representation of ethnic and minority groups;
   (c) that it preserves a real link between the member and his/her constituency;
   (d) that it is as simple as possible to understand;
   (e) that it ensures adequate representation of less populous areas; and
   (f) that the system be designed to place the greatest possible power in the hands of the electorate.
3. Having secured the firm commitment of all the major participants in the Convention to these principles, including equality of representation of men and women, the Convention will seek to identify the precise electoral system which best meets these criteria.

(Scottish Constitutional Convention 1990: 17)

The 1991 Scottish conferences of the Liberal Democrat and Labour parties gave their representatives within the Convention powers of negotiation on an electoral system, but early agreement appears unlikely. The Labour party at the British level, for instance, has set up a working party on electoral reform, chaired by Professor Raymond Plant, and with a wide remit to examine electoral reform options for the UK as well as Scotland. The Plant Committee produced a preliminary report in July 1991, but its final report is not likely to appear until 1992 (*Guardian* 1991). It is not clear whether agreement on a system of election for a Scottish parliament will await the final report of the Plant Committee or not. An Alternative Vote or AMS system appears to be emerging as Labour's preferred option, while the Liberal Democrats could now find a form of AMS acceptable. But as Alice Brown has commented, 'The options favoured by the different political parties reflect their anxiety about the potential outcome of any electoral change. To a large extent the question of equal representation has been subsumed under this debate' (Brown 1991b: 16).

Nonetheless, *Towards Scotland's Parliament* makes a clear commitment to equality of representation. Yet given Liberal Democrat hostility, the fate of the 50:50 option is uncertain and the vagueness of Labour's 1991 Scottish Conference pledge 'to take account of the party's declared support for the equal representation of men and women' in arriving at a final choice of electoral system is worth noting. A possible outcome may be agreement on a form of AMS with two-member constituencies in the first-past-the-post constituency section. This would allow the parties to arrive at their own answer to pursuing equal representation in their own selection arrangements. For instance, a party could impose 50:50 on its own selection procedures for a Scottish parliament. That is, a man and a woman would have to be selected as candidates for the party in each of the two-member constituencies. A similar arrangement would be made for the top-up list, such as listing woman, man, woman, man. Such an agreement may well boost women's representation in a Scottish parliament without bringing about the overnight sensation of equal representation.

The attitudes of the parties outside the Convention will become more important as the Convention package is tested at the next general election. Although not directly participating in the Convention the SNP and the Conservative party have been unable to avoid responding to Convention discussions thus far but their contribution to the debate on women's representation has been minimal. The parties within the Convention have been put into the position of having to define a position on women's representation. The resulting proposals have presented a challenge to the parties themselves and may have an influence outside Scotland.

– CONCLUSION –

Can women lose out of this? Time will tell. The brief review of the history of Scottish women's representation at Westminster reveals a gloomy picture of under-representation. The figures for women's representation in Scottish local government are better and have shown a steady line of increase. Since 1974 the proportion of women councillors in Scottish District Councils has risen from 12.9% in 1974 to 19.6% in 1988, clearly an improvement on the Westminster figures.[10] These figures offer some support for the view that, even if nothing is done to try to ensure that more women are elected to a Scottish parliament, there will be more women than at Westminster because a Scottish parliament is likely to have several features in common with local government. The Westminster record, however, offers a telling answer on what happens if women's representation is left to rise naturally. The lessons from the setting up of new Parliaments in

Eastern Europe also underline the need to plan for increased women's representation. Despite the introduction of PR electoral systems, women's representation tumbled in the new democracies – from 32.2% to 20.5% in the then GDR, from 21% to 8.5% in Bulgaria, from 20.9% to 7% in Hungary, from 29.5% to 6% in Czechoslovakia, and from 34.3% to 3.5% in Romania (*Guardian* 1990).

Yet the setting up of a Scottish parliament offers an exciting opportunity to involve women from the outset. The Green, Labour, and Liberal Democrat parties have committed themselves to improving their record on putting up women candidates. The Constitutional Convention has provided a platform for a wide-ranging debate on how best to involve women in a Scottish parliament. Equal representation of men and women has been set as one of the criteria to be met by an electoral system. These are positive developments for women's representation.

Some urgency, however, attaches to the final outcome of the Convention negotiations. The next general election must take place by 1992. In the event of a Labour victory a Scottish parliament could be in place within a year. Such a timescale must concentrate minds. And if a Scottish parliament is to be in place by 1993 then the parties would begin the candidate selection process some months earlier. If the final choice of an electoral system involves some compulsion on the parties to put up women candidates then in their parties women will be sought out. There will be places for women. If it is left to the parties to resolve in their own way then historical experiences suggest that women will lose out. Even so, in the first round of selections there would be the rare advantage of a clear slate – no sitting members in place. But if the first election to a Scottish parliament reproduces the 93:7 male:female ratio presented by Westminster then the golden opportunity of making a Scottish parliament a place for women as much as for men would have turned to dross. The same uphill struggle to increase women's representation would have to be faced in a Scottish parliament as in other areas. The moral must be that if women want to make sure of places in a future Scottish parliament, **now** is the time to do so. There will never be a better time.

– NOTES –

1. The information in Table 14.1 is drawn from House of Commons data.
2. This calculation is based on election statistics drawn from F. W. S. Craig (1989) and Scottish Conservative & Unionist Central Office (1966).
3. For a comparative overview of women's representation see Lovenduski, Joni and Jill Hills (eds) (1981).
4. Figures drawn from Lovenduski & Hills (1981) and F. W. S. Craig (1989).
5. Interview with Maidie Hart, cited in Emma Simpson (1990).
6. Information supplied to the author by Yvonne Strachan and Jane MacKay of the STUC Women's Committee.

7. Information supplied to the author by Irene Brandt of the Scottish Green Party.
8. Sheila Ritchie speaking at meetings of the Scottish Constitutional Convention in April and June 1990.
9. Executive Statement passed at Scottish Labour Party Conference, Aberdeen, March 1991.
10. Information provided by the Scottish Local Government Information Unit based on statistics compiled by John Bochel and David Denver following the 1988 District Council elections.

– REFERENCES –

Beddoe, Deirdre (1989), *Back to Home and Duty*, London: Pandora.

Bochel, John, David Denver and Allan Macartney (eds) (1980), *The Referendum Experience: Scotland 1979*, Aberdeen: Aberdeen University Press.

Breitenbach, Esther (1989), 'The Impact of Thatcherism on women in Scotland', in Alice Brown and David McCrone (eds) *The Scottish Government Yearbook 1989*, Edinburgh: Unit for the Study of Government in Scotland, University of Edinburgh.

Breitenbach, Esther (1990), ' "Sisters are doing it for themselves": The Women's Movement in Scotland', in Alice Brown and Richard Parry (eds) *The Scottish Government Yearbook 1990*, Edinburgh: Unit for the Study of Government in Scotland, University of Edinburgh.

Brown, Alice (1991a), 'Thatcher's Legacy for Women in Scotland', in *Radical Scotland*, Apr–May.

Brown, Alice (1991b), 'Women in Scottish Politics', paper presented to ECPR Conference, University of Essex, 22–28 March.

Craig, F.W.S. (1989), *British Electoral Facts 1832–1987*, Aldershot: Parliamentary Research Services.

Fyfe, Maria (1989–90), 'Women's Voice – Equal Representation', in *Equal Voice*, Winter.

The Guardian (1990), 25 July.

The Guardian (1991), 12 July.

House of Commons *Women in the House of Commons*, Factsheet No 5, undated. *Labour Research* (1991), January pp. 9–11.

Lee, Jennie (1981), *My Life with Nye*, Harmondsworth: Penguin.

Levy, Catriona (1992), 'The Long Slow March: Scottish Women MPs 1918–45', in Esther Breitenbach and Eleanor Gordon (eds) *Against the Grain: Women in the Public Domain in Scotland*, Edinburgh: Edinburgh University Press.

Lovenduski, Joni and Jill Hills (eds) (1981), *The Politics of the Second Electorate: Women and Public Participation – Britain, USA, Canada, Australia, France, Spain, West Germany, Italy, Sweden, Finland, Eastern Europe, USSR, Japan*, London: Routledge & Kegan Paul.

Mann, Jean (1962), *Woman in Parliament*, London: Odhams.

Phillips, Kate (1989), Letter to *Radical Scotland*, 38, Apr/May.

Radical Scotland (1989), 38, Apr/May.

Roddick, Jackie (1989–90), 'Women and Voting Systems', in *Radical Scotland*, Dec/Jan.

Scottish Conservative & Unionist Central Office (1966), *The Year Book for Scotland 1966*, Edinburgh: Scottish Conservative & Unionist Central Office.

Scottish Constitutional Convention (1989), 'Women and a Scottish Parliament', in *Towards Scotland's Parliament, Consultation Document and Report to the Scottish People*, October, Edinburgh: CoSLA.

Scottish Constitutional Convention (1990), *Towards Scotland's Parliament, A Report to the Scottish People*, November, Edinburgh: CoSLA.

Scottish Liberal Democrats' Women's Commission (1990), *Report of the Scottish Liberal Democrats' Women's Commission*, November.

Simpson, Emma (1990), ' "Mainly Manly": The Scottish Constitutional Convention and the implications for women's representation', University of Edinburgh, unpublished Politics Honours dissertation.

Strachey, Ray (1979 reprint), *The Cause*, London: Virago.

The Scotsman (1918), 10 December.

The Tribune (1991), 12 April.

Vallance, Elizabeth (1988), 'Two cheers for equality: Women candidates in the 1987 General Elections', in *Parliamentary Affairs*, January.

Woman's Claim of Right Group (1989), 'A Scottish Woman's Claim of Right', unpublished submission to Scottish Constitutional Convention.

Woman's Claim of Right Group (eds) (1991), *A Woman's Claim of Right in Scotland*, Edinburgh: Polygon.

CHAPTER 15

Gender Goes Top of the Agenda

TOM NAIRN

'Gender Goes Top of the Agenda', *The Scotsman*, 28 December 1994.

Some years ago I attended a seminar addressed by the historian Eric Hobsbawm. His subject was nationalism. The professor had just come back from a conference in Valencia, Spain, a region famed for oranges but with a capital city so ravaged by modernity that it might be anywhere: 'Wolverhampton-on-Sea', as he called it. It also happens to be a borderland between Catalonia and the Spanish heartland, Castile. There, his audience of trade unionists and Socialist Party militants had gone through the motions over official conference topics like Socialism and Europe but 'you could tell there was only one thing people really wanted to talk about, and that was, whether Valencia should be Catalan or Spanish'.

Something similar happened a few weeks ago at the Scottish Constitutional Convention meeting in Edinburgh. The reforming worthies had gathered to discuss a number of recommendations on the shape of a future Scottish parliament, but there was only one thing they really wanted to discuss: the proposal that 50% of the Parliament's members should be women. This was what had seized the imagination, or in some cases the indignation. Cannier worthies were expending much pech over all the practical problems. There are, in truth, a fair number of these. Yet they were really wasting their time. Nothing, but nothing, will now cause this issue to go away. It has become a small-'n' nationalist banner – an emblem of the kind of country and the style of nationalism people really want. Something fundamental has been stirred by it. The reticence of the Scots has been awakened (as perhaps it could only be awakened) by a missionary idea. Unlike its Catalan equivalent, Scottishness has never been ethno-linguistic or 'cultural' in a folkish sense. It is more like a consciousness of a people who have unaccountably lost their way in history. Now at last a rallying cause has been disclosed: the world can again be shown the way, via a new start – by the first legislature of modern times fully to acknowledge the equality of genders and build an authentic constitution around that act of liberation. Say it lichtly, gin ye daur:

this would lift our country and justify its return. What stronger indication could there be of a civil identity, of a belonging unmarked by mythologies of blood and vengeance? In Scotland great countermyths of enlightenment and civil society would also be forged and, in this new light, would appear as still native to its rediscovered nationhood. The long patience of the Scots might also be justified by it: after 1989's second springtime of nationalism, they waited for a truer path of their own – distinctive yet non-ethnic. Especially in George Robertson's party, the elders are still trying to depict all this as just a passing fad. They could not be more mistaken. The famous obstacles of which so much is made (not enough 'suitable' women, unfair to some men, interminable time needed, etc.) are really chaff in the wind.

Some interesting recent descriptions give a clearer sense of what is at stake. On Boxing Day, a letter in *The Scotsman* reminded readers of the first ordination of women priests at St Mary's Cathedral, and of how unexpectedly moved most of the congregation were. The *Independent on Sunday* columnist, Neal Ascherson (a stout non-believer), had witnessed the same process in King's College Chapel, Cambridge: 'I was unprepared for what I felt then – a rush of joy – the instinct that recognises the fall of a Bastille is never wrong.' A church cannot help being transformed by the embrace of all people, rather than all men. The change strikes through to the common heart (and this is what the traditionalists most fear). How much more would a nation be transformed by comparable solemn ordination? This is what was really being debated at that Convention meeting.

In its day, socialism began as a universal credo but had to become national, and sometimes nationalist, in order to get anywhere. The same will probably be true of feminism. And its appeal may turn out to be strongest in those nations most darkened by male authoritarianism – in our case, the pernicious inheritance of 'daeing as ye're telt' or (Murray Grigor's great phrase) 'cock-a-doodle-don't'. The democratic side to Calvinist Election was always dragged down by a fearful, Hyde-like social culture for which, as Satan's chosen entry to the kingdom, the female soul was a potential enchantress or witch. Emancipation from this past shame is only one of the formidable advantages of the 50% proposal. It also strikes at Westminster's pitiable record over the same issue: a supposedly more liberal society which manages just 6% representation for women. It argues (with common sense) that such a change is far easier in a new polity than for one already entrenched in misrepresentation. It evokes a salutary vision of self-rule not just 'in Europe' but in one important way ahead of the European Union – ahead and (one would think) certain to win wide support there. Fifty years from now, 'gender balance' will probably be taken for granted. Today, anticipation of this future state of nature would also serve to reassure all the existing minorities in Scottish society and invite their active participation in the new Government.

CHAPTER 16

Women and Politics in Scotland

ALICE BROWN

'Women and Politics in Scotland' (1996), *Parliamentary Affairs*, 49 (1).

The role of women in Scottish politics has been a relatively neglected area of academic enquiry. The 1980s and 1990s have, however, witnessed a growing interest, which has in turn led to a number of research projects and publications. As a result, work is now available on the history of women's involvement in politics, on the role of women in local government, on the women's movement and on the involvement of women in the constitutional debate; a comparative study of the participation of women in politics in Scotland and the Republic of Ireland has also been conducted.[1]

While women involved in politics in Scotland share similar experiences and concerns with those in other parts of the United Kingdom and elsewhere, it can be argued that the politics of Scotland have impacted in a particular way on their political participation. More specifically, the challenge to the current constitutional arrangements and the campaigns for a Scottish parliament have provided a political opportunity for women to articulate their own demands. The movement for constitutional change has included policies for electoral reform, for the 'democratisation' of the parliamentary process, and for more openness and accountability in decision-making. Women have added their voice to these campaigns and have incorporated their claim for equal representation as an integral part of the proposals for radical change in the government of Scotland.

The mobilisation of women in Scotland behind the critical mass of opinion in favour of constitutional reform has been significant. It provides an example of a form of coalition and agenda-building politics which has proved one of the most successful strategies for women's advancement. Other examples can be found in the gains made in the mid-1960s in the United States, which can be explained partially as a result of the political legacy of the civil rights movement; in the European Union, where women were able to take advantage of attempts to harmonise labour costs and put forward their own claim for equal pay; and in Britain, where the modernisation process taking place within the Labour Party allowed women to push for a greater say in the running of the party and for the policy of all-women short-lists in half of the vacant, winnable, parliamentary seats. Similarly, the strategies adopted by political activists in Scotland can be analysed within the theoretical frameworks of the activities of political movements and the role of specific political opportunity structures.

Here we outline the involvement of women in contemporary Scottish politics and their networking both within and outside the formal structures of political power. Evidence is drawn from interviews carried out with activists in the political parties, the trade unions and local government, and with women involved in the wider women's movement in Scotland. It is argued that, although women in Scotland are poorly represented in top posts in key political institutions, they are actively engaged in the political life of the country. Reflecting the experience of women in other countries and cultures, political activists in Scotland have seized the chance to advance their demands as part of a broad coalition and pressure for change.

– Women's political representation in Scotland –

It has been possible for women in Scotland, as in other parts of the UK, to stand for election to the House of Commons since 1918, the same year as women over the age of 30 were first given the right to vote. Since that time, just 24 have represented Scottish constituencies at Westminster. The pattern has been one of fluctuation around a low level and, unlike other European countries, the level of representation has not risen significantly in the postwar period. At the General Election in 1992, five women MPs were elected from a total of 72 Scottish MPs, the same number as were elected at the 1959 and 1964 General Elections. The election of two more women at by-elections in Scotland in 1994 (Labour) and 1995 (SNP) brought the number to a record level of seven.

Table 16.1
Women MPs at the General Election and Following By-Elections

| | 1992 | | 1995 | |
	UK	Scotland	UK	Scotland
Conservative	20	0	20	0
Labour	37	3	39	4
Liberal Democrats	2	1	2	1
SNP	1	1	2	2
Total	60	5	63	7
	(9.2%)	(6.9%)	(9.7%)	(9.7%)

At local government level, the representation of women is higher. Under the old two-tier system of local government, around 22% of councillors elected at the District elections in 1992 were women and some 17% at the Regional elections in 1994. In the first elections for the new unitary authorities in Scotland, held in April 1995, just over one in five of the new councillors were women. The results of the elections for the shadow councils were a disappointment for women activists who had campaigned for more equal representation, especially as the next local elections will not take place until 1999. Finally, the representation of Scottish women MEPs at the European level dropped from two to one in 1994, against the trend in all other European countries except Portugal.

Table 16.2
Elections for Shadow Unitary Authorities in 1995

	% Women Candidates	% Women Elected
Conservative	26	27
Labour	27	24
Liberal Democrats	33	29
SNP	24	20
Ind./Other	18	13
Total	26	22

Growing awareness of the relatively low level of women's representation in Scotland, and knowledge of the experience of improved representation in other West European countries, has led to claims for gender balance with positive action to effect change. Such demands run in parallel to claims in other spheres in Scottish society for greater equality and autonomy. Women are under-represented in all areas of decision-making, including business, the trade unions, the judiciary, the media and public bodies; and they are disadvantaged in terms of their labour market position, levels of income, poverty, housing and health (Engender 1993, 1994, 1995). Strategies by women in the political parties for equal representation should be interpreted within wider economic, social and political changes in Scotland and the UK, but also as part of a broader movement by women in Europe and beyond for a greater say in decision-making bodies and for an equal share of resources. However, the prospects of constitutional change and the establishment of a parliament in Scotland have provided a specific set of political opportunities for women in Scotland. Similar debates are taking place in Wales.[2]

Political pressure to improve representation has not been confined to women within the political parties; it is apparent in the trade union movement and local government, and significantly within the various women's groups and organisations in Scotland. Writing in 1990, Esther Breitenbach argued that 'the current political situation in Scotland provides an opportunity for a resurgent feminism to organise anew and to act more effectively on political institutions and ideologies'. Evidence of this resurgence can be found in the creation of a new women's organisation, Engender, and the publication of a new feminist magazine, *Harpies & Quines*, in 1992; the achievements of feminists within local government in initiatives such as the Zero Tolerance Campaign; and the coming together of women from different feminist perspectives around the issue of women's representation. Feminists in Scotland have demonstrated their willingness to engage with wider political developments, the state and other formal political power structures in order to make their claim in Scotland.

– WHY SO FEW SCOTTISH WOMEN MPs? –

The low number of women recruited to the House of Commons and other levels of government raises an obvious question, and that is, why has representation in Scotland and other parts of the UK remained so low? No simple answer to this question can be provided. Explanations are, in part, linked to the more general reasons cited for the poor representation of women in legislatures throughout the world. At the UK level, the most comprehensive summary of the potential reasons can be found in the survey of candidates for the 1992 General Election carried out by Pippa Norris and Joni Lovenduski, who analyse the influences on participation and recruitment at three different levels. The first level, or 'systematic factors', relate to the broad context in which recruitment of political candidates will take place in a country, and will include the legal system, electoral system, party system and structure of opportunities. The second context involves 'political party factors', such as party organisation, rules and ideology. The third influence will be 'individual recruitment factors' which will include factors determining the supply of candidates (for example the resources and motivation of aspirants) and the demand factors (such as the attitudes and practices of 'gatekeepers').[3]

Interviews with ten women activists in each of the main political parties in Scotland in 1994 revealed that they perceived that the reasons for poor participation are interrelated in a complex way and operate on all three levels identified by Norris and Lovenduski. At the 'systematic' level, the women interviewed highlighted the particular practical difficulties imposed by the location of Parliament in London, and the unsocial hours of parliamentary meetings. Added to this, the first-past-the-post electoral system was believed by some to disadvantage women, as is the adversarial nature of the party system and the dominance of the two main parties, Conservative and Labour. The career structure for elected office, with recruitment in the main from the party, local government or trade unions, was considered to work to the advantage of men within the parties.

Barriers to involvement in politics were also identified at the 'political party' level. Party rules and organisation, the timing of meetings, ways of conducting political business, and method of political appointments within the party were not viewed as conducive to the equal participation of women. Some, particularly those in the Scottish Liberal Democrats and the SNP, felt their party was doing more to actively involve women. In contrast, women in the Scottish Labour Party were most critical of the rate of change within their party, while in the Conservative Party they were inclined to the view that able women would succeed in spite of the obstacles which they face.

Both supply and demand factors were specified as influencing 'individual recruitment'. Women's role in the family was considered to be a key factor limiting the supply or participation of women in Scottish political life. Even where the reality of women's lives is that they combine paid work with family responsibilities, or indeed do not have a family of their own, those interviewed felt that traditional attitudes towards women as home-makers and men as decision-makers continue to influence the expectations of both women and men. Responsibility for the family came first, and before political ambition, for most of the women in the different parties, some interviewees arguing more positively that after women had raised their children they brought an added understanding to politics and had more to offer. However, there was an acknowledgement amongst some women that family responsibility was a relatively 'easy' explanation for the low representation of women which avoided analysing potentially more contentious reasons such as discrimination against them. If women in modern Scotland are expected to combine a full-time paid job with looking after a family, then the question remains as to why specifically a parliamentary career is relatively closed to them.

Contrary to the findings of Norris and Lovenduski that-the lack of resources was a key determinant, few women in the Scottish study volunteered finance as a serious barrier for women (the financial assistance offered through Emily's List in the Labour Party was not taken up in Scotland). This does not necessarily mean that resources are not important, rather that other barriers were seen as more pressing: for example, lack of confidence including inexperience in public speaking, or fear of making a fool of themselves, were cited as important factors which prevented women from putting themselves forward. In arguing that men are 'more likely to put themselves forward', a number of women noted the importance of being asked to consider themselves as candidates.

The individual factors relating to the supply of women available for political positions were therefore accompanied by an identification of demand side factors and party variables which interviewees believed also played a role in deciding the level of women's political participation. A number of those who had stood for office had been encouraged to do so by a male colleague. Indeed, somewhat ironically, some, particularly those in the Conservative Party, identified other women in their parties as more biased against promoting and selecting women candidates. However, women within the Scottish Labour Party were much more likely to explain exclusion from selection to safe seats in terms of the reluctance of men in the party to give up power.

With regard to demand factors and the actual selection process, responses from the Scottish activists varied across party. Women in the Scottish Liberal Democrats and SNP did not identify any specific problems for women at the selection stage, although they saw it as more of a problem in the Conservative Party in Scotland and particularly for women in the Scottish Labour Party. They considered that men and women in the Conservative Party were more inclined to hold traditional views on the role of women in society and that the Scottish Labour Party was very male and trade union dominated. Some women in the Conservative Party agreed that women often faced problems at the selection stage in their party because of the attitudes of both male and female selectors. Although at a national level the policy of the party has changed, they considered that women were disadvantaged because power over selection still rests in the hands of the local party.

Women in the Scottish Labour Party believed there were great difficulties for women in being selected, partially as a result of Labour's dominance in Scottish politics. As the party with 49 of the 72 parliamentary seats in Scotland following the 1992 election, Labour holds a considerable degree of power. In the first-past-the-post electoral system, incumbency is also an important factor. When Labour seats do become available, then the competition for them is fierce. The party now has a policy that there should be all-women short-lists in half of the vacant winnable seats in Scotland. (Some women activists in the Scottish Labour Party proposed that there should be all-women lists in all vacant seats in Scotland because of the slow rate of seats becoming available, but this was rejected by the party Conference.) Given the slow rate of turnover, it will be some time before women in the party gain equality as Westminster parliamentarians.[4]

The Labour women interviewed gave specific examples where they or other experienced women candidates had not been short-listed for the selection interview, or had been disadvantaged at the selection meeting. For them it was clearly an issue of power and the refusal of many men to share power with women in the party. There is a strong sense of injustice that often very able and high profile women, who have worked in the party for twenty or more years and have considerable experience, are not being selected for parliamentary seats. Thus, although men in the Labour Party employ the rhetoric of women's equality, it was felt that these principles were not always practised within the party.

An important influence which operated at all three levels was the political culture in Scotland and, more specifically, in the House of Commons. The predominantly male culture in which politics is conducted was cited across the party divide as a key inhibiting factor for women. Some made the link between women's apparent lack of confidence and their reluctance to participate in what many described as the macho, adversarial style of politics which they consider dominates parties and the Parliament in Britain. Thus the whole political culture and way in which politics is conducted is perceived as a disincentive to women's participation and a more subtle way of excluding them from the political process. The women who do reach high office are those who are most able to fit in with the male culture which predominates. (Studies, mainly in Scandinavia, suggest that culture is unlikely to change until there is a critical mass of women, 30% or more.)

Women activists in Scotland, therefore, referred to factors operating at the systematic, political party and individual recruitment level. The many and varied explanations demonstrate that participants perceive a complex interplay between the three dimensions, and also between the supply of and demand for potential candidates. Although the views of these in the survey do not provide concrete evidence of the actual existence of barriers to women's political participation, such views are important and can prevent women, both directly and indirectly, from taking part in conventional politics. If women believe they will be discriminated against at the selection stage, or will be treated as inferior because of their sex, or if they are simply not encouraged to see themselves as potential candidates, it is not surprising that they are less inclined to put themselves forward.

Many of the views expressed were shared by women across the party divide. However, there were also differences between the four main political parties. These differences are significant and affect the proposals for change advocated by the women involved, and the policies which they believe are necessary to improve women's representation. The contrast in approach can be illustrated through examining the involvement of women in the constitutional debate in Scotland.

_ Campaigns for a Scottish parliament _
with gender equality

Electoral support for the Conservative Party in Scotland has declined rapidly from the 1950s, and fell further under the administrations of Margaret Thatcher and John Major. In the 1950s, it stood at just over 50%. By the 1992 General Election it had dropped to under 26%. At the elections for the new shadow local authorities in 1995 it reached an unprecedented low of 11%.[5] In the 1987 General Election, when the Conservatives won only 10 of the 72 parliamentary seats, strength was added to the argument that the Conservative Government did not have a mandate to rule in Scotland. It was contended by the Government's opponents that Scotland was suffering from a democratic deficit. The campaign for a Scottish parliament gathered force within the opposition political parties and through such organisations at the Campaign for a Scottish Assembly (later to become the Campaign for a Scottish Parliament). Some women activists held that they were experiencing a 'double democratic deficit', first on the grounds that they supported political parties which favoured an independent or devolved Scottish parliament, and second because as women they were grossly under-represented as MPs.

Following publication of the document, *A Claim of Right for Scotland*, by the Campaign for a Scottish Assembly in 1988, and the establishment of the Scottish Constitutional Convention in 1989, working groups were established by the latter to prepare options for the future devolved Government of Scotland. Membership of the Convention included representatives from the Scottish Labour Party, the Scottish Liberal Democrats, the Scottish Trades Union Congress, the Campaign for a Scottish Parliament, and others from local government, the churches, small political parties and civic organisations including the Scottish Convention of Women. The Scottish National Party decided not to join because it advocates an independent Scottish parliament within Europe, and the Conservative Party declared its total opposition to constitutional change. One of the groups set up by the Convention was the Women's Issues Group, chaired by the Labour MP, Maria Fyfe. The agreement to have a group looking specifically at women's representation in a Scottish parliament was a significant step forward. It was made possible because of pressure from women representing political parties, the trade union movement, and women's groups, together with the support of some men within the Convention (Brown 1995a).

It was at this early stage that other women activists in Scotland entered the debate and formed the Woman's Claim of Right Group. This comprised women from different political parties, but predominantly the Scottish Green Party, in addition to women who were not formally involved in party politics. They came together mainly in protest at the small number of women, some 10%, who had been nominated for membership of the newly established Scottish Constitutional Convention: 'Once again, major proposals and decisions affecting the life and well-being of Scottish people would be made with women being significantly under-represented.' The group monitored the work of the Convention and submitted a separate document to the Women's Issues Group, later publishing a book of the same title (Woman's Claim of Right Group 1991).

The Women's Issues Group invited submissions from women in Scotland, and the question of representation within a new Scottish parliament was discussed amongst women in political parties, trade unions, local government, women's organisations, community groups and the voluntary sector. Reaction to the constitutional debate in the 1980s can be contrasted to involvement in the

1970s. Both Esther Breitenbach and Catriona Levy discuss the role of women in the devolution debate in the 1970s and the division between them on the issue (Beitenbach 1990, Levy; 1992). While some took an active part in the campaigns for a Scottish Assembly, others felt that such a body could be more reactionary in its attitudes and policies towards women than the Westminster Parliament. Catriona Levy quotes the feminist journal, *MsPrint*: 'On the whole the women's movement ignored the referendum or saw it as irrelevant.' An attempt by the Scottish Convention of Women to raise the issue of women's representation by distributing a questionnaire to the political parties met with little success.

By the late 1980s the political situation had changed in Scotland. Women activists across the party divide and outside party politics became increasingly aware that women's representation was extremely low and that it compared unfavourably with most other European countries. They began to ask why. The possibility of a new Scottish parliament which was to be run on a radically different basis from the Westminster Parliament added impetus to demands for change and provided a common focus for political action. In contrast to the 1970s, there was broad agreement that such a parliament could act as a progressive force for women and the campaign to ensure more equal representation gathered steam. The reasons for this change of strategy are discussed in more detail elsewhere (Brown, McCrone and Paterson 1996) and relate to the impact of Thatcherism on women in Scotland; the increase in political involvement of women in the political parties, local government and trade unions in the 1980s and 1990s; their growing frustration with the British political system, the Westminster style of government and the slowness of change; a dislike for the adversarial nature of party politics and the political behaviour of MPs; and the realisation that as women they had to be involved in shaping the plans for the new Parliament for their perspectives to be taken into account.

The aim of gender balance and fair representation of others traditionally excluded from elected office thus became intertwined with plans to build a more democratic new parliament. In its first report, *Towards Scotland's Parliament*, in 1990, the Scottish Constitutional Convention committed itself to the principle of equal representation. It set up two new groups to undertake more detailed work on the *Procedures and Preparations for Scottish Parliament* and the *Electoral System for Scottish Parliament*. The group examining the electoral system had to take into account the need for gender balance and fair representation of ethnic minority groups. Although there was general agreement that something had to be done to ensure that the Scottish Parliament did not repeat the Westminster pattern, there was no consensus on the policies needed to ensure gender balance. In particular, the two main parties within the Convention divided along ideological lines, the Scottish Labour Party favouring positive discrimination, which the Scottish Liberal Democrats opposed. The Scottish Labour Party adopted a proposal for 'active intervention', first put forward by the Scottish TUC's Women's Committee, that there should be a statutory imposition on the political parties to select a man and a woman for each of Scotland's 72 constituencies – the 50:50 option. For their part, the Liberal Democrats were totally opposed to any form of statutory restriction on the freedom of parties to select and voters to elect their Members of Parliament. Instead they proposed electoral change on the basis of 'STV-plus', arguing that under a list system and with other 'promotional' policies the representation of women would improve.[6]

While women were involved directly in the Constitutional Convention as representatives from the political parties or other organisations, they were also actively engaged in the debate within Scottish civil society and in organising women's conferences and other events (Brown 1992). Their aim was to widen the debate to include women in parties not involved in the Convention and from outside the formal political structures with the objective of maintaining pressure on the main parties. There was a broad consensus within and outside the parties that women should be more equally represented within a new Scottish parliament. The increased involvement of women was also reflected in the setting up of a new research and campaign organisation, Engender.

In the run-up to the General Election in 1992, the need for the parties within the Convention to reach a compromise position became more urgent if they were to present a united opposition to the Government. Just before the election, the Convention was able to announce an agreed scheme: an Additional Member System for elections, an obligation on parties to select an equal number of men and women candidates, and the use of the additional list of the Additional Member System to achieve gender balance if this was not achieved through the constituency elections. This settlement did not mean full endorsement of the '50:50' option proposed by the Scottish Labour Party, nor acceptance of the 'Single Transferable Vote-plus' electoral system advocated by the Scottish Liberal Democrats. Nevertheless, it represented a significant compromise by the parties involved and a leap forward in guaranteeing more equal representation for women within a future Scottish parliament. These plans received an enormous setback when the Conservative Party was re-elected in 1992, although in Scotland with just eleven MPs.

Following the Conservatives' return to office, some commentators anticipated that the demands for constitutional change would be shelved, and with it the campaign for equal representation, at least until the run-up to the next general election. However, as the parties which supported either a devolved or an independent parliament for Scotland obtained 75% of the vote, it was unlikely that the pressure for constitutional change would immediately evaporate.

After the election, campaign groups were formed to keep demands for a Scottish parliament on the political agenda, including Common Cause, Scotland United and Democracy for Scotland. Continued commitment to the campaign for democratic renewal was illustrated in the well-attended Democracy demonstration organised to coincide with the European Summit held in Edinburgh in December 1992. Despite some initial difficulties, the Scottish Constitutional Convention also continued in existence, and established a Scottish Constitutional Commission in 1993 to examine the issues left unresolved before to the 1992 election. In 1993 the Coalition for Scottish Democracy was also formed, bringing together many political activists in the different pressure groups and political parties. It put forward the case for a Scottish Senate to allow civic organisations a positive input into the debate about the future governance of Scotland and was successful in setting up a Scottish Civic Assembly. The first meeting of the Assembly took place in March 1995; reflecting the broader campaign for gender equality, it operated a 50:50 gender representation policy in inviting a wide range of non-party organisations to attend.

The women's movement maintained its pressure on the political parties and trade unions for equal representation and formed the Women's Co-ordination Group drawn from the main women's groups. Its objectives were to co-ordinate campaigns and political action, and to lobby the Scottish Office and the parties in Scotland on the issue of women's representation. It organised discussions and conferences on strategies for improving representation both within party structures and in a future Scottish parliament, and it published reports from women in Scotland to the UN Conference in Beijing in 1995 and the European Union's Fourth Action Programme.

The Scottish Constitutional Commission delivered its report to the Scottish Constitutional Convention at the end of 1994. The Commission's task was to make recommendations on an electoral system with gender balance provisions, and consider the constitutional implications at UK level and for local government of the establishment of a Scottish parliament. Its report recommended a Scottish parliament of 112 members elected by the Additional Member System, of which 72 constituency members would be elected on a first-past-the-post basis using the existing Westminster parliamentary constituencies, and an additional 40 on a proportional basis from party lists using the eight European Parliament constituencies. In order to achieve greater gender balance, it proposed that parties should be asked to achieve a target of 40%-plus representation of women in the parliament within the first five years, taking into account both the constituency and list seats. It advocated the removal of social, economic and other barriers to women's political participation through measures such as: changing parliamentary working hours and meeting times, facilities for caring, and attendance and carer allowances; changing the adversarial style and ethos of parliamentary behaviour; and encouraging participation of women in parliamentary committees. The establishment of a Public Appointments Commission to ensure the full participation of women and others in public bodies was recommended in addition to a Parliamentary Equal Opportunities Commission.

In making these recommendations, the Commission rejected the adoption of a statutory scheme for the equal representation of women, but it acknowledged that a 'dual ballot' system which gave political parties the opportunity to put forward an equal number of female and male candidates on a 50:50 basis was 'the most straightforward way of ensuring equal representation of men and women in the Scottish parliament'. It also noted that in the event of voluntary targets not being reached in the five year period, the Parliamentary Equal Opportunities Commission should re-examine statutory means of ensuring gender balance and fair representation of minorities. In making this recommendation the Commission referred to the UN Charter on the Rights of Women which makes provision for 'temporary special measures' to redress the inequality experienced by women.

The Commission's report was strongly criticised by activists who had campaigned long and hard for a firm and statutory commitment to gender equality for the first Scottish parliament. But it also did not attract endorsement from those supporting a more voluntarist approach. The report had one, perhaps unintended, consequence and that was in bringing women together to put forward an alternative scheme of their own. Talks between women within the two parties and the Women's Co-ordination Group took place to find an alternative solution to that of the Scottish Constitutional Commission. All involved agreed that it was vital to begin with equal representation because it is much more difficult to reform a political institution once it is well established and parliamentary seats are already occupied. They drew up an Electoral Contract for consideration by the executives and conferences of the Labour and Liberal parties. On the understanding that the Contract would pertain only to the first Scottish parliamentary elections, the parties were asked to endorse the principle that there should be an equal number of men and women members in that Parliament. This aim was to be achieved by fielding of an equal number of male and female candidates, the fair distribution of female candidates in winnable seats, and the use of the Additional Member System.[7] It was agreed that the detailed mechanisms for ensuring the selection of an equal number of women in winnable seats, and their distribution between the constituency and list seats, should be left to the discretion of each party.

The consensus reached between Labour and Liberal Democrat women activists reflects the importance they attached to the opportunities which a Scottish parliament could offer. The strategic importance of the new Parliament was also reflected in interviews with the women activists both inside and outside the parties. Their vision of a parliament which is located in Scotland, has equal numbers of men and women, a more proportional electoral system, meeting times compatible with family life, payment of carer allowances, and which is more accountable to Scottish society, has acted as a strong mobilising force in campaigns. Women across the party divide and non-party women strongly believed that more women in parliament will make a substantial difference to political life in Scotland. Women would bring their specific life experiences and expertise to the job, and would alter the style of political debate. Often used phrases were 'women are more consensual', 'women are less confrontational and better at getting things done', 'women have a much more open and sharing approach', or 'with more women the whole political ethos would change'. There was also a broad consensus that the policies of a new Scottish parliament would be different with the equal participation of women. The Child Support Act was quoted as legislation which would not have passed through Parliament in its original form if more women had been involved in the drafting. Others cited the influence women would have on education, health and housing policies, in addition to economic and taxation decisions. There was a widely held belief that current policies tend to be seen as 'gender neutral' and thus fail to reflect the specific impact they could have on women's lives. In summary, there was general agreement that politics and political decisions are the poorer for the absence of women.

The view that women have an important contribution to make to political life is not confined to political activists. In an opinion poll survey carried out by ICM for *The Scotsman* in 1994, there was strong support for the proposition that more women should be involved in politics. Of those questioned, 85% agreed that there were not enough women participating in politics, and 76% thought that political parties should make special efforts to involve more women. A majority of 72% believed that governments would make better decisions if more women were in politics, and 75% disagreed with the statement that men are better at politics than women.

It is interesting to note that in their desire for a Scottish parliament with equal representation, the potential problems for women associated with direct involvement in formal political structures appear to have been put in the background by women activists and have ceased to be crucial to the debate. Instead, the key objective has been to put the issue of women's access to political power high on the political agenda in Scotland on the assumption that significantly more women within the Parliament will make a difference. The success of women activists in Scotland in achieving their objective has met with some reactions, particularly from some men who consider that their political careers will suffer as a result of women-only short-lists for Westminster and 50:50 gender balance in a Scottish parliament. One male Labour activist is reported as saying that the 'parade of quota queens' would shut out a whole generation of male politicians. Echoing the fears expressed by men when women campaigned for the right to vote at the beginning of the century, some male activists would appear to fear that more women politicians will 'upset' the political balance and bring instability to the current (predominantly male) structures of power.

– CONCLUSION –

It has been demonstrated above that Scottish women are under-represented at the political elite level but are active in politics across different political parties, institutions, organisations and groups. In this respect the women's movement in Scotland is alive and well. In their study of contemporary feminist politics and the influence of the women's movement in Britain, Joni Lovenduski and Vicky Randall put forward the view that the feminist movement had declined, that activists were fewer and that old networks had broken down (Lovenduski and Randall 1993). However, they observed that Scotland was different and did not fit this pattern, as they noted evidence of a resurgence from 1987 onwards. This resurgence can be linked to campaigns for constitutional reform. While in the past, the women's movement in Scotland has very much paralleled the development of the women's movement in Britain as a whole, as Esther Breitenbach has argued, a distinctive Scottish identity has become more pronounced over time and women have formed new alliances and networks (Breitenbach 1990). This can be explained partly as a result of a growing perception of a distinctive Scottish identity more generally and because of the context of the politics of Scotland. In addition, women's involvement in the relatively small political and policy community in Scotland has helped to facilitate the networking between women in different spheres.

Women activists in Scotland have taken part in the broad coalition for constitutional change and have added their voice to the debate. In adopting this strategy, they have been successful in pushing the issue of equal representation high up the political agenda. In Scotland, the real possibility of establishing a completely new parliament has offered a historic political opportunity for the advancement of women, and one in which activists have mobilised in order to ensure gender balance. Recognising the difficulties of reforming an institution once it is established, they have campaigned for equal representation from day one of the Parliament. Their concern to begin with a fundamentally different model from Westminster is reflected in their willingness to put aside party, ideological and policy differences in drawing up plans for the first Parliament. The consensus is also based on the belief that a Scottish parliament with gender equality will foster a more representative, accessible, accountable and democratic form of government which will work to the benefit of Scottish society.

The Scottish case illustrates what has been referred to as the 'Third Wave of Feminism'[8] and the way in which women from different political arenas and sections of the women's movement have campaigned together to improve women's representation. They have been successful in combining their knowledge of political institutions and their experiences of autonomous working in other groups and organisations. Working together, they have developed a mutual respect for the contribution and role of different women, and through their activities they have challenged the traditional view that politics is confined to party politics. It can also be argued that they have mounted a challenge to the traditional political culture which has existed in Scotland and which has been hostile to the involvement of women in the formal arenas of power. Through their campaigns, Scottish women have demonstrated a vision of a different kind of politics and have succeeded in laying the foundations for a Scottish parliament with gender equality.

– NOTES –

1. E. Breitenbach, (1990, 1993, 1995); Brown (1995, 1996 [unpublished], 1996); Brown and Galligan (1993, 1995); Henderson and Mackay (1990); Kelly, E. (1992, 1995 [unpublished]); Liebermann (1989); Levy (1991, 1992); Woman's Claim of Right Group (1991).
2. See Osmond, J. (ed.) (1994), especially ch. 8.
3. See Norris, P. and Lovenduski, J. (1995). For 'supply' and 'demand' factors see also Randall, V. (1987).
4. For the effect of turnover rates see Norris, P. (1993). For the Labour Party's policy on quotas see Lovenduski, J. (1994).
5. For the General Election result in Scotland see Mitchell, J. (1992) and Paterson, L., Brown, A. and McCrone, D. (1992).
6. See model outlined in Brown and Galligan (1993).
7. For the Electoral Contract see Brown, A. (1995).
8. 'The Third Wave of Feminism' was the title of a book edited by Helena Kennedy, Caroline Ellis, Yasmin Ali and Christine Jackson in 1995. The idea for the book developed from a conference on Women's Representation held in London. In the event, the book was not published.

– REFERENCES –

Breitenbach, Esther (1990), ' "Sisters are doing it for themselves": The Women's Movement in Scotland' in Alice Brown and Richard Parry (eds) *The Scottish Government Yearbook 1990*, Edinburgh: The Unit for the Study of Government in Scotland, University of Edinburgh.

Brown, Alice (1992), 'Plans for a Scottish Parliament: Have Women Made a Difference?', paper given at Gender and Power Workshop, ECPR, University of Limerick.

Brown, Alice (1995a) 'The Scotswoman's Parliament', *Parliamentary Brief*, April.

Brown, Alice (1995b), 'Plans for a Scottish Parliament: Did Women Make a Difference?', New Waverley Papers, Edinburgh: Department of Politics, University of Edinburgh.

Brown, Alice and Yvonne Galligan (1993), 'Changing the Political Agenda for Women in the Republic of Ireland and in Scotland', *West European Politics*, 16 (2) April.

Brown, Alice, McCrone, David and Paterson, Lindsay (1996), *Politics and Society in Scotland*, Basingstoke: Macmillan.

Engender (1993), *Gender Audit 1993*, Edinburgh: Engender.

Engender (1994), *Gender Audit 1994*, Edinburgh: Engender.

Engender (1995), *Gender Audit 1995*, Edinburgh: Engender.

Levy, Catriona (1992), 'A Woman's Place? The Future Scottish Parliament', in Lindsay Paterson and David McCrone (eds) *The Scottish Government Yearbook 1992*, Edinburgh: Unit for the Study of Government in Scotland, The University of Edinburgh.

Lovenduski, Joni (1994), 'Will Quotas Make Labour More Woman-Friendly?', *Renewal*, 2 (1), January.

Lovenduski, J. and V. Randall (1993), *Contemporary Feminist Politics: Women and Power in Britain*, Oxford: Oxford University Press.

Mitchell, James (1992), 'The 1992 Election in Scotland in Context', *Parliamentary Affairs*, 45 (4).

Norris, Pippa (1993), 'Slow Progress for Women MPs', *Parliamentary Brief*, Nov/Dec.

Norris, Pippa and Lovenduski, Joni (1995), *Political Recruitment: Gender, Race and Class in the British Parliament*, Cambridge: Cambridge University Press.

Osmond, J. (ed) (1994), *A Parliament for Wales*, Ceredigion: Gomer.

Paterson, Lindsay, Alice Brown and David McCrone (1992), 'Constitutional Crisis: The Causes and Consequences of the 1992 Scottish General Election Result', *Parliamentary Affairs*, 45 (4).

Randall V. (1987), *Women and Politics*, Basingstoke: Macmillan.

Woman's Claim of Right Group (eds) (1991), *A Woman's Claim of Right in Scotland*, Edinburgh: Polygon.

Chapter 17

Deepening Democracy: Women and the Scottish Parliament

Alice Brown

'Deepening Democracy: Women and the Scottish Parliament' (1998), *Regional and Federal Studies*, 8 (1), pp. 103–19, Frank Cass & Co. Ltd.

One of the striking features of the current debate on home rule in Scotland that contrasts with the devolution debate in the 1970s is the inclusion of a significant gender dimension. This dimension relates both to the way in which women political activists have become involved in the debate and to the fact that equality of representation in a Scottish parliament has been pushed up the political agenda in an unprecedented way. The explanations for this shift can be found in developments both within and outside Scotland. They include wider campaigns by women across the world for greater equality and for improved representation in political institutions and public bodies[1] and the specific aspects of the campaign for constitutional change in Scotland which are grounded in the arguments for creating a new form of democratic political system and legislature.

The support for constitutional change in Scotland gathered force during the administrations of the Conservative Government in the 1980s and 1990s. In the run-up to the 1997 General Election, all the major political parties, with the exception of the Conservative Party, stated their commitment to the establishment of a Scottish parliament – the Scottish Labour Party and the Scottish Liberal Democrats favouring a devolved parliament within the UK, along the lines advocated in the final report of the Scottish Constitutional Convention (1995), and the Scottish National Party (1995) arguing instead for an independent parliament within the European Union. The case for a Scottish parliament contains within it a critique of the Westminster style of government and of an electoral system that has consistently returned a party to power with just over 40% of the popular vote. The argument had particular resonance in Scotland, where support for the then party of government, the Conservative Party, fell from a peak of over 50% in the 1950s to 25% in the 1992 General

Election and just 11% in the 1995 elections for the new shadow local authorities, fuelling claims of a 'democratic deficit' in Scotland. The British system of government is charged by its critics with being undemocratic, unrepresentative, inaccessible, highly centralised and secretive. A claim has been made for the establishment of a parliament in Scotland which is run on fundamentally different lines from Westminster, which has a more proportional and representative electoral system and which engenders a new democratic political culture (Scottish Constitutional Convention 1990).

As the campaign for a Scottish parliament has developed, women political activists in Scotland have entered the debate to make their own specific claim for improving democracy and for the equal representation of women within the new legislature. In sharing the general critique of the Westminster Parliament and style of government, they have added a further criticism of the existence of a predominantly male political culture which they perceive as hostile to the participation of women in politics. They see the setting up of a new parliament as a unique opportunity for radical change and the chance to have an institution in which women can participate equally, contributing to new democratic practices and procedures that they hope will fundamentally alter the political culture of politics in Scotland.

This chapter outlines the way in which women have become involved in the politics and discourse of constitutional reform and have made their claim to play an equal part in the future governance of Scotland. Women political activists from the political parties, trade unions, local government, the voluntary sector and a broad range of organisations and women's groups have seized the political opportunity opened up by the constitutional debate in order to make their own proposals for deepening democracy. They have networked and formed coalitions and alliances around their shared objective of improving the representation of women. They hold similar perceptions and experience of a political system that has failed to deliver equality and to be responsive to the needs of women and others, articulating instead their desire for a different type of parliament and politics in Scotland.[2]

– CONTEXT –

Key factors influencing the constitutional debate are the decline in electoral support for the Conservative Party in Scotland and the unwillingness of the party leadership during the 1980s and 1990s to concede the case for significant constitutional reform. Electoral support for the Conservative Party in Scotland has been in decline since the mid-1950s, reaching a low level at the 1987 General Election when the party gained only 10 of the 72 parliamentary seats in Scotland and just 24% of the vote. With no change in policies that had proved to be unpopular in Scotland and the persistence of the Prime Minister of the time,

Margaret Thatcher, and other Cabinet ministers in criticising the Scots for their 'dependency culture', support for the Conservatives in Scotland continued to deteriorate. In the run-up to the 1992 General Election, commentators predicted a humiliating defeat for the Conservative Party in Scotland with the loss of more parliamentary seats. Against these expectations, the party returned 11 MPs to the House of Commons and enjoyed a short-lived increase in their share of the vote (Bochel and Denver 1992; Mitchell 1992; Paterson, Brown and McCrone 1992). The 1997 General Election was to prove disastrous for the Conservative Party, as they lost every parliamentary seat in Scotland when their vote collapsed to 17.5%. Such a wipe-out had not been predicted (Brown 1997).

Within this broader picture, the number of women MPs from Scottish constituencies has remained relatively low. At the General Election in 1992, the number rose to five women from a total of 72 Scottish MPs, a representation rate of less than 7%. However, the same number of women were elected at the General Elections in 1959 and 1964, demonstrating that little progress had been made for women's representation in the intervening years.[3] Following two by-elections in 1994 and 1995, Helen Liddell was elected to represent the Labour Party in Monklands East and Roseanna Cunningham to represent the SNP in Perth and Kinross. This brought the total number of women MPs to seven, a representation rate of just under 9.7%. This all-time record was broken by the return of 12 women MPs at the 1997 General Election, nine from the Labour Party, two from the SNP and one from the Liberal Democrats, increasing the representation rate to 16.6%.

At local government level, the Conservative Party has also experienced a fall in electoral support. Following plans to re-organise local government in Scotland from a two-tier to a unitary system, elections were held for the new shadow authorities in April 1995, with the new unitary authorities taking control in April 1996. At these elections the Conservative Party gained just 11% of the vote and failed to win control of any of the 32 new local authorities. The elections did not result in a significant improvement in the representation of women to the new councils. Although the participation of women in local government is greater than at central government level, the representation rate rose marginally to 22.35%, an increase of some half a per cent on the 1992 district council elections (Bochel and Denver 1995; Brown 1996). The failure of the parties to select significantly more women for election did not go unnoticed by those women campaigning for equality in the Scottish Parliament.[4]

The pattern of low electoral support for the Conservative Party in Scotland and low representation of women politicians is repeated at the level of the European Parliament. At the European Elections in 1994, the Conservative Party failed to win any of the eight vacant seats, and, against the trend in most other European countries, the number of women MEPs fell from two to one (Denver 1994).

It is within this electoral and political context that the campaign for constitutional change in Scotland has taken place. The campaign has involved a number of groups and organisations including the Campaign for a Scottish Assembly (CSA) which was formed in 1979 following the setbacks in proposals for devolution at that time, as a cross- and non-party body established to campaign for and co-ordinate the pressure for constitutional reform. Following the so-called 'doomsday scenario' in 1987, a phrase coined by opponents of the Government to describe the situation where the collapse of electoral support in Scotland coincided with the return of a Conservative majority government to Westminster, the movement for constitutional reform intensified (Lawson 1988). In response to the re-election of a third Thatcher government, the CSA published a document in 1988, A *Claim of Right for Scotland*, in which it supported the sovereign right of the Scottish people to govern themselves. It recommended the establishment of a Scottish Constitutional Convention as a forum for discussing the future government of Scotland.

A Scottish Constitutional Convention was created and held its first meeting early in 1989, at which it adopted the *Claim of Right* document and its three key proposals: first, to draw up and agree a scheme for a Scottish parliament; second, to mobilise Scottish opinion and ensure the approval of the Scottish people for the scheme; and third, to assert the right of the Scottish people to secure the implementation of the scheme (Scottish Constitutional Convention 1990). Membership of the Convention included representatives from the Scottish Labour Party, the Scottish Liberal Democrats, the Scottish Trades Union Congress (STUC), the CSA (later to change its name to the Campaign for a Scottish Parliament, CSP), and others from Scottish local government, the churches, small political parties and other civic organisations including the Scottish Convention of Women (SCOW). After attending the first meeting, the Scottish National Party decided to withdraw from the Convention and opposed plans for a devolved parliament, advocating instead an independent Scottish parliament within the European Union. Officially declaring its opposition to constitutional change, the Conservative Party in Scotland was not represented in the Convention, although some well-known members of the party voiced their support for some form of devolved power.

Despite the non-participation of two of the main political parties in Scotland, the Scottish Constitutional Convention represented a broad alliance of Scottish institutions and organisations in favour of the establishment of a devolved Scottish parliament. The case for a parliament was based on the view that Scotland was suffering a 'democratic deficit' in that the Conservative Party did not have a mandate to rule and impose policies on a Scottish electorate while it had minority electoral support in Scotland. As a result, criticisms of the first-past-the-post electoral system increased while support for some form of proportional representation grew and the political system was charged with being undemocratic and unrepresentative. Other attacks on the Westminster style of government surrounded its highly centralised decision-making, secrecy and lack of accessibility and accountability, as well as other practical considerations such as the hours of meetings and the geographical location of Parliament. According to the Convention, such conditions were not conducive to modern, open and effective government and democracy, and operated against the participation and recruitment of a wider spectrum of the Scottish population, to the particular disadvantage of women. The Convention began its work by establishing working groups which had the task of drawing up options for the future government of Scotland. A Women's Issues Group was formed as a result of pressure from women activists and from men in the Convention who gave their support to increasing the representation of women.

– Women's role in the constitutional debate –

In contrast to the devolution campaigns in the 1970s, women political activists in Scotland formed a broad alliance in support of a Scottish parliament and have been successful in placing the issue of gender balance in representation in the new Parliament high on the political agenda. Catriona Levy (1992) notes that the feminist journal, Msprint, reported that the women's movement ignored the referendum or saw it as irrelevant. Others feared that a parliament in Scotland could be a backward step for women, with Westminster providing an opportunity for more progressive social policies (Breitenbach 1990). Yet by the late 1980s women recognised that they had to be involved in the preliminary stages of the discussions surrounding the proposed Scottish Parliament to ensure that the key decisions were not taken by men and that the needs and priorities of women were not marginalised. One of the immediate responses by some women activists was to form A Woman's Claim of Right Group, partially as a response to the composition of the newly established Scottish Constitutional Convention which was predominantly (90%) male: 'Once again, major proposals and decisions affecting the life and well-being of Scottish people would be made with women being significantly under-represented' (A Woman's Claim of Right Group (eds) 1991: 1). The group published a separate document entitled A Woman's Claim of Right in Scotland, which was submitted to the Women's Issues Group of the Convention[5], in which they put forward their proposals for improving the representation of women stating that 'as few elements of the male "pub culture" should be allowed to surround the operation of the Assembly as is humanly possible' (Women's Claim of Right 1989: 5).

When the Convention published its first report in 1990, Towards Scotland's Parliament, the efforts of the women activists were very much reflected in the document. The Convention noted the 'failure of the British political system to face the issue of women's representation', and in stating that the Scottish

Parliament offered the 'opportunity for a new start' it committed itself to the 'principle of equal representation' (Scottish Constitutional Convention 1990: 12). Two additional groups were then established by the Convention to undertake more detailed work on parliamentary procedures and the electoral system. The recommendations of these groups also reflected an awareness of the gender dimension. Recognising that many women are politically active in their communities rather than at the political elite level, the procedures group considered ways in which the new Parliament could be more accessible and accountable to all members of the community. It outlined plans for meetings of parliamentary committees to be held in communities affected by proposed policy changes and ways in which women's and other groups could be involved in initiating legislation and giving evidence to these committees. The removal of practical barriers to women's participation were also agreed. It was proposed that the Parliament should meet at times compatible with family life and that carer and travel allowances should be provided. Similarly, the group responsible for proposing an electoral system for the Parliament was asked to consider a scheme which would result in a truly representative assembly based on certain principles including gender equality: 'that it ensures, or at least takes effective positive action to bring about, equal representation of men and women, and encourages fair representation of ethnic and other minority groups' (Scottish Constitutional Convention 1992).

Although there was wide acceptance of the view that women are under-represented in political elites and that steps needed to be taken to redress the gender imbalance, there was no consensus on the mechanism for ensuring gender equality. It was at the point of agreeing a precise mechanism that the ideological differences between the women in the different parties emerged. For example, the Scottish Labour Party's official policy was statutory 50:50, a policy that had originally been developed by the women's committee of the STUC. It was argued that the easiest and fairest way to achieve the objective of equal representation was to have a man and a woman Member of Parliament for each constituency in Scotland. It was further argued that, given the failure of voluntarism in the past, the scheme should be statutory so that all political parties would have the opportunity to field both a female and male candidate for each of Scotland's 72 constituencies. This scheme was opposed by the Scottish Liberal Democrats, on the grounds that it was being adopted by the Labour Party as a way of avoiding a more proportional electoral system and, crucially, on democratic grounds. It was contended that it was inherently undemocratic to 'force' political parties to select and the electorate to choose a man and a woman and in addition that it was not the place of the state to interfere with the democratic process within political parties themselves.

Another area of contention between the parties was the disagreement on the precise electoral system to be adopted in the new Parliament. The Liberal Democrats advocated the use of the Single Transferable Vote system with modifications. For its part, the Scottish Labour Party had some difficulty in persuading some of its members of the advantages of changing to a proportional electoral system. After all, given the strong support for the Labour Party in Scotland, they had much to gain by retaining the first-past-the-post elections in a four-party system.

In spite of these differences, the broad consensus for change and pressure to create a more democratic and representative parliament kept the Convention discussions alive. It is widely acknowledged that the active participation of women in the Convention's Working Groups was crucial in ensuring that the issue of equal representation stayed on the agenda. In attempting to reach a compromise between the main political parties in the Convention on an agreed scheme, there was always the danger that the objective of equal representation would be sacrificed, particularly as the mechanism for achieving equity was a key area of contention between the main players. As one woman activist commented: 'Their (the men's) agenda was different and we had to keep raising the issue. Although some men on the Electoral Reform Group were supportive and sympathetic to our demands, we doubt whether they would have pursued the issue. We were the ones who had to argue the case again and again.'

Prior to the 1992 General Election a compromise was reached and the Scottish Constitutional Convention issued its agreed proposals for a Scottish parliament which included acceptance of an Additional Member System (AMS) for elections and a statutory obligation on parties to put forward an equal number of men and women candidates.[6] The debate surrounding gender balance went beyond the two main parties in the Convention. The fact that the Convention members had addressed the issue and had made commitments to ensure equal representation almost inevitably meant that the other two main political parties in Scotland, the SNP and the Conservative Party, were forced to respond. As Hayes and McAllister (1996) argue, the political representation of women became one of the key and divisive issues among the Scottish political parties at the 1992 General Election and 'women's representation as well as constitutional reform were heavily influenced both by party ideology and political pragmatism'.

_ THE OPPORTUNITIES FOR WOMEN IN A _
SCOTTISH PARLIAMENT

Following the re-election of the Conservative Government in 1992 which meant that proposals for a Scottish parliament with gender balance were not going to be realised in the immediate future, campaign groups were formed to keep the constitutional question alive, including Common Cause, Scotland United and Democracy for Scotland. In spite of political difficulties, the Scottish Constitutional Convention remained in existence, setting up a Scottish Constitutional Commission in 1993 to examine the issues left unresolved prior to the General

Election and to make specific recommendations regarding gender balance with regard to the electoral system for a Scottish parliament. In the same year the Coalition for Scottish Democracy was formed, bringing together many political activists in the different pressure groups and political parties with a view to establishing a Civic Assembly.[7] Women activists were involved in all of these organisations. In addition, the women's movement in Scotland maintained political pressure on the political parties and trade unions by forming the Scottish Women's Co-ordination Group with representatives from the main women's groups in Scotland, the CSP and the churches. Its main function was to ensure that the recruitment of women in a Scottish parliament was kept high on the political agenda.

After taking oral evidence and written submissions from a wide range of individuals, groups and organisations in Scotland, the Commission delivered its report to the Convention in 1994 (Scottish Constitutional Commission 1994). The Commission recommended a Scottish parliament comprised of 112 members elected on the Additional Member System with 72 constituency members elected on a first-past-the-post basis using the existing Westminster parliamentary constituencies and an additional 40 members elected on a proportional basis from party lists using the eight European constituencies. To achieve greater gender balance, the Commission recommended a voluntary scheme in which parties should be asked to meet a target of at least 40% representation of women in the Parliament taking into account both the constituency and list seats under the AMS electoral system. It recommended further that the target should be achieved within five years of the setting up of a Scottish parliament with targets being set for the fair representation of minority ethnic groups. To encourage more women to stand as parliamentary candidates, recommendations were made for the removal of social, economic and other barriers to women's participation.

The Commission's proposals were not well received. Those women activists who had campaigned long and hard for a firm and statutory commitment to gender equality for the first Scottish Parliament and for 50:50, saw the 40% voluntary target as a weak substitute. Others who had advocated a more voluntary approach were also dissatisfied with the Commission's recommendations. It was at this point that the campaign for gender equality took an unexpected turn. The Scottish Women's Co-ordination Group facilitated talks between women within the two main political parties in the Convention – Labour and Liberal Democrats – to see if there was a way of resolving their differences and finding an alternative solution to that proposed by the Scottish Constitutional Commission.

The women involved accepted that it was vital to begin with a parliament of equal representation, in recognition that it is much more difficult to reform a political institution once it is well established and parliamentary seats are already occupied. In spite of their political differences, and reflecting the importance they attached to the issue, they sought a compromise which built on their shared objective to break the mould of under-representation. They agreed a scheme for the first Scottish Parliament that would satisfy their different perspectives and drew up an Electoral Contract for consideration by the executives and conferences of the Labour Party and Liberal Democrats. On the understanding that the Electoral Contract would pertain only to the first elections of the Scottish Parliament, the parties agreed to endorse the principle that there should be an equal number of men and women MSPs and to approve the selection and fielding of an equal number of male and female candidates, the fair distribution of female candidates in winnable seats, and the use of the AMS system in a parliament large enough to facilitate effective democratic and representative government (Brown 1995). Within this scheme the parties were free to find their own mechanism for fulfilling their commitment to gender balance, recognising their different electoral positions in Scottish politics.[8]

The proposals for gender balance recommended by the Commission in 1994 had not been the only factor to cause discontent. The size of the Parliament with 112 members was argued to be insufficient to allow the type of proportionality and representation that had been envisaged. The Scottish Liberal Democrats stated that they were only willing to accept the Electoral Contract if the minimum number of Scottish MSPs was 145. In another unexpected turn, the leaders of the Scottish Labour Party and the Liberal Democrats announced plans in September of 1995 for a parliament of 129 members (73[9] to be elected on the constituency side by FPTP and the other 56 on the additional member list with seven members from each of the eight European constituencies). After some opposition from the STUC and other organisations, not least from within the two political parties themselves, agreement was reached and the Scottish Constitutional Convention endorsed the proposal. The agreement on the size of Parliament and provisions for gender equality were then written into the final scheme drawn up by the Convention and launched on St Andrew's Day 1995 (Scottish Constitutional Convention 1995).[10]

Having agreed to a smaller parliament, the possibility of operating the 50:50 scheme as originally planned was not open to the Scottish Labour Party. A 50:50 constituency balance plus a top-up for proportionality would necessitate a parliament of around 200 members, far in excess of the 129 agreed with their Convention partners. Women within the party were anxious that the commitment to equality should not be diluted, and the Women's Caucus Group which had been formed following the 1992 General Election took a particularly radical stance on the issue. The party then considered operating all-women short-lists in selection of candidates, a policy that had been adopted at the British level to improve women's representation at Westminster (Lovenduski 1994; Norris 1993).[11] When the Industrial Tribunal ruled against the use of all-women short-lists at the end of 1995, this presented a problem not only for the party in Britain but for the plans in

Scotland, especially as the leadership of the party made the decision not to challenge the ruling just prior to a general election. Another option being considered by the Scottish Labour Party is that of twinning or pairing constituencies.[12] It is likely that the Liberal Democrats will use the top-up list on the additional member electoral system to redress any gender imbalance and will adopt other promotional strategies such as training and encouraging women to stand as candidates and support constituencies in selecting women. The precise mechanism to be adopted by the parties has still to be announced.

There have been significant political developments since the publication of the SCC report in 1995 including the controversy that followed Labour's decision in 1996 to introduce a referendum on constitutional change and not least the General Election campaign in 1997. In this climate the debate on gender balance was somewhat overshadowed. However, it has re-emerged as a result of the positive reaction to the increase in the number of women MPs elected to the House of Commons[13] and in the context of the new Government's plans for constitutional reform. Immediately after the election, the Government announced a referendum in Scotland on 11 September 1997, in which 'Voters will be asked whether they agree that there should be a Scottish Parliament and whether they agree that such a Parliament should have powers to vary tax' (Scottish Office 1997: 34). The women activists joined in the broad-based campaign for a 'Yes'/'Yes' vote organised by Scotland Forward, holding a conference immediately after the General Election at which the new Minister for Women, Henry McLeish, gave a keynote address.

– A LEARNING EXPERIENCE? –

It could be argued that the 1980s and 1990s have been something of a learning experience for political activists in Scotland as they have worked together to achieve constitutional change. The campaign has not been confined to the political parties and has involved a broad range of civic organisations and groups such as the Civic Assembly, the Campaign for a Scottish Parliament, Charter 88, Scottish Education and Action for Development (SEAD) and the Women's Co-ordination Group. They have played their part in widening and deepening democratic participation. As discussed above, the involvement of women has been an important aspect of this process. A number of factors can help explain why women activists have decided that constitutional reform is such a crucial political issue.

First, one can draw on political developments in the 1980s and 1990s which help to explain why women activists appear to have changed their political strategy since the devolution debate of the 1970s. The factors that might provide such an insight have been discussed elsewhere (Brown, McCrone and Paterson 1996), and they include the impact of Thatcherism in Scotland and on women in particular; the experience gained by women through working within political parties, trade unions and local government during the period; women's growing frustration with the slow pace of change for women within the Westminster Parliament; the dislike articulated by women for the hostile and adversarial way in which they consider politics is conducted and the belief that women themselves have to be involved directly in making plans for the Scottish Parliament in order to ensure that their voices are heard.

Second, the constitutional campaign in Scotland and women's direct involvement in it has impacted on the level of awareness of the under-representation of women from the existing legislature. Participation in the debate has led to questions being asked about the reasons for the relative exclusion of women from political recruitment to parliament, a problem common to women in all the political parties in Scotland and in comparisons being drawn with women in other legislatures.[14] The experience of women in Europe, the United States and other countries such as Australia, has been charted and lessons drawn.[15] An interview survey of women political activists in Scotland carried out in 1993/4 helped to identify their views on legislative recruitment and their perceptions of the reasons for the low representation of women in political office.[16]

Third, in spite of their differences of view on the mechanisms for increasing the number of women in a Scottish parliament, women activists in Scotland have campaigned together in support of the principle of equal representation and have transcended some of the boundaries that have existed between different feminist strategies. Traditionally, the claim for equal representation was assumed to be the preserve of liberal feminists, being rejected by socialist-Marxist feminists on the grounds that it would do little to change the nature of capitalist society, and by radical feminists who preferred to put their energies into autonomous women's groups and to bring such issues as domestic violence on to the political agenda. With growing recognition that these strategies are not necessarily in conflict, there has been a coming together of women from different perspectives with the aim of getting more women into key decision-making bodies, including Parliament – a trend that is not confined to Scotland or the UK. Getting women in is not seen just as an end in itself but as a means of achieving other objectives such as enhancing the political life and culture of the country and delivering resources and policies which will help women in the community.[17]

In Scotland, this coming together of women within political parties, trade unions and local government with other women in women's groups, the voluntary sector and organisations around a common agenda has helped strengthen the campaign for a more democratic and woman-friendly Scottish parliament. They have also been mobilised by their belief that a Scottish parliament where half the members are women will be 'different' and will deliver not only a more representative and democratic system of government but also one which encourages the participation of women and others in the community and which delivers the type of policies which people in Scotland want.

The strategic importance of the new Parliament was reflected in the interviews with the women political activists. Their vision of a parliament which is located in Scotland, has equal numbers of men and women, a more proportional electoral system, hours and meeting times compatible with family life, payment of carer allowances and which is more accessible and accountable to Scottish society, has acted as a strong mobilising force in their campaigns. Women across the party divide hold strong perceptions that significantly more women in Parliament will make a substantial 'difference' to political life in Scotland. The view was expressed that women would bring their specific life experiences and expertise to the job and would alter the style and behaviour of political debate. Phrases such as 'women are more consensual', 'women are less confrontational and better at getting things done', 'women have a much more open and sharing approach' or 'with more women the whole political ethos would change' were often used.

There was also general agreement between the women activists that politics is the poorer for the absence of women. With more women politicians, not only would the Parliament operate more effectively but society in general would be improved. They justified this view on the grounds that there would be different policy priorities, more directed at those in need in society, and also different perspectives on the same policies.

These views could appear at first sight to be essentialist and to endorse theories of biological determinism that have been rejected by some feminists. Also they could be interpreted as logically inconsistent in that the women activists are arguing both for equality and difference. However, feminist theory has developed to incorporate the desire to achieve both equality and assert women's difference from men and the differences between women and to move away from rather narrow debates surrounding so-called 'women's issues'.[18] For example, Deborah Rhode argues that women are both the same and different but that the salient issue is not difference per se but the consequences of addressing it in particular social and historical circumstances. She puts forward the view that women's political strategies must rest on feminist principles and not feminine stereotypes: 'The issues of greatest concern to women are not simply 'women's issues'. Although the feminist agenda incorporates values traditionally associated with women, the stakes in its realisation are ones that both sexes share' (Rhode 1995: 158).

– CONCLUSION –

Until recently no feminist in her right mind would have thought liberal democracy could deliver the goods. (Phillips 1994: 195)

The above quotation from Anne Phillips is a useful reminder that campaigning for gender equality in liberal democracies has not always been a political strategy advocated by feminists. In Scotland, a broad consensus now exists that increasing the representation of women is one way to ensure a more equal and democratic society (Breitenbach 1995). The 'constitutional question' facilitated a discourse around issues of democracy, representation, proportionality and accountability. It also opened up an opportunity for women to enter the debate and make their specific claims for a parliament which reflected their priorities. As Catriona Burness (1995) has argued, women's representation is now intrinsically linked with wider campaigns for devolution and improved democratic participation.

Inevitably, the raising of demands for equal representation within the new Scottish Parliament has led to an examination of the policies of the political parties on gender equality and the asking of the question, 'How democratic and representative are the parties themselves?' Although women form almost half of the membership of the political parties in Scotland, they are significantly under-represented in the top posts. Women activists are increasingly aware that the political parties themselves have to change if women are to play an equal part in political life in Scotland. Women across the party divide support the view that the political culture in Scotland is predominantly male, a culture that needs to alter if more women are to become involved in the party and political system. Drawing on the experience of women in the Scandinavian countries in particular, women activists argue that a 'critical mass'[19] of women in a new Scottish parliament will help engender a new political culture.

The Government's White Paper on devolution endorses the Scottish Constitutional Convention's proposals for a parliament with 129 MSPs elected on a version of the Additional Member System. In posing the question of who will be eligible for selection and election to the Scottish Parliament, the Government state that they are 'keen to see people with standing in their communities and who represent the widest possible range of interests in Scotland putting themselves forward for election. In particular the government attach great importance to equal opportunities for all – including women, members of ethnic minorities and disabled people'. The Government urges 'all political parties offering candidates for election to the Scottish Parliament to have this in mind in their internal candidate selection processes' (Scottish Office 1997).

On reflection, it is perhaps surprising that women have managed to make so much progress on the question of gender balance, although it would be difficult for those advocating the case for improving democracy to deny, at least publicly, the right of women to have an equal share in the future governance of Scotland. Writing in 1994, Tom Nairn noted that the 'elders (in the Labour Party) are still trying to depict all this as just a passing fad. They could not be more mistaken. The famous obstacles of which so much is made (not enough "suitable" women, unfair to some men, interminable time needed, etc.) are really chaff in the wind'. [See Chapter 15, this collection.] The proposals for gender balance can be argued to be one of the most radical aspects of the plans for constitutional change. However, the opposition to such plans should not be under-estimated. In moving towards a more proportional electoral system in which the Labour Party is unlikely to have an overall majority in the new Parliament, the competition for constituency seats and places on the additional top-up lists will be intense. In such a climate, advocates of gender balance will have to work hard to ensure that the commitments to equality made by the political parties are met.

With the overwhelming Yes vote in the referendum of 11 September 1997, it seems likely that a parliament will be established by the year 2000, as planned by the Government. Selection of candidates for seats and for the top-up lists will begin in 1998, with the first elections for the Parliament being held in 1999. It will not be long, therefore, before we can judge whether women have achieved their goal of gender balance in Scotland's first Parliament since 1707. The greatest fear of women activists is that they will have campaigned long and hard for a new democratic institution but that it will be dominated by old politics.

– NOTES –

1. One of the key outcomes of the United Nations Fourth World Conference on Women held in Beijing in 1995 was the demand for a significant improvement in the representation of women in decision-making bodies. It was also one of the three elements of the submission by Scottish women to Beijing, the other two being the elimination of poverty and violence against women (Scottish Women's Co-ordination Group 1995).

2. Much of the material that follows is necessarily descriptive and draws on accounts to be found in Brown (1996) and Brown, McCrone and Paterson (1996), Chapter 8.

3. It has been possible for women to stand for election since 1918. From 1918 to 1997 a total of just 28 women have represented Scottish constituencies at Westminster.

4. For example, Engender, the women's research and campaigning organisation, held a press conference publicising the election results and the effect on women's representation. They also published a survey of the impact of local government reform on women in the *Gender Audit 1996* (Engender 1996).

5. The group published a book of the same title, *A Woman's Claim of Right in Scotland*, in 1991 (Woman's Claim of Right Group (eds) 1991).

6. This statutory obligation did not imply a complete acceptance of the 50:50 proposal, and the wording of the document was kept somewhat vague. The mechanism for ensuring equal representation was not spelled out. Following the 1992 General Election, the Convention established a Scottish Constitutional Commission to take the issues forward. At this stage the Scottish Liberal Democrats noted their intention to withdraw from the 'statutory' clause in the Convention's document published in 1992.

7. The Civic Assembly held its first meeting in 1995 and operated the principle of gender balance by requesting the groups participating in the forum to ensure that they sent equal numbers of female and male representatives.

8. Given the difference in electoral support for the two parties in Scotland, it is estimated that Labour will obtain most of its parliamentary seats through the

constituency side of the elections, while the Liberal Democrats will have to rely more heavily on the top-up list. The compromise meant that the parties could take this into account in drawing up their own particular mechanism for meeting their side of the Electoral Contract.

9. The increase from 72 to 73 constituencies resulted from the Boundary Commission's decision to divide the constituency of Orkney and Shetland.

10. The SNP and the Conservative Party re-stated their own plans on the same day. The SNP's proposals include a commitment to 'guarantee geographical and gender balance in SNP representation' by using the party lists. They propose a single chamber, with 200 members; 144 members are to be elected by the alternative vote system (two from each constituency) and 56 selected from party lists under the additional member system (SNP 1995). The Conservative Party made their case for protecting the Union.

11. All-women short-lists were to operate in 50% of the winnable vacant seats for the 1997 General Election. Consensus meetings were held within the party to identify the constituencies that would select a woman candidate from an all-woman short-list. Norris (1993) reminds us that although this sounds like a very radical policy, given the low turnover of MPs at any given election the actual increase in women MPs is likely to be more modest than many anticipate.

12. Under this proposal, women and men will be invited to stand as candidates for a pair of twinned constituency seats. The woman who receives the most votes from the list of women candidates will be selected for one seat and the man who receives the most votes from the male list will be selected for the other.

13. A record number of 160 women were elected as MPs at the 1997 General Election – 102 Labour, 14 Conservatives, 2 Liberal Democrats and 2 SNP – a representation rate of 18.2%. The Scottish figures are 9 Labour, 1 Liberal Democrat and 2 SNP (16.6% representation rate).

14. Parallels can be drawn with the politicisation of women in the civil rights movement in the United States in the 1960s.

15. The Scandinavian countries in particular, with representation rates of around 40% women, attracted interest.

16. This survey was conducted by Alice Brown with the support of research grants from the Leverhulme Trust and the ESRC.

17. For a discussion on the consensus built around representation and other issues, see Breitenbach (1996).

18. See, for example, the contributions in Bock and James (1992).

19. A 'critical mass' is said to exist when there is around 25–30% representation of women.

– REFERENCES –

Bochel, John and David Denver (1992), 'The 1992 General Election in Scotland', *Scottish Affairs*, 1.

Bochel, John and David Denver (1995), 'The Elections for the Shadow Local Authorities', *Scottish Affairs*, 13.

Bock, Gisella and Susan James (eds) (1992), *Beyond Equality and Difference*, London: Routledge.

Breitenbach, Esther (1990), ' "Sisters are doing it for themselves": The Women's Movement in Scotland' in Alice Brown and Richard Parry (eds) *The Scottish Government Yearbook 1990*, Edinburgh: Unit for the Study of Government in Scotland, University of Edinburgh.

Breitenbach, Esther (1995b), 'The Women's Movement in Scotland in the 1990s', *New Waverley Papers*, Edinburgh: Department of Politics, The University of Edinburgh.

Brown, Alice (1995c), 'The Scotswoman's Parliament', *Parliamentary Brief*, April.

Brown, Alice (1996), 'Women and Politics in Scotland', *Parliamentary Affairs*, 49 (1).

Brown, Alice (1997), 'The 1997 General Election in Scotland: Paving the way for a Scottish Parliament?', *Parliamentary Affairs*, 50 (4).

Brown, Alice, David McCrone and Lindsay Paterson (1996), *Politics and Society in Scotland*, Basingstoke: Macmillan.

Brown, Alice and Yvonne Galligan (1993), 'Changing the Political Agenda for Women in the Republic of Ireland and in Scotland', *West European Politics*, 16 (2), April.

Burness, Catriona (1995), 'Will Scotland Lead the Way for Women?', *Parliamentary Brief*, March.

Crick, Bernard and David Miller (1991), *Standing Orders for a Scottish Parliament*, Edinburgh: John Wheatley Centre.

Crick, Bernard and David Miller (1995), *To Make the Parliament of Scotland a Model for Democracy*, Edinburgh: John Wheatley Centre.

Denver, David (1994), 'The 1994 European Elections in Scotland', *Scottish Affairs*, 9.

Engender (1996), *Gender Audit 1996*, Edinburgh: Engender.

Hayes, Bernadette and Ian McAllister (1996), 'Political Outcomes, Women's Legislative Rights and Devolution in Scotland', in D. Broughton, D. Farrell, D. Denver and C. Rallings (eds) *British Elections and Parties Yearbook 1995*, London: Frank Cass.

Lawson, Alan (1988), 'Mair nor a rauch wind blawin' in David McCrone and Alice Brown, *The Scottish Government Yearbook 1988*, Edinburgh: Unit for the Study of Government in Scotland, University of Edinburgh.

Levy, Catriona (1992), 'A Woman's Place? The Future Scottish Parliament', in Lindsay Paterson and David McCrone (eds) *The Scottish Government Yearbook 1992*, Edinburgh: Unit for the Study of Government in Scotland, University of Edinburgh.

Lovenduski, Joni (1994), 'Will Quotas Make Women More Woman-Friendly', *Renewal*, 2 (1), January.

Lovenduski, Joni and Pippa Norris (eds) (1993), *Gender and Party Politics*, London: Sage.

Mitchell, James (1992), 'The 1992 Election in Scotland in Context', *Parliamentary Affairs*, 45 (4).

Nairn, Tom (1994), 'Gender Goes Top of the Agenda', *The Scotsman*, 28 December.

Norris, Pippa (1993), 'Slow Progress for Women MPs', *Parliamentary Brief*, Nov/Dec.

Norris, Pippa and Joni Lovenduskii (1995), *Political Recruitment: Gender, Race and Class in the British Parliament*, Cambridge: Cambridge University Press.

Paterson, Lindsay, Alice Brown and David McCrone (1992), 'Constitutional Crisis: The Causes and Consequences of the 1992 Scottish General Election Result', *Parliamentary Affairs*, 45 (4).

Phillips, Anne (1994), 'The Representation of Women', in *The Polity Reader in Gender Studies*, Cambridge: Polity Press.

Rhode, Deborah (1995), 'The Politics of Paradigms: Gender Difference and Gender Disadvantage', in Gisella Bock and Susan James, *Beyond Equality and Difference*, London: Routledge.

Scottish Constitutional Commission (1994), *Further Steps: Towards a Scheme for Scotland's Parliament*, October, Edinburgh: CoSLA.

Scottish Constitutional Convention (1990), *Towards Scotland's Parliament, A Report to the Scottish People*, November, Edinburgh: CoSLA.

Scottish Constitutional Convention (1992), *Electoral System for Scottish Parliament*, February, Edinburgh: CoSLA.

Scottish Constitutional Convention (1995), *Scotland's Parliament, Scotland's Right*, November, Edinburgh: CoSLA.

Scottish National Party (1995), *Programme for Government*, Edinburgh: SNP.

Scottish Office (1997), *Scotland's Parliament*, Cmmd. 3658, July, Edinburgh: HMSO.

Scottish Women's Co-ordination Group (1995), *Report and Recommendations to the UN 4th World Conference on Women, Beijing 1995*.

Woman's Claim of Right Group (1989) unpublished, *Submission to Scottish Constitutional Convention*.

Woman's Claim of Right Group (eds) (1991), *A Woman's Claim of Right in Scotland*, Edinburgh: Polygon.

CHAPTER 18

Networking for Equality and a Scottish Parliament: the Women's Co-ordination Group and Organisational Alliances

RONNIE MCDONALD, WITH MORAG ALEXANDER
AND LESLEY SUTHERLAND

The Women's Co-ordination Group, created in 1992, played a central role in ensuring that debate and dialogue on the issue of women's representation continued to take place throughout the 1990s. This group was a loose alliance of women's organisations and individuals. It organised meetings and conferences to keep women's issues on the agenda and, as well as promoting the 50:50 campaign, it identified priority areas of concern to women in Scotland and contributed to the debate about equality structures in the Parliament and about the need for the Parliament to operate in woman-friendly ways. The Scottish Trade Unions Congress (STUC), building on a tradition of work on women's issues, took on the role of administering the work of the Co-ordination Group, and worked closely with the Equal Opportunities Commission in Scotland and Women's Forum Scotland, and with other organisations such as the Scottish Joint Action Group, Engender, the Church of Scotland Women's Guild, and Scottish Education and Action for Development. This chapter brings together contributions which focus on the role of the STUC and trade union movement, the EOC in Scotland, and Women's Forum Scotland in networking for equality and a Scottish parliament. As with other contributions to this book, this is only a partial story: other organisations and individuals played a part alongside those mentioned here.

For the best part of 100 years, the STUC has been a fervent advocate of devolution and greater autonomy in Scottish affairs, and has an acknowledged and creditable place as a prime mover of devolution and a Scottish parliament. Though the trade union movement is rarely credited for its dynamism and leadership in the advocacy of rights for women, as far back as 1926 the STUC created a Women's Advisory Committee to advise the General Council – the key trade union decision-making body in Scotland on issues affecting women workers. That Committee's work provided the STUC with a focus and a clear steer on women's issues throughout the twentieth century, with many trade union campaigns for improvements in women rights at work achieving considerable success.

The equality agenda of the 1970s promoted significant legal changes for women with the enactment of the Equal Pay and Sex Discrimination Acts. This legislation also created in 1975 the Equal Opportunities Commission (EOC), with its headquarters in Manchester. In 1978 a Scottish office of the EOC was opened in Glasgow, but it was not until 1993, when Morag Alexander was appointed as Director and there was an increase in staff resources, that the office in Scotland had the capacity to promote equality of opportunity in Scotland effectively. The main areas in which the EOC works are in law enforcement and the provision of information and advice; training lay advisers, trade unionists, and lawyers; promoting understanding of women's role in economic development and training through the Fair Play consortium; and promoting gender equality policies in education and training.

Within the Scottish trade union movement, following on from the legislative advances of the 1970s, the 1980s represented a period of immense change in answer to a profound challenge within its ranks to represent, and be seen to represent, all of its members. The movement was male-dominated – there were very few women in any of its key positions or committees. Campaigns by women in the movement for equality crystallised at this time and positive action was promoted as the only way to transform and create a body which would be relevant to women as well as men. In addition to campaigning for greater representation of women in decision-making bodies within the trade union movement, women trade unionists took up the campaign for improved representation of women in public life in Scotland, a campaign in which the STUC Women's Committee has played a significant role. It was perhaps to be expected, then, that the Women's Committee would take a dynamic approach to women's representation in a Scottish parliament, and, indeed, in the Scottish Constitutional Convention (SCC).

It was seen as imperative for women to be involved in the SCC so that its culture could embrace the women's agenda, particularly in the early days, and we owe a debt of gratitude to the women who helped make the difference in all the debates within the Convention. When the working group of the Campaign for a Scottish Assembly was establishing the framework for the SCC, the STUC was consulted about women's involvement and proposed that the Scottish Convention of Women (SCOW), as a broadly representative women's organisation in Scotland, should be part of the SCC. At about the same time, the STUC Women's Committee took a lead role in bringing together women from a range of organisations to develop Women's Forum Scotland. This organisation was established in 1990 to provide a network for women's organisations in Scotland, to act as a communication channel, and to lobby, influence and inform institutions and policy makers on matters of concern to women. The establishment of a Scottish parliament with equal representation was a primary objective of the STUC and of WFS, inherited from its predecessor body, SCOW. The other main stimulus to the establishment of WFS was the increasing recognition of the impact of Europe on women in Scotland, and WFS is a link to and participates in the European Women's Lobby. WFS's main means of participation and contribution to the campaign for women's representation was through the SCC (as one of the signatory organisations), in working with other women's organisations and participating in the Women's Co-ordination Group, and interacting with sister organisations in the UK and Europe.

– EQUAL REPRESENTATION FOR WOMEN AND MEN – 50:50 –

The STUC was represented on the SCC, and worked in common purpose with other members of the Convention to devise a blueprint for a Scottish parliament. That the blueprint included the equal representation of women and men in the Parliament is credited to the STUC Women's Committee who, in their submission to the SCC Working Party on Women's Issues in August 1989, put forward a radical agenda of measures including the proposal that the Scottish Parliament should represent women and men equally, i.e. that 50% of elected representatives should be women and 50% men.

The proposal was greeted with a mixture of excitement and disbelief: excitement that at last women could have the opportunity to play an equal role with men in the government of Scotland and that the time was right to push for that agenda, and disbelief that such a preposterous idea could see the light of day. Despite comments such as 'Are there enough women who could stand for the Parliament?', 'Do we need to introduce chromosome tests for candidates?', or 'They would need special training', the proposition did indeed see the light of day and ignited one of the most strategic campaigns for equality for women in Scotland.

The Women's Committee recognised that the proposal was radical, and were keenly aware that any campaign for 50:50 had to attract the broadest possible support. The strategy was therefore firstly directed to mobilising the key partners in the SCC and thereafter towards building and sustaining support for the campaign. Initially, the support of the STUC General Council and the Scottish Labour Party was seen as crucial. Women trade unionists and women in the Scottish Labour Party took the case for 50:50 to the leadership of their respective organisations, to union and party branches. Various conferences and meetings were arranged and in the spring of 1991 both the STUC Annual Congress and the Annual Conference of the Labour Party adopted the 50:50 proposal as policy.

Meanwhile, the case for 50:50 was being debated in the SCC itself, and in its working groups. The STUC established a parallel working group involving key members and women campaigners, such as Alice Brown, Maria Fyfe, Isobel Lindsay, and Yvonne Strachan, to develop models illustrating how 50:50 could operate in an electoral system which was likely to embrace an element of proportional representation. A pamphlet was produced, 'Say "Yes" to 50:50: How it will work with PR', and was circulated widely to the SCC, political parties and politicians, trade unions, women's organisations and to academics. And although the SCC accepted the principle of equal representation in its first report, there was a long way to go to secure a means of implementing it in the electoral system.

The Women's Committee sought the support of key institutions in Scotland, such as local authorities, and many did give their tacit support, while others regretted they were unable to accept the principle. Their first approach to the Electoral Reform Society about the proposal was met with the view that to offer one man and one woman for election would deprive the electorate of choice: an observation which seemed to the Women's Committee wholly contradictory and certainly did not deter them from campaigning.

– BUILDING A 50:50 NETWORK –

Very few people would say publicly that women and men should not be equal, but the Women's Committee knew from experience that they had to get the 50:50 proposal talked about and that the more it was in the public domain, the harder it would be for the fairness of the proposal to be refuted. That was an essential part of the strategy. Another essential part of the strategy was to ensure that the issue of women's representation in the Parliament was interwoven within the fabric of the debate around a new democracy for Scotland.

In March 1991, the Women's Committee organised a Parliamentary Debate by Women involving the political parties in Scotland around the theme 'An Equal Voice for Women'. One hundred women were invited, on the basis that they would be representative of half the Parliament, with each party entitled to appoint a proportionate number of members to reflect proportionality within Westminster. Although not members of the SCC, the SNP and the Scottish Conservatives participated in this debate. This event was vitally important to the campaign for equal representation, and in opening the door to discussions with women from all parties.

While the campaign began with the STUC Women's Committee, it quickly attracted the support of a broad coalition of women and women's organisations. Along with the John Wheatley Centre (now the Centre for Scottish Public Policy), the Unit for the Study of Government in Scotland at the University of

Edinburgh, and the Scottish Convention of Women, the Women's Committee organised a major conference entitled 'Changing the Face of Scottish Politics' in March 1992. That was the last major public event on women's representation before the general election of May 1992: an issue which was not a key part of any of the political parties' election campaigns. However, at this conference an undertaking was given to organise some publicity during the election and to have a recall event following the election. A financial appeal was launched to those who had attended the conference, to the STUC General Council, trade unions, selected members of the SCC, and to selected members and prospective Members of Parliament, and as a result two equality adverts were placed in *The Herald* and the *Evening Times*.

_ THE EMERGENCE OF THE SCOTTISH WOMEN'S _ CO-ORDINATION GROUP

The promised recall conference was held in June 1992, and from this event the Scottish Women's Co-ordination Group emerged: a voluntary group involving representatives from the STUC Women's Committee, Women's Forum Scotland, the Scottish Joint Action Group, Engender, and the Church of Scotland Women's Guild, as well as a few individual women. The Group was joined later by the Equal Opportunities Commission Scotland, and Scottish Education and Action for Development. The STUC agreed to administer the work of the Co-ordination Group and did so throughout the entire campaign for 50:50.

The Group gave the lead in two significant campaigns: to raise the awareness of women in Scotland and of government – at a national, European and international level – of the need for equal representation of women in decision-making; and to provide women with a means of communication to government in Scotland. With regard to the former, the Group conducted two consultation exercises with women and women's organisations in Scotland in relation to the United Nations Fourth World Conference on Women (the Beijing Conference in 1995) and the 4th European Union Action Plan on Equal Opportunities for Women and Men of 1996. Reports were prepared following open and accessible local consultations with women in Scotland, and endorsed at consultative conferences. The issues which women in Scotland identified as their key concerns were women's representation, violence, and poverty.

The Beijing report was submitted to the United Nations as the *Scottish Women's Report*, separate from the UK Government report, which had not been based on any similarly consultative process, and a handful of women from Scotland participated in the Beijing conference itself. The Scottish report on the EU 4th Action Plan was incorporated within the national EOC Report. Subsequently, the EOC, working with the STUC Women's Committee and Women's Forum Scotland, organised a number of special seminars around the joint Equal Opportunities Commission/Women's National Commission Agenda for Equality, which provided the opportunity to get equality on to the general election agenda. The promotion of the National Agenda for Action, drawn up by the Women's National Commission and the EOCs for Great Britain and Northern Ireland, has been one of the main aspects of the EOC's work in recent years. The National Agenda provided a basis for UK implementation of the Global Platform for Action agreed at the 1995 United Nations Fourth World Conference on Women in Beijing. In the same year the STUC, the EOC, the Women's Co-ordination Group and other women's organisations were invited to take part in meetings at the Scottish Office to discuss how it could respond to, and recognise the contribution of, women's organisations in Scotland.

In this context the EOC in particular was well placed to put the case for more research and gender disaggregated statistics, on the strength of its own record. EOC-commissioned research has been, and was intended to be, a catalyst to encourage other institutions and organisations to carry out research on gender issues. The EOC in Scotland has played this catalytic role through commissioning two research reviews on gender equality issues (Brown et al. 1994; Myers and Brown 1997) and setting up the Scottish Gender Equality Research Network. It has also from time to time been able to make a modest financial contribution to the production of the *Gender Audit* published by Engender.

The STUC and the Women's Co-ordination Group had devoted considerable time and energy to the campaign to give women a direct means of communication with government, and tried to inject the politics of issues affecting women into the discussions with the Scottish Office. Separately, the STUC and the Women's Co-ordination Group developed a case for the establishment of a Scottish Women's Council, to be funded by government, and whose purpose would be to give women access to government and government access to the views of women. This process was important in opening up a dialogue within the Scottish Office and within the civil service, and was the forerunner to the establishment of an informal women's advisory group to the Labour Minister for Women's Issues, to the creation of the Women in Scotland Consultative Forum and to the appointment of a Women's Issues Research Consultant.

_ Raising the campaign's profile within the _ political parties

In tandem with these activities and events, the campaign for equal representation led to a series of round table discussions with women from political parties, organised by the Women's Co-ordination Group. The first of these took place in January 1994. With the exception of the Conservatives, all the main parties participated and a women's political coalition emerged, supporting improved women's representation, although there was no consensus of view amongst the parties on the strategies to be adopted in their respective parties to achieve this. These dialogues were, however, a vital part in the process of maintaining the momentum for gender balance in a Scottish parliament.

A sub-group of the Women's Co-ordination Group, involving Ronnie McDonald, Alice Brown and Yvonne Strachan, was established to have separate dialogues with women in the Scottish Labour Party and the Scottish Liberal Democrats to see if women in the parties could bring forward a consensus for the electoral system which could be adopted by the SCC. This dialogue resulted in the Scottish Labour Party and the Scottish Liberal Democrats signing in 1995 an Electoral Agreement which accepted the principle that there should be an equal number of men and women as members of the first Scottish Parliament. It also set the groundwork for further discussions with the Scottish Labour Party on how gender balance could be achieved in the electoral context, specifically, as it turned out, with the twinning of constituencies. Separate discussions were established with women in the SNP about how gender balance could be taken forward within the electoral mechanisms to be adopted by the SNP. And the STUC separately initiated meetings with the leadership of the parties, including the Scottish Conservatives, about gender balance and other key issues.

In November 1996, the Women's Co-ordination Group organised its last major public event before the General Election in 1997: a conference, co-funded by the European Commission, involving speakers from European countries and bringing together for the first time the leaders of the three main parties in Scotland at that time: George Robertson, Alex Salmond and Jim Wallace. The remainder of the campaign for equal representation took place during a period in which there was a Labour Government and a commitment to getting more women into Parliament. However, the Women's Co-ordination Group continued to campaign, organising a conference only four weeks after the General Election at which the newly appointed Minister for Women's Issues, Henry McLeish, was the key speaker. Shortly after this a Women's Advisory Group to the Minister was established, involving some members of the Women's Co-ordination Group. The Women's Advisory Group continued to develop the case for 50:50 with the Minister, including the issue of exemption from the Sex Discrimination Act of the first round of elections to the Scottish Parliament.

The STUC and the Women's Co-ordination Group also played a role, together with trade union women and others, in campaigning with Scotland Forward for a 'double yes' vote in the referendum of September 1997, disseminating information and encouraging member organisations to participate. The Women's Co-ordination Group produced a leaflet, Vote for Women: Vote for Scotland, encouraging women to vote in the referendum, and more than 40,000 leaflets were distributed as part of the referendum campaign.

Following the referendum, the EOC took action over the issue of the legality of measures promoting the selection of women as parliamentary candidates. The

Commission was concerned that the law was unclear as to whether or not selection procedures were covered by the Sex Discrimination Act, and took the step of encouraging political parties to use legal means including positive action to tackle the under-representation of women. The EOC in Scotland wrote to all political parties seeking a meeting to discuss the application of equal opportunities principles to selection procedures, and subsequently met with Scottish Labour Party and Scottish Liberal Democrat representatives. The STUC also conducted meetings with all the political parties to promote the work of the Consultative Steering Group (CSG), and to seek commitment to fielding equal numbers of men and women candidates.

As well as the campaign for equal representation, there were discussions on the kind of structures the Parliament should have, how it should function, and what might be policy priorities for the Parliament to promote women's participation and take account of their concerns. Various members of the Women's Co-ordination Group, and EOC staff, contributed to the development of proposals on structures and policy priorities through a John Wheatley Centre commission on equal opportunities. Subsequently, women members of the CSG successfully put the case for the inclusion of equal opportunities as one of the four founding principles of the Scottish Parliament. Recommendations were also made by the STUC and the EOC on parliamentary structures, contributing to the recommendations of the CSG that there should be a standing committee on Equal Opportunities, that a mainstreaming approach should be adopted and an Equality Unit established in the Scottish Executive, and that Parliament should operate in a 'family-friendly' manner.

– Shaping our history –

In the first Scottish parliamentary election, Labour was the only party to deliver 50:50, electing equal numbers of women and men MSPs, though a significant number of SNP MSPs are also women. The new Scottish Parliament has 37.2% women members – not the 50% that many women had campaigned for, but more than the 'critical mass' thought necessary to ensure that the Parliament takes a different approach to issues and policies. The campaign for 50:50 undoubtedly made a difference, without which there might otherwise have been little change.

One of the key factors which contributed to the qualified success achieved in the representation of women and the higher profile of women's issues on the political agenda has been the capacity of women's organisations across a wide range to work together. This can be illustrated by the STUC Women's Committee's success in persuading the STUC General Council to back the 50:50 proposal, which ensured that, instead of being sidelined as a women's issue, it became an issue of equality, of equity and fairness: a democratic issue. Nor should the significance of the dialogue between women's organisations and women in political parties be overlooked. It played a hugely important part in widening and deepening the basis of support for equality in representation.

Since the election, the Scottish Parliament has endorsed the recommendations of the Consultative Steering Group. The Scottish Executive has an Equality Unit which is reaching out to women and other members of Scotland's diverse community. A commitment has been made to mainstreaming equality throughout all policy areas and the Executive's legislative programme. The Executive is supporting the Women in Scotland Consultative Forum. There is a Minister in Cabinet and Deputy Minister for Equalities. However, the activities of the Scottish Executive and its Equality Unit, the Scottish Parliament and all its committees, particularly the Equal Opportunities committee, will need to be monitored and evaluated. Campaigning for equality of women in decision-making needs to be sustained and developed to meet new challenges and circumstances. Joint activity must be built on.

Women's and equality organisations have continued to be active in putting forward their views and proposals to MSPs and to the Scottish Executive. For example, since the establishment of the Parliament the EOC has facilitated the setting up of a cross-party group on women's issues; has taken part in a briefing session for MSPs organised by the Scottish Parliament Information Centre; and has responded to numerous consultation documents. It has called for a duty on public sector bodies to promote equality, including conducting pay audits, target setting, monitoring and evaluation, and annual reporting to the Scottish Parliament. It has also called on the Parliament to tackle gender stereotyping through a lifelong learning strategy. The STUC Women's Committee has produced a Women's Agenda for Scotland, which has been presented to the Deputy Minister for Communities, and the Committee will continue to campaign in the Parliament to achieve this agenda. Several of the members of the Women's Co-ordination Group continue to play a high profile role on women's issues within the Scottish political system. For its part, WFS has actively pursued the establishment of the Scottish Civic Forum. This was preceded by the Scottish Civic Assembly, of whose council WFS has been a member from the outset. WFS takes the view that if the representation of women is to be further advanced there needs to be activity both inside and outwith the Parliament, and WFS has therefore continued to advocate on behalf of women in the Civic Assembly, and now in the Civic Forum.

Aspirations and expectations of all those who campaigned for the Parliament are high, and there are concerns that these aspirations might not be met. A primary concern is that there should not be a retreat from the position that has so far been achieved in terms of women's representation, a concern shared by women's organisations and women in political parties. A further concern is that consultative processes for women in Scotland should be effective. WFS has stated that while the continuance of the Women In Scotland Consultative Forum at this stage is welcome, it has to be recognised that in its present form it has its limitations, as it does not have independent status. It therefore has a different capacity and relationship to the government from that of a non-governmental organisation (NGO). In particular, WFS's European links have made it aware of the different models of women's NGOs' relationships with their governments. The problem encountered in the main by women's NGOs is lack of resources. The STUC is committed to the development of an independent women's organisation, but in the meantime, along with the EOC, has also argued for realistic support for the Women in Scotland Consultative Forum.

All the organisations discussed here will continue to have a role to play, in supporting the work of the Equality Unit and Equal Opportunities Commitee, and in monitoring progress and putting forward proposals. The women's groups that have campaigned for equality to be a founding principle of the Scottish Parliament will continue to campaign to ensure that the new Equality Unit is well resourced and staffed, so that it can play a real role in assisting the creation of an equal Scotland. In the forthcoming period a central matter for women's organisations to discuss will be how to strengthen women's structures, and whether current arrangements should be developed, changed or totally transformed. It would be welcome if such initiatives were to be met with a commitment from the Scottish Executive to the value of the independent expression of women's voices. For such progress as has been made has been achieved largely through the interaction and common purpose of many women and their organisations.

– References –

Brown, Alice, Esther Breitenbach, and Fiona Myers, (1994), *Equality Issues in Scotland: A Research Review*, Manchester: EOC.

Engender (1993–2000), *Gender Audit*, Edinburgh: Engender.

Myers, Fiona and Alice Brown (1997), *A Research Review Update*, Manchester: EOC.

Powney, J., J. McPake, L. Edwards and S. Hamilton (2000), *Gender Equality and Lifelong Learning in Scotland*, Manchester: EOC.

CHAPTER 19

Taking their Place in the New House: Women and the Scottish Parliament

ALICE BROWN

'Taking their Place in the New House: Women and the Scottish Parliament'
(1999), *Scottish Affairs*, 28, Summer.

– INTRODUCTION –

At the first meeting of the Scottish Parliament on 12 May 1999, the number of women taking their seats as newly elected members (MSPs) brought Scotland into line with countries such as Sweden and Norway, which are top of the league in terms of women's representation. The total of 48 women MSPs breaks all records in Scotland.[1] This figure is all the more remarkable when one considers that in the first democratic elections to Scotland's new Parliament, the number of women elected in one day exceeds the total number of women elected to represent Scottish constituencies in general elections to the House of Commons over the past 80 years, that is since 1918 when women were first eligible to stand for election to parliament. At 37%, the percentage of female MSPs falls well short of the 50:50 representation for which many women activists campaigned. Nevertheless, it is a major step forward for supporters of gender balance and is substantially more than the 22% women councillors elected at the local government elections on the same day.[2] Even at the 1997 Westminster election, when there was a much publicised rise in the number of women MPs elected, the representation rate of women for the whole of the UK was around 18%. For Scotland it was less than 17% with just 12 women being elected from Scotland's 72 constituencies.

This chapter places the election of Scotland's first women MSPs within the context of the selection processes of the different political parties and the wider campaign to represent the interests of women in the Scottish Parliament.

– SELECTING WOMEN CANDIDATES –

In the year prior to the Scottish elections on 6 May 1999, when the political parties were engaged in selecting candidates, all parties stated their concern to see more women in politics and their intention to encourage women to come forward for selection. A research report (Innes 1999) published by Engender and based on work conducted in co-operation with the Heinrich Böll Foundation in Berlin outlines the different approaches taken by the political parties in Scotland both to encourage women to stand for election and in implementing specific mechanisms to help ensure greater gender balance. The Scottish Labour Party offered preparation courses for women which included assertiveness training and public speaking, as well as financial support from the (UK) Emily's List. The Scottish Liberal Democrats organised a series of training days and seminars for women and offered support for childcare for those attending. The Scottish National Party held a women's training day for potential candidates. Lack of resources prevented the Scottish Green Party from undertaking a specific programme and, according to Engender (1999), when asked what they were doing to encourage women to come forward as candidates, the Conservative and Unionist Party said 'we're waiting for it to evolve and it's evolving nicely'.

Although equal representation was a significant part of the debates in the Scottish Constitutional Convention and the subject of an Electoral Agreement between the two main political parties participating in the Convention – Labour and the Liberal Democrats – the Scottish Labour Party was the only party to operate a specific mechanism to achieve gender balance in representation (Brown 1998). Recognising that, under the Additional Member System agreed for elections to the Parliament, most of its seats would be obtained on the first-past-the-post or constituency elections, a scheme was designed to 'twin' constituencies to allow both men and women to stand for election. Under this scheme, the woman with the highest number of votes would be selected as the Labour candidate for one of the twinned seats, at the same time as the man with the highest number of votes would be selected for the other. The twinning mechanism was used to select Labour candidates for all constituencies with the exception of four Highlands and Islands constituencies (McKenna 1998).

The Scottish Liberal Democrats signed the Electoral Agreement published in the Convention's final publication, *Scotland's Parliament, Scotland's Right*, in which they committed the party to the principle of gender equality in the new parliament and to achieve greater balance under the Additional Member System. The party initially proposed that two men and two women should stand for selection in each constituency, and that the additional or 'top up' seats should be 'zipped'[3] to achieve gender balance and redress any imbalance in the constituency selection and election process. However, the party ran into some difficulty in fielding an equal number of men and women for constituency seats and later decided not to implement the proposed 'zipping' mechanism at their conference in March 1998, despite the support given to this strategy by the leader, Jim Wallace. The stated reason was that the party had taken legal advice to the effect that the policy of 'zipping' would be vulnerable to an appeal to the Industrial Tribunal under the terms of the Sex Discrimination Act, and reference was made to the legal challenge to the Labour Party's policy of all-women shortlists for the 1997 Westminster elections. Pressure and attempts from different quarters to find ways of exempting the selection processes of political parties from this legislation by inclusion of an appropriate clause in the Scotland Act (1998) were unsuccessful.

In contrast to the Scottish Labour Party, the Scottish National Party was always likely to get most of its seats in the regional or 'top up' lists under the new electoral system. Thus the party stated its intention to use the additional seats and, like the Liberal Democrats, to use 'zipping' as a way of ensuring greater gender balance. However, this approach was also rejected by the party conference in May of last year. Nevertheless, the party did place women at the upper end of their regional party lists.

For their part, the Conservative Party continued to express their opposition to special measures to increase the representation of women. Writing in his capacity at the time as Deputy Chairman of the Scottish Conservative Party's Policy Commission and a prospective candidate, the current leader David McLetchie argued that the 'Scottish Conservatives resolved to have no truck with rules and procedures which would create an artificial gender balance among the candidates selected . . . Our candidates will be selected entirely on merit regardless of race, religion or sex and we are confident that among them will be a number of talented women who will be a credit to the Scottish Parliament' (McLetchie 1998).

– THE RESULTS –

The results of the election in terms of the distribution of votes and seats between the political parties and independent candidates are discussed in detail by Denver and MacAllister (1999). The gender composition of the new Parliament and the relative performance of the political parties in achieving gender balance are illustrated in Table 19.1.[4]

In assessing the overall performance of the different political parties, it is clear that Labour is the only party to have achieved 50:50 representation, closely followed by the SNP at 43% representation of women. The main disappointment for those seeking equal representation lies with the Liberal Democrats, especially because of their involvement in the Convention's plans and the fact that they had signed the Electoral Agreement to ensure greater gender equality in the new Parliament. As the Conservative Party had stated their opposition to any form of positive action to achieve gender parity, the results are perhaps of no great surprise. It can be argued, therefore, that the increase in the number of women taking their place in Scotland's first democratically elected Parliament has not happened 'naturally'. It has involved the implementation of specific mechanisms and the use of the new electoral system. In addition, the sustained efforts of many women activists who worked together across different political party lines and across numerous groups and organisations to take forward the common aim of giving women an equal voice in Scotland's new Parliament should not be discounted (Brown 1998a).

Table 19.1

Gender Composition of the Scottish Parliament

Political Party	Elected MSPs (number of seats)		Elected MSPs (% of seats)	
	women	men	women	men
Conservative	3	15	17	83
Labour	28	28	50	50
Lib Dem	2	15	12	88
SNP	15	20	43	57
Others[a]	0	3	0	100
Total	48	81	37	63

[a] Includes two male representatives from the Scottish Socialist Party and the Scottish Green Party and one male Independent MSP (Dennis Canavan).

The high number and percentage of women elected in the new Parliament has not, however, been reflected in the ministerial appointments that followed the election. As expected, no single party achieved an overall majority in the Parliament and, after days of speculation, a Partnership Agreement was finally reached between the Scottish Labour Party and the Scottish Liberal Democrats. In selecting his Cabinet and deciding on other ministerial posts, the new First Minister, Donald Dewar, selected five women in making a total of 22 appointments. Wendy Alexander is Minister for Communities, while Jackie Baillie has responsibility as Deputy Minister for Social Inclusion, Equality and the Voluntary Sector. Susan Deacon is Scotland's Minister for Health and Community Care, and Sarah Boyack has been appointed Minister for Transport and the Environment. The fifth ministerial appointment went to Rhona Brankin as Deputy Minister for Culture and Sport. There is some way to go, therefore, before gender balance is achieved in key government positions in Scotland.

– REPRESENTING WOMEN –

While the representation of women as MSPs is considered important in itself, the representation of women's interests and concerns is also of relevance to women activists. Thus the campaign to get more women into the Parliament was not seen solely as an end in itself, but as a means to achieve other aims. It was considered necessary for women to have equal access to government and the policy making process, in order that their diverse needs and experiences could be taken into account. For campaigners, there were positive developments in this regard prior to the elections in 1999 which have continued after the opening of the Scottish Parliament.

Soon after taking up his appointment as the new Minister for Women in 1997, Henry McLeish announced the decision to establish a consultative forum for women and to appoint a Women's Issues Research Consultant to gather information and data on women's organisations. The Women in Scotland Consultative Forum was then established and several conferences and meetings have been held since 1997. The newly elected Minister responsible for equality issues in the Scottish Parliament has indicated her support for the continuation of the Forum. In addition, Equal Opportunities was one of the key principles adopted by the Consultative Steering Group (CSG) which was established by the Secretary of State at the end of 1997 to help draft Standing Orders and Procedures for the Parliament. The four key principles – Sharing of Power, Accountability, Access and Participation and Equal Opportunities – have subsequently been endorsed by the members of the new Parliament. Under the Standing Orders and Procedures the Parliament meets at times that are more compatible with family life and recognises Scottish school holidays. The new parliamentary arrangements also allow the potential for the views of women in the community or from different groups and organisations to be fed into the consultative channels envisaged for the parliamentary committees and the pre-legislative process. It has also been agreed that the Parliament should have an Equal Opportunities Committee, that the Scottish Office (now retitled Scottish Executive) should establish an Equality Unit, and that equal opportunities should be mainstreamed in all aspects of the work of the Parliament and the Scottish Executive. There is evidence to suggest, therefore, that the extension of the campaign from getting more women representatives to ensuring that the interests of women are represented in other ways has had some success.

– CONCLUSION –

Following the elections on 6 May 1999, it is clear that the increase in women's representation to 37% exceeds the 'critical mass' of around 25–30% considered necessary for women to have an impact on the political process.[5] The substantial rise can also be interpreted as going some way to meet symbolic arguments for the increased representation of marginalised groups. Symbolic arguments draw a link between social representation and concerns about justice and political legitimacy. In terms of justice, it is contended that it is not acceptable or fair to exclude some groups from public life. All citizens should have the equal opportunity to participate in politics and stand for elected office. In terms of legitimacy, it is argued that the presence of members of all significant social groups in roughly proportionate numbers in political assemblies is seen to signal fairness and is an indicator of a healthy democracy (Phillips 1995).

Arguments for increasing the number of women in politics on symbolic grounds are often linked to substantive arguments. Claims of substantive presence are based upon predictions that the inclusion of under-represented groups will lead to direct change in political agendas and policy outcomes. This 'rhetoric of difference' has more commonly been used in political debates in Scandinavia, particularly in relation to women. It is based on ideas of representing women's interests and the added resources, in terms of experience, knowledge, values and skills, that women can bring to politics, complementing those of male politicians.

There are high expectations amongst activists that the new Scottish Parliament will provide a genuine opportunity for the participation of women in the democratic process, not just as elected members, and that there will be different channels and avenues through which the voices of women in Scotland can he heard and can have an impact. A new political institution, together with other plans for new parliamentary arrangements, policy-making and consultation mechanisms certainly offer greater potential for moving beyond symbolic to substantive differences. Future research will be able to judge whether such aspirations have been realised.

– NOTES –

1. In the first elections to the Welsh National Assembly, 24 women were elected from a total of 60 members, a proportion of 40%. This was largely due to the 'twinning' mechanism operated by the Labour Party in Wales and the willingness of Plaid Cymru to place women high on the regional party lists. In the past, the representation of women in Wales has been lower than that for women in Scotland. It is one of the ironies of politics that the representation rate of women is now slightly higher in Wales than in Scotland, especially as the policy of 'twinning' was strongly opposed in some quarters of the Welsh Labour Party, with threats of a legal challenge being made.
2. Data compiled by the Scottish Local Government Information Unit shows that 276 women or 22.6% were elected on 6 May 1999 in the elections to Scottish local government. This is around the same percentage of women elected in the previous elections in 1995.
3. Under the particular form of AMS designed for elections to the Scottish Parliament

'zipping' would involve the political parties alternating female and male candidates in drawing up the order of candidates on their lists for the 'additional' or 'top up' seats.

4. It should be noted that, in spite of efforts to have representatives from minority ethnic groups in the Parliament, all the MSPs are white. This has led to pressure to consider special measures in the future.

5. There is evidence to suggest that a certain proportion of women – a critical mass – needs to be present in a political institution before they are able to make a difference and to challenge the dominant male culture. Research into women politicians in Scandinavian countries which have relatively high levels of representation indicates small but significant differences between male and female politicians in terms of interests, policy orientation and style.

– REFERENCES –

Brown, Alice (1998), 'Representing Women in Scotland', *Parliamentary Affairs*, 51 (3), July.

Brown, Alice (1998a), 'Deepening Democracy: Women and the Scottish Parliament', *Regional and Federal Studies*, 8 (1) Spring.

Denver, D. and I. MacAllister (1999), 'The Scottish Parliament Elections 1999: an Analysis of the Results', *Scottish Affairs*, 28, Summer.

Innes, Sue (1999), *Keeping Gender on the Agenda*, Research Report, Edinburgh: Engender.

McKenna, R. (1998), 'Selection Procedures for the Scottish Labour Party Panel for the Scottish Parliamentary Elections', *Scotland Forum*, Edinburgh: HMSO.

McLetchie, D. (1998), 'Made in Scotland – Scottish Conservatives for the Scottish Parliament', *Scotland Forum*, Edinburgh: HMSO.

Phillips, A. (1995), *The Politics of Presence*, Oxford: Oxford University Press.

Scottish Office (1998), *Shaping Scotland's Parliament*, Report of the Consultative Steering Group the Scottish Parliament, December, Edinburgh: HMSO.

CHAPTER 20

'Quietly Thrilling': Women in the New Parliament

SUE INNES

This piece was originally written in 1999 for the short-lived London-based feminist magazine *Sybil*. The magazine folded before it could be published.

The new Scottish Parliament sat for the first time on May 12th. Since then I have been urging women I know to slip into the public gallery just to see what a parliament with 37.2% of its members women looks like. In the abstract 37.2% is a fine achievement; it places Scotland fourth highest in the world in terms of women members, behind Sweden (42.7%), the Welsh Assembly (40%) and Denmark (37.4%) (using Inter-Parliamentary Union figures). But actually to *see* a parliament with so many women is quietly thrilling, in a way that percentages are not. It is to see a new stage in the movement for women's suffrage and full participation in public life that began more than 200 years ago.

Although 37.2% is not 50%, there are nevertheless enough women for their participation to seem not exceptional but normal. That is why it is *quietly* thrilling. I expected the Parliament to look different, but it doesn't. It looks like the rest of life, where women and men are present in roughly equal numbers except when gender segregation is imposed – openly and otherwise – for a special reason. To see a parliament where women's participation is relatively high is to kill off the last remnants of the belief that lingers and colours perception, because it is what we have seen for years almost every time Westminster is on TV, that senior roles in public life are for people who are male, older, authoritative and, above all, *not like me*.

The most important step towards gender equality in representation at the Scottish Parliament was that once we started talking the language of democracy, it was very evident that some groups suffered a 'double deficit'. The full participation of women rapidly came to symbolise inclusion and radical difference. It came to stand for the kind of democratic regeneration that the Scottish Constitutional Convention, which created the blueprint for the new Parliament, called for. Scotland likes to think of itself as inherently egalitarian, and women's arguments for a greater political voice capitalised on that. Both men and women argued for gender equality in the Parliament, and say they are proud of the results. But what if those women want to take things further, get *really* uppity? It is going to be very interesting to see whether the relatively high number of women makes a real difference or whether it remains a symbol without much meaning in practice.

Numbers do matter. Women's political participation is a matter of civil rights and representative government should reflect a population of which women form half. Research shows that a 'critical mass' of around a third women makes a difference to political priorities, though Norwegian studies suggest that real change to political culture needs more than just the presence of women, which some exaggerated expectations may suggest. The women's movement in Scotland is not exactly over the moon about the new women MSPs. Pleased, yes – but a lot of women are waiting to see what they actually do. Cynicism about politics and politicians remains a factor, especially outwith the 'chattering classes', and disappointment expressed about Labour women at Westminster has affected the Scottish debate. One of the major disappointments is that the Parliament does not include any members of Scotland's ethnic minority communities – none were selected to stand for a winnable seat.

The ten-year-long campaign for gender equality in the Parliament was about not just a bigger slice of the cake, but changing the recipe. Doing that is actually a great deal more difficult than adding only a gendered flavouring. We should not be too quick to judge – making a difference takes time. The experience of the European Parliament (with a third of its members women) is that women are more able to bring their interests forward in ways that change the political agenda. The problem women face in mainstream politics is no longer of formal or even effective exclusion but of inclusion on different terms and the requirement to line up with malestream values in order to have power and influence. The central political dilemma of how differences among women can be acknowledged without diluting feminist claims is also very much at issue. The high proportion of women should mean that the women MSPs can be different from one another, that we will not assume that they have a necessarily shared agenda or political style.

Just as the full participation of women came to symbolise the kind of different politics Scotland wanted, so it was part of a deeper debate on the renewal of democracy that defines the new politics in three main ways: as including people – through, for example, the open availability of most parliamentary information and a pre-legislative process that civic groups will play a role in; as a more consensual style of politics; and in terms of the sharing of power, so that backbenchers and the committees of the Parliament will play a much greater role – which is arguably the most important change. Election by PR is also about better democracy; the consequences of no one party having an overall majority are modified by the partnership agreement between Labour and the Liberal Democrats but may yet prove interesting.

The – admittedly duller – debate about the detailed procedures of the Parliament that are creating its structures and its political culture is at least as important to gender equality as the question of representation. Commitments have been made to a parliament characterised by openness, accessibility and equality of opportunity. Working practices and political culture are crucial because it is no longer explicit barriers that keep women out of, or less powerful within, existing political institutions, but the hidden barriers created by 'how things are done'. It will take time for new approaches to bed in, and there will be a continuing tension between new ideals and 'politics as usual' – openness, accessibility and equality of opportunity do not sit easily within a political process that is, in the end, about money and power, wherever it is. But in the first debates of the Parliament the commitment to a new politics was repeatedly expressed – if, ironically, it was often used adversarially to accuse politicians of other parties of not acting in the spirit of the new politics. If politics is about personal and party rivalries and holding on to power, nevertheless there are people ready to remind the politicians that there are other ways, based in constituencies of support and giving meaning to inclusiveness. Of particular importance are the recommendations of the Consultative Steering Group on how the Parliament would manage its day-to-day business, including such issues as budgetary processes and accountability, a Code of Conduct for MSPs, use of IT, establishing a Civic Forum etc. Its proposals, now being put into practice, include an equalities committee as mandatory, procedures that make possible a participative approach to the development, consideration and scrutiny of policy and legislation, and that all bills be accompanied by a memorandum detailing consultation undertaken and a check for impact in terms of gender equality, human rights and sustainable development, as appropriate. The arguments for the new politics are seen by some as wildly idealistic, but they have helped shape the Parliament's standing orders – and when can you have high ideals if not when you are creating something new?

Seating in the Parliament's main chamber is arranged in a horseshoe – also a symbol of new politics, although again it remains to be seen how much it will mean. Within it, where the women members are sitting is worth noting: they are mainly on the SNP (15 women out of 35 MSPs) and Labour benches (28 out of 56 – exactly half); on the front bench three of the ministers (25%) are women and two of the 10 junior ministers. The Conservatives have only three women among their 18 members. The Liberal Democrats have only two out of 17; they rescinded an earlier commitment to a mechanism to achieve gender balance at their annual conference before the election, claiming that in a modern equal society this was unnecessary and anyway it might be illegal. The grey suits in their segment of the horseshoe are a reminder that society is not yet so equal that these things can be left to chance. The Green Party and the Scottish Socialist Party also made commitments to gender equality but in the event both got a single candidate in via the regional lists, and both are men. One of the two deputy presiding officers (the Speaker's role) is a woman, Patricia Ferguson. Six of the 16 committee conveners – a crucial role – are women. All the party business managers – an even more crucial role, managing parliamentary business through the Bureau – are men, as are the MSP members of the Scottish Parliamentary Corporate Body.

The experience of campaigning for gender equality was itself a learning curve. There isn't much complacency, even in the Scottish Labour Party, which achieved most. Some Labour women still don't quite believe it and see the 50:50 result as 'a miracle'. At a cross-party Engender forum soon after the election, SNP MSP Fiona Hyslop commented on how different, welcoming, open and accessible the atmosphere of the new Parliament is. The campaign for gender equality in representation had been as successful as it has, she said, because women had expected more and demanded more. We should not become defensive now but go on demanding more, continue to have high expectations. There was general agreement that the twinning mechanism introduced by the Labour Party had been essential – 'if things had been left to take their course it would have been just jobs for the boys' – as had the long women's movement campaign and that women in and outside the political parties had worked together. Finding ways to continue to do so will be important to translating greater gender equality in the Parliament into action to create greater gender equality in Scottish society. That will mean taking on the major issues of gendered poverty and social exclusion and their link to women's family roles, and also the paucity of women in other areas of public life. Although there is a clear role for the women's movement in monitoring the Parliament, supporting sympathetic MSPs with research and feedback, and contributing to committees, the shoestring budgets that all its organisations survive on mean that, frustratingly, they do not have the capacity to respond fully to the opportunities now available.

At another recent Engender event Nuala Ahern, the Irish Green MEP, commented that although the European Parliament is around a third women, that is treated as if it is equality 'and the men feel outnumbered'. It is possible that 37.2% will be seen as equality and not as what it is: a good starting point for achieving equality both in the Parliament and, through it, in Scottish society. The comment of Swedish women MPs when asked why their numbers fell in the early 1990s is also worth remembering: 'because we took our eye off the ball'. We need to watch out for a covert sense that 'this nonsense has all gone far enough' – a view that surfaced occasionally during the selection processes.

The achievement so far is worth celebrating, but it must also be only the start –

the basis of a continuing campaign for a parliament characterised by gender equality, by the inclusion of other previously under-represented groups and one that will give the highest priority to creating a society notable for equality and inclusion. If the Parliament finds the right ways to include women from all classes and ethnic backgrounds as representatives and in promoted posts and if it finds ways to listen to and take into account the experience and understanding of women throughout Scotland in its policy development, that will be much more than a symbol of equality – a sign that the promised new politics and deepened democracy are real.

Biographies

In the following section we give brief biographical details of the 48 women who were elected as Members of the Scottish Parliament (MSPs) in the first Scottish Parliamentary elections in May 1999, together with a list of members of the parliamentary Cross-Party Group on Women. We also provide information on the 12 women currently serving as Members of Parliament for Scottish constituencies at Westminster and the two female Members of the European Parliament representing Scotland.

The biographies have been derived from publicly available sources and details are provided at the end of the piece. It was not possible within the scope of the current book to conduct additional research but it is clear this in an area in which more work needs to be done in order to record the backgrounds, pathways to office and achievements of women politicians. What can be noted is both the unevenness of the information available and the general lack of information about women politicians.

– Holyrood Women: MSPs –

Wendy Alexander (Labour) is constituency MSP for Paisley North and Minister for Social Inclusion, Local Government and Housing. Born in Glasgow in 1963, she was educated at Park Marns High School, Erskine and Pearson College. She is a graduate of Glasgow and Warwick Universities and holds an MBA from the INSEAD business school in France. She has worked as a management consultant in Europe, America and Asia. She has also worked as a research officer for the Labour Party. Most recently she was a special adviser to the Secretary of State for Scotland and helped shape all aspects of the legislation in the establishment of the Scottish Parliament. She has also worked specifically on policy areas including women's issues, social exclusion and industry.

She was appointed Minister for Social Inclusion, Local Government and

Housing in 1999. As part of her portfolio, she has lead responsibility for Executive policy on equality issues and the voluntary sector.

She is a member of TGWU and Amnesty International.

Jackie Baillie (Labour) is constituency MSP for Dumbarton and Deputy Minister for Communities. Born in 1964 in Hong Kong, she was educated at St Anne's School, Windermere, Cumbernauld College and the University of Strathclyde. She is currently studying towards an MSc in Local Economic Development at the University of Glasgow. She previously worked as a Community Economic Development Manager with East Dunbartonshire District Council and a resource centre manager at Strathkelvin District Council.

She has held a number of positions within the Labour Party, including Branch Chair and Secretary, Constituency Chair and Education Officer. She is a former Chair of the Scottish Labour Party and is a member of the National Executive.

Appointed Deputy Minister for Communities in 1999, she has particular responsibility for social inclusion, equality and the voluntary sector.

Sarah Boyack (Labour) is constituency MSP for Edinburgh Central and Minister of Transport and Environment. Born in 1961, she was educated at Glasgow University (MA(Hons)). A former lecturer in planning at Edinburgh College of Art, Heriot Watt University, she is a member of the Royal Town Planning Institute. She was Convener of the RTPI, Scotland and chaired its women's panel in 1997. She has also worked as a senior planning officer for Central Regional Council.

She has held a number of positions within the Labour Party including Branch Secretary, Constituency Secretary and Deputy Election Agent. She has previously contested local government elections. She was Chair of the National Organisation of Labour Students in 1985 and previously served on the Executive of the International Union of Socialist Youth.

Appointed Minister of Transport and Environment in 1999, her responsibilities include the development for integrated transport policies for rural areas, the environment, natural heritage, sustainable development, strategic environmental assessments and the land-use planning system.

She is Scottish co-ordinator of the Socialist Environmental Resource Association and a board member of the Scottish Centre for Public Policy. She is a member of the National Transport Forum for Scotland.

Rhona Brankin (Labour) is constituency MSP for Mid Lothian and Deputy Minister of Culture and Sport. Born in 1950, she was educated at the University of Aberdeen. She previously worked as a Lecturer in Educational Needs at Northern College and is also a former teacher.

She has held a number of Party positions including Chair of the Scottish

Labour Party (1995–96) and spokesperson of the Scottish Labour Party. She has been a member of the Executive for 16 years. She has previously contested local government elections.

She was appointed Deputy Minister of Culture and Sport in 1999.

Cathie Craigie (Labour) is constituency MSP for Cumbernauld and Kilsyth. Born in Stirling in 1954, she was educated at Kilsyth Academy. She was formerly an accountant. She has also been a parliamentary assistant to an MP (1992–97).

She was a councillor at Cumbernauld and Kilsyth District Council from 1984–96 and Council Leader from 1994–96. She served as Chair of Planning, Housing, Policy and Resources and Equal Opportunities Committees. She was also a member of North Lanarkshire Council (1985–99) where she was Vice-Chair of Housing, Chair of Environmental Services and Chair of Kilsyth Local Area Committees. She chaired Cumbernauld Housing Partnership and served as a representative of Council on the Convention of Scottish Local Authorities. She has held the position of Constituency Secretary and has served on the Labour Party National Policy Forum.

She is a member of the Parliamentary Audit Committee and the Social Inclusion, Housing and Voluntary Sector Parliamentary Committee; and is a member of the Cross-Party Group in the Scottish Parliament on Animal Welfare.

She is a member of the AEEU.

Roseanna Cunningham (SNP) is constituency MSP for Perth. Born in Glasgow in 1951, she was brought up in Perth, Australia, before returning to Scotland in 1976. She has also been Westminster MP for the constituency since a by-election in 1995 (see MPs' biographies for details). She has degrees from the University of Western Australia (Hons Politics) and the University of Edinburgh (Law), and also obtained a Diploma in Legal Practice from the University of Aberdeen. She worked in the SNP research department from 1977–79, then as a solicitor for Dumbarton District Council and for Glasgow District Council. From 1989, she worked in private practice as a solicitor, and became an Advocate in 1990. She is a member of the SNP National Executive.

She is SNP Spokesperson on Justice, Equality and Land and Convener of the Justice and Home Affairs Parliamentary Committee.

She is a former NALGO convener and shop steward. She is a member of the National Union of Journalists and the Faculty of Advocates.

Margaret Curran (Labour) is constituency MSP for Glasgow Ballieston. Born in 1958, she is a history and economics graduate from the University of Glasgow. She worked previously as a Lecturer in Community Education at Strathclyde University and also acted as an Election Agent in the 1997 General Election.

She has wide-ranging experience of local government and community education work and is particularly interested in education and economic and urban regeneration.

She is Convener of the Social Inclusion, Housing and Voluntary Sector Parliamentary Committee and is Deputy Member of the Scottish Parliamentary Bureau, and a member of the Cross-Party Group in the Scottish Parliament on Women.

Susan Deacon (Labour) is constituency MSP for Edinburgh East and Musselburgh and Minister for Health and Community Care. Born in Musselburgh in 1964, she was educated at Musselburgh Grammar School and the University of Edinburgh (MA (Hons) Social Policy and Politics; MBA). She has worked as a business consultant and has held various research and management positions in local government and higher education. She has also been a tutor for the Open University and a voluntary welfare rights worker.

She has held a number of positions within the Labour Party including Branch Chair and Vice-Chair, Treasurer, member of Constituency Executive and the Party Executive and Party spokesperson. She has previously contested local government elections.

She was appointed Minister for Health and Community Care in 1999. Her political interests include health, social inclusion, family and childcare policy, education and training, public management and business and enterprise.

She is a member of the Institute of Personnel and Development, and the Transport and General Workers Union. She is also a member of the National Trust for Scotland, National Childbirth Trust and War on Want.

Helen Eadie (Labour) is constituency MSP for Dunfermline East. Born in Stenhousemuir, she was educated at Larbert Village, Larbert High, Falkirk Technical College and the London School of Economics where she gained a Certificate in Trade Union Studies. She has previously worked in a laundry, a supermarket and a TV outlet. She has been a full-time administrator for GMB in Glasgow, then in London as Equal Opportunities and Political Officer. She has worked as an assistant to two MPs and was a member of James Callaghan's general election campaign team. A local government councillor in Fife from 1986–99, her key responsibilities included: Chair of Equal Opportunities Committee; Depute Leader; Spokesperson on roads and transport; Senior Vice-Chair Strategic Development Committee. She has also served as the CoSLA representative to Channel Tunnel Initiative; Vice-Chair of South East Scotland Partnership in Transport (now known as SESTRAN); Vice-President of the North Sea Commission (comprises 100 member local authorities around the North Sea in seven European countries); Chair of the Business Development Group of North Sea Commission; and Member of the Political Bureau of the

Conference of Peripheral and Maritime Regions. She is a past Chair of STUC Youth Advisory Committee.

She has served as a Branch secretary, a member of the Constituency Executive, Constituency Vice-Chair and as an election agent. She also contested the Roxburgh and Berwickshire seat in the 1997 General Election.

She is a Member of the Public Petitions Parliamentary Committee; and the Transport and Environment Parliamentary Committee. She is also a member of the Cross-Party Group in the Scottish Parliament on Borders Rail; and the Cross-Party Group in the Scottish Parliament on Oil and Gas.

She is a member of the GMB, the Co-operative Party, the Fabian Society, Edinburgh Labour Business Forum, Labour Movement in Europe and the European Movement.

Dorothy Grace Elder (SNP) is a List MSP for Glasgow. A first-time candidate, she was previously a freelance journalist and a campaigning columnist. She has worked as a reporter, news feature writer, leader writer and columnist for a range of newspapers, including *Scotland on Sunday, Daily Express, Scottish Daily Express, Sunday Mail* and *The Herald*. She won the UK Reporter of the Year in the 1997 Press Awards and was an Oliver Award-winning columnist in 1995–96. She was awarded a Citation for Humanitarian Aid Work by the City of Pushkin in Russia 1997–99. She has also worked as a television scriptwriter and producer.

She is a member of the Health and Community Care Parliamentary Committee and is a member of the Cross-Party Group in the Scottish Parliament on Animal Welfare and the Cross-Party Group in the Scottish Parliament on Borders Rail.

She is a Trustee of Yorkhill Children's Fund, Royal Hospital for Sick Children, Glasgow, and is a member of ACHE UK Committee (opposing child pornography). She is a member of the National Union of Journalists.

Margaret Ewing (SNP) is constituency MSP for Moray. Born in 1945 in Lanark, she was educated at Biggar High School and later Glasgow University (MA in English and History), Strathclyde University (BA in Economic History), and Jordanhill College of Education. She has worked as a Secondary teacher, as a freelance journalist, and as Co-ordinator of the West of Scotland Certificate in Social Service Scheme. She has also qualified as a teacher of special needs. She has been Westminster MP for Moray since 1987 and was MP for East Dunbartonshire from 1974 to 1979. (See MPs' biographies for details.)

She was a member of the SNP NEC from 1974–80; Vice-President of the Party from 1981–3; and Senior Vice-Convener of the Party from 1983.

She is Convener of the Cross-Party Group on Strategic Rail Services for Scotland, and a member of the Cross-Party Group in the Scottish Parliament on Oil and Gas.

Dr Winnie Ewing (SNP) is a List MSP for the Highlands and Islands. Born in 1929, she was educated at Queen's Park Senior Secondary School and Glasgow University (MA, LLB). She also holds the degrees of Doctor of the Open University, and Doctor of Laws. She is a qualified solicitor and Notary Public and was Secretary of the Glasgow Bar Association from 1962–67. She has served as both an MP and an MEP. She was MP for Hamilton from 1967–70 and MP for Moray and Nairn from 1974–79. She was a Member of the European Parliament from 1975–99. She was a member of the Rainbow Group of the European Parliament, and was Chair of the European Free Alliance from 1991. She sat on a number of European Parliamentary committees, and has also served as Chair and Vice Chair of Committees.

She has served as Vice-President of the Scottish National Party since 1979 and was elected Party President in 1987.

She is a member of the European Committee of the Scottish Parliament and is a Vice-Convener of the Cross-Party Group in the Scottish Parliament on Animal Welfare. Her special interests include fishing, agriculture, EEC regional policy, aid to minority languages such as Gaelic, animal welfare and Third World development.

She is an FRSA. She is a member of the Law Society, Scotland, and has been President of the Glasgow Bar Association.

The *Scottish Biographical Dictionary* notes that her by-election victory in 1967 'established the SNP as a major political force'. It also notes that her energetic work on behalf of constituents in the European Parliament earned her the title 'Madame Ecosse'. It attributes her high profile as an SNP figure to her 'flamboyant electioneering style and combative debating techniques'.

Linda Fabiani (SNP) is a List MSP for Central Scotland. Born in Glasgow in 1956, she was educated at Hyndland School in Glasgow, Napier University, Edinburgh (SHND SEC Studies) and Glasgow University (Diploma in Housing Studies). A first-time candidate, she was previously Director of East Kilbride and District Housing Association. She has served as party Branch Treasurer. Her interests include housing, social policy, environment and women's issues.

She is the SNP deputy spokesperson on culture, she is also a member of the Transport and Environment Committee of the Scottish Parliament.

She is a member of the Institute of Housing and the TGWU (ACTS).

Patricia Ferguson (Labour) is constituency MSP for Glasgow Maryhill. Born in Glasgow in 1958, she was educated at Garnethill Convent Secondary School and Glasgow College of Technology. She has an SHNC in Public Administration.

She has served in various positions in the Labour Party including: Scottish Officer for the Labour Party, Branch Chair, Secretary, Constituency Secretary and Woman's Section Secretary. She has also been a community councillor.

She was appointed Deputy Presiding Officer of the Parliament in 1999. She is a Member of the Standards Parliamentary Committee and a member of the Cross-Party Group in the Scottish Parliament on Tobacco Control.
She is a member of GMB/APEX.

Karen Gillon (elected as Karen Turnbull) (Labour) is constituency MSP for Clydesdale. Born in Edinburgh in 1967, she was educated at Jedburgh Grammar School and Birmingham University (Certificate in Youth and Community Work). She previously worked as Community Education Worker for North Lanarkshire Council before leaving to become Personal Assistant to Rt Hon. Helen Liddell MP in 1997.

She has held a number of positions within the Labour Party, including Branch Secretary and Constituency Youth Officer, and has served on the Party Executive. She is Deputy Convener of the Education, Culture and Sport Parliamentary Committee and is a member of the Standards Committee. She is also a member of the Cross-Party Groups in the Scottish Parliament on Borders Rail and on Older People, Age and Ageing.

She is active in the trade union UNISON and was union representative for Lanarkshire.

Trish Godman (Labour) is constituency MSP for West Renfrewshire. Born in 1939, she was educated at St Gerard's Senior Secondary School. She later went on to Jordanhill College, Glasgow as a mature student where she obtained a Certificate of Qualification in Social Work. A former social worker, she has been a Strathclyde Regional councillor and a member of City of Glasgow Council.

She is Convener of the Local Government Committee of the Scottish Parliament and is a member of the Subordinate Legislation Parliamentary Committee. She is also a member of the Cross-Party Groups in the Scottish Parliament on Children, and on Epilepsy.

She is a member of the trade union, MSF.

Annabel Goldie (Conservative) is a List MSP for West of Scotland. Born in Glasgow in 1950, she was educated at Greenock Academy and Strathclyde University. She has an LLB. Self-employed as a partner in a law firm since 1978, she is a member of the Law Society and the Scottish Law Agents' Society.

She has served in a number of positions in the Conservative Party including Branch Chair, Constituency Chair, Party Chair, Party Deputy Chair and Party Vice-Chair.

She is Deputy Leader of the Conservative Party and is Conservative Spokesperson for Industry, Economy and Finance. She is Deputy Convener of the Enterprise and Lifelong Learning Parliamentary Committee and a member of the Audit Parliamentary Committee.

She is a director of the Prince's Scottish Youth Business Trust, and Vice-Chairman of the West Scotland Salvation Army Advisory Board. She is a member of the Royal Automobile Club, the National Trust for Scotland, the Church of Scotland, Scottish Wildlife Trust and RSPB.

Christine Grahame (elected as Christine Creech) (SNP) is a List MSP for South of Scotland. Born in Burton-on-Trent in 1944, she was educated at Boroughmuir School, Edinburgh, Edinburgh University and Moray House, Edinburgh (MA, LLB, Dip Education and Dip Legal Practice). She worked as a secondary school teacher before qualifying as a solicitor in 1986.

She joined the SNP in 1969 and has served on the SNP Party Executive and the Party National Council. She has stood as a prospective candidate for Tweeddale, Etterick and Lauderdale in the 1992 General Election and later as a candidate for South of Scotland in elections to the European Parliament.

She is SNP Shadow Deputy Minister for Older People. She is a Member of the Public Petitions Parliamentary Committee and the Justice and Home Affairs Parliamentary Committee. She convenes the Cross-Party Group in the Scottish Parliament on Borders Rail; and is a member of the Cross-Party Groups on Animal Welfare and on Older People, Age and Ageing.

Rhoda Grant (Labour) is a List MSP for Highlands and Islands. Born in Stornoway in 1963, she was brought up in Kenmore in Wester Ross. She was educated at Inverness College of Further and Higher Education and through the Open University. (BSc Hons in Social Science and an HNC in Public Administration.) She has worked in various administrative and clerical posts in the private sector and has also worked for Highland Regional Council and UNISON where she was Office Manager.

A member of the Labour Party since 1991, she is the Labour Group representative on Labour Party Scottish Executive. She is also the Inverness East Branch Secretary, Local Government Committee Secretary and a member of the Constituency Labour Party Executive.

She is a member of both the Finance Parliamentary Committee and the Rural Affairs Parliamentary Committee. She is also a member of the Cross-Party Groups in the Scottish Parliament on Women, on Children and on Oil and Gas.

Her political interests include social exclusion in rural areas, transport and employment. She was part of the Scotland Forward campaign.

Janis Hughes (Labour) is constituency MSP for Glasgow Rutherglen. Born in 1958, she was educated at the Western College of Nursing (State Enrolled Nurse). She worked in the NHS for 19 years, initially as a nurse and then as an administrator at Glasgow Royal Infirmary.

She has served in various Labour Party positions, including Branch Treasurer and Constituency Vice-Chair. She has also served as a member of the Labour Party Executive.

She is Deputy Convener of Procedures Parliamentary Committee and a Member of the Transport and Environment Parliamentary Committee.

She is an active member and Lay Officer of UNISON.

Fiona Hyslop (SNP) is List MSP for Lothians. Born in 1964, she was educated at Ayr Academy and Glasgow University (MA Hon in Economic History and Sociology). She also has a Post Graduate Diploma in Industrial Administration from the Scottish College of Textiles. She formerly worked as Marketing Manager for Standard Life.

She joined the SNP in 1986 and is a member of the Party's National Executive. She has previously stood as candidate for Edinburgh Leith in the 1992 General Election and Edinburgh Central in the 1997 General Election. She also stood as a candidate for Edinburgh District Council and Lothian Regional Council in 1988, 1990 and 1994.

She is SNP Spokesperson on Housing and Social Justice and is Deputy Convener of the Social Inclusion, Housing and Voluntary Sector Committee in the Scottish Parliament.

Dr Sylvia Jackson (Labour) is a constituency MSP for Stirling. Born in Lincolnshire in 1946, she was educated at Briggs Girls High School, Hull University (BSc Hons, PGCE (Sec) and BPhil (Ed)) and University of Stirling (PhD Education). A former Chemistry teacher before becoming involved in education research, she has been an Education adviser to both Lothian Regional and Edinburgh District Councils and was a Lecturer in Education at Moray House, Edinburgh.

She is a member of the European Parliamentary Committee and the Local Government Parliamentary Committee. She convenes the Scottish Parliament Renewable Energy Group (SPREG). She is also a member of the Cross-Party Groups in the Scottish Parliament on Women, Animal Welfare, Children, Epilepsy, Older People, Age and Ageing, Media, Tobacco Control and Sports.

Cathy Jamieson (Labour) is constituency MSP for Carrick, Cumnock and Doon Valley. Born in 1956, she was educated at James Hamilton Academy in Kilmarnock; Glasgow School of Art, (BA (Hons) in Fine Art); Goldsmiths College, London/(Higher Diploma in Art); Glasgow University (Certificate Qualification in Social Work); and Glasgow Caledonian University (Certificate in Management). Originally trained as an Art Therapist, her career developed into work with young people at risk. She was Principal Officer of Who Cares? Scotland, the advocacy organisation for young people in care. She was a member of the Edinburgh Inquiry into Abuse in residential care and has served on Management and Advisory Committees of several child care agencies.

She has served as a Constituency Chair and is a member of Labour's Scottish and National Executive Committees. She has also been an election agent for an MEP.

She is Deputy Convener of the European Parliamentary Committee and a member of the Transport and Environment Parliamentary Committee. In addition, she is Convener of the Cross-Party Groups in the Scottish Parliament on Children and on Citizenship, Income, Economy and Society (CIES). She is also Vice-Convener of the Cross-Party Group on Animal Welfare. She is a member of the Cross-Party Groups on Women, Epilepsy, Older People, Age and Ageing, Media, Tobacco Control and Sports. She is a member of the Scottish Parliament Renewable Energy Group (SPREG).

Her interests include social economy and co-operatives, social inclusion, youth and children's issues. Cathy Jamieson is a member of the TGWU.

Margaret Jamieson (Labour) is constituency MSP for Kilmarnock and Loudon. Born in Kilmarnock in 1953, she was educated at Grange Academy and Ayr College, where she gained a City and Guilds in catering. After leaving college she worked in public sector catering until she joined the National Union of Public Employees (now UNISON) as its first female full-time officer in 1979.

A former chair of Scottish Labour's Women's Committee, she has held various branch, constituency and Party executive positions.

She is a member of the Audit Parliamentary Committee; and the Health and Community Care Parliamentary Committee. She is also a member of the Cross-Party Groups in the Scottish Parliament on Women, on Children, and on Citizenship, Income, Economy and Society (CIES). Her interests include education, equal opportunities, health and planning.

Margaret Jamieson is a member of UNISON. She is a board member of East Ayrshire Employment Initiative and is Chairperson of Gargieston School Board.

Johann Lamont (Labour) is constituency MSP for Glasgow Pollock. Born in Glasgow in 1957, she was educated at Woodside Secondary and Glasgow University (MA (Hons)). She gained a Postgraduate teaching qualification at Jordanhill College of Education in Glasgow and a Certificate of Guidance from Strathclyde University. She previously worked as a teacher in Rothesay and later Glasgow.

She has served in a number of Party positions at branch, constituency and national level. She is a former chair of the Scottish Labour Party and member of the national executive.

She is Deputy Convener of the Scottish Parliament Local Government Committee and is a Member of the Equal Opportunities Parliamentary Committee. She is Treasurer of the Cross-Party Group in the Scottish Parliament on Shipbuilding; and is a member of the Cross-Party Groups on Animal Welfare, Children, Older People, Age and Ageing, Media and Sports .

Her political interests include education, women's rights, equal opportunities and social exclusion. She is an active campaigner on women's issues. She is a member of teaching union EIS, the Scottish Co-operative Party, Oxfam, Amnesty International and NSPCC.

Marilyn Livingstone (Labour) is a constituency MSP for Kirkcaldy. Born in 1952, she was Head of the Fife College Business School and has previously worked as a lecturer. A councillor with Fife, she was responsible for vocational education and training strategy. She has been involved in the Fife New Deal Steering group, and is a member of the National New Deal Steering Group for the Voluntary Sector.

She is a member of the Equal Opportunities Parliamentary Committee; and the Enterprise and Lifelong Learning Parliamentary Committee. She is also a member of the Cross-Party Groups in the Scottish Parliament on Women and on Children. Her political interests include education, equal opportunities, social inclusion, economic development and local government.

She is a member of the Co-operative Party, the EIS and UNISON.

Margo MacDonald (SNP) is List MSP for Lothians. Born in 1944 in Bellshill, she was educated at Hamilton Academy and Dunfermline College, Aberdeen (Diploma in Physical Education).

She has previously worked as a teacher; a barmaid; Director of Shelter in Scotland; a Chief Executive of a communications company; and as a freelance broadcaster and journalist. She devised and established Drugline, Smokeline, and NHS Patients' Helpline. She managed and re-organised National AIDS Helpline, and managed and updated Training Access Points service for Local Enterprise Companies (LECs) during the early 1990s.

She was MP for Govan from November 1973 – February 1974. She contested Govan in 1974, and Hamilton in May 1978. She also contested Paisley in 1970. She served as SNP Deputy Leader from 1974 to 79, and Party Vice-Chair from 1972–9.

She is a member of the European Parliamentary Committee; and the Enterprise and Lifelong Learning Parliamentary Committee.

The *Scottish Biographical Dictionary* has described her as a 'bullish advocate for Scottish Nationalism' and also describes her 1973 by-election victory as 'momentous'. Ideological differences in the SNP led to a temporary retreat from party politics from 1982, and she subsequently made a career as a radio and TV presenter. With the advent of the Scottish Parliament, she has returned to the political arena.

Irene McGugan (SNP) is List MSP for North East Scotland. Born in Angus in 1952, she was educated at Forfar Academy; Robert Gordon University; Aberdeen (CQSW and Diploma in Social Work); and Dundee University (Advanced Certificate in Child Protection). After working for a year in a school in rural India with Voluntary Service Overseas, she continued her voluntary work in Scotland for a number of years before taking up studies as a mature student. Most recently, she was a Childcare Manager for Angus Council Social Work.

A first-time candidate, she has been an SNP member and activist for over 20 years. She has been an active campaigner against the tolls on the Skye Bridge.

She is a member of the Equal Opportunities Parliamentary Committee and the Rural Affairs Parliamentary Committee. She is also a member of the Cross-Party Groups in the Scottish Parliament on Children and on Oil and Gas.

She is a member of Rural Forum and One Parent Families Scotland. She is also a Church of Scotland Elder.

Lyndsay McIntosh (Conservative) is List MSP for Central Scotland. Born in Glasgow in 1955, she was educated at Duncanrig Senior Secondary in East Kilbride; Langside College (HNC in Secretarial Studies); and Dundee College of Commerce and Dundee College of Technology (Postgraduate Diploma in Management Studies). A formerly self-employed business consultant, she began work as a Legal Secretary before joining the Civil Service. She then took a sabbatical to gain her Diploma. She lived in Saudi Arabia for two years and upon her return to Scotland joined the Ladies Circle, Parent Teachers Association and the Conservative Party.

She was appointed Justice of the Peace in 1993 and Lay Inspector of Schools in 1994.

Lyndsay McIntosh stood as candidate for Fallside at local council elections in 1992 and 1999. She stood as candidate in three by-elections, Greenfaulds in 1997, Condorrat in 1998 and Whinhall, also in 1998.

She is Conservative Deputy Spokesperson on Home Affairs (with specific responsibility for drugs policy) and a member of the Justice and Home Affairs Parliamentary Committee. She is also a member of the Cross-Party Groups in the Scottish Parliament on Animal Welfare and on Children.

She is a former member of the Inland Revenue Staff Federation.

Kate MacLean (Labour) is constituency MSP for Dundee West. Born in Dundee in 1958, she was educated at Craigie High School. She then trained as a nurse. A former local government councillor, she served as Leader of Dundee City Council from 1992–99. She was Vice-President of CoSLA from 1996–99. She joined the Labour Party after the miners' strike of 1983–84.

She is Convener of the Equal Opportunities Parliamentary Committee; and a member of the Justice and Home Affairs Parliamentary Committee. She is also a member of the Cross-Party Groups in the Scottish Parliament on Women and on Animal Welfare. Her political interests include equal opportunities, social inclusion, housing and public finance.

She is a member of the T&G Union and CND.

Fiona McLeod (SNP) is List MSP for West of Scotland. Born in Glasgow in 1957, she was educated at Bearsden Academy in Glasgow; the University of Glasgow (MA (Hons) in Medieval and Modern History); and Strathclyde University (Postgraduate Diploma in Librarianship). A formerly self-employed library and information consultant, she has worked in education and the health service and has also done voluntary work with young people.

She stood as candidate for Bearsden and Milngavie District Council in 1984, 1988 and 1992. She also stood as candidate for Strathclyde Regional Council in 1986. She is a former Community Councillor.

She is a member of the Education, Culture and Sport Parliamentary Committee in the Scottish Parliament. She is also a member of the Cross-Party Groups in the Scottish Parliament on Women and on Children.

She is a Chartered Librarian and an Associate of the Library Association. She is also a member of Historic Scotland.

Maureen Macmillan (Labour) is List MSP for Highlands and Islands. Born in Oban in 1943, she was educated at Oban High School; Edinburgh University (MA Hons English); and gained a teaching qualification at Moray House, Edinburgh. She returned to full time employment in 1983 as Teacher of English and Senior Teacher with an Equal Opportunities remit. She has been active in politics for 25 years. She has served as Secretary and Treasurer at Labour party branch level and as Constituency Secretary and Women's Officer. She has also been Chair of a Community Council.

She is a member of the European Parliamentary Committee, and the Justice and Home Affairs Parliamentary Committee. She is Vice-Chair of the Cross-Party Group in the Scottish Parliament on Oil and Gas, and a member of the Cross-Party Group on Women.

Co-founder of Ross-shire Women's Aid, she is a member of Highland Domestic Abuse Forum. She is a member of the teaching union, EIS.

Pauline McNeill (Labour) is constituency MSP for Glasgow Kelvin. Born in 1962, she qualified as a graphic designer at Glasgow College of Building and Printing. She is currently studying Law at Strathclyde University. She has previously worked as a graphic designer and was a regional organiser for the GMB in the health service for ten years. She has extensive experience in health, strategic planning, education and law.

A long-time campaigner for devolution, she was a member of the Committee of the Campaign for a Scottish Parliament. She is a former President of the National Union of Students, Scotland.

She has held various Labour party positions including Branch and Constituency Education Officer and Constituency Vice-Chair.

She is Deputy Convener of the Public Petitions Parliamentary Committee and a member of the Justice and Home Affairs Parliamentary Committee. She is also a member of the Cross-Party Group in the Scottish Parliament on Epilepsy.

A member of the GMB union, she also sits on the Board of the 'Routes Out of Prostitution' Social Inclusion Partnership and is Chair of Glasgow Joint Trades Union Committee.

Tricia Marwick (SNP) is List MSP for Mid Scotland and Fife. Born in Cowdenbeath in 1953, she previously worked as a Public Affairs Officer for Shelter Scotland.

Currently a member of the SNP National Executive Committee, she has held a number of Party positions at branch, constituency and national level. She has previously contested both General Elections and local government elections. She stood as a candidate for Central Fife in the 1992 and 1997 General Elections. She also stood as a candidate for Fife Regional Council in 1990.

She is Deputy Convener of the Standards Parliamentary Committee and a Member of the Equal Opportunities Parliamentary Committee. She also serves as SNP Deputy Member of the Scottish Parliamentary Bureau. She is a member of the Cross-Party Groups in the Scottish Parliament on Animal Welfare.

She is an unpaid member of the Advisory Board for the World Development Movement Scotland (from 1999) and is a member of the Transport and General Workers Union.

Mary Mulligan (Labour) is constituency MSP for Linlithgow. Born in Liverpool in 1960, she was educated at Notre Dame High School and the University of Manchester (BA Hons in Economic and Social Studies). After graduating, she worked in Retail Management, but left to have children.

A former councillor, she has served on Edinburgh District Council and then City of Edinburgh Council since 1988. She is a former chair of the housing committee. She has been a member of the Labour Party since 1983. At branch level she has been Chair, Vice-Chair and Secretary. She has been Vice-Chair and Women's Officer in her constituency. She was Election Agent at local elections in 1990 and 1994, and at the 1997 General Election. She is a past member of the District, Region and City Party.

She is Convener of the Education, Culture and Sport Parliamentary Committee. She is a member of the Cross-Party Groups in the Scottish Parliament on Children, Sport and Epilepsy.

She is a member of USDAW and an active member of her local Parent Teacher Association.

Dr Elaine Murray (Labour) is constituency MSP for Dumfries. Born in Hitchin, Hertfordshire in 1954, she was educated at Mary Erskine School, Edinburgh and then at Edinburgh University (BSc (Hons) Chemistry) and Cambridge University (PhD Chemistry). A former research scientist and a part-time lecturer with the Open University, she has also worked as an assistant to an MEP.

She was a councillor at Strathclyde Region (1994–96), where she was chair of the Women's Advisory group, and at South Ayrshire (1995–99) where she convened the Education Committee. She was CoSLA spokesperson on cultural issues (1996–99). She has held a number of Party positions, including those of Branch Secretary and Branch Treasurer.

She is a member of the Enterprise and Lifelong Learning Parliamentary Committee, and the Rural Affairs Parliamentary Committee. She is also a member of the Scottish Parliament Renewable Energy Group (SPREG). She is a member of the Cross-Party Group in the Scottish Parliament on Animal Welfare; the Cross-Party Group in the Scottish Parliament on Borders Rail; and the Cross-Party Group in the Scottish Parliament on Older People, Age and Ageing, and the Cross-Party Group in the Scottish Parliament on the Media.

She is a member of TGWU, AUT, OXFAM and RSPB.

Irene Oldfather (Labour) is constituency MSP for Cunninghame South. Born in Glasgow in 1954, she was educated at Irvine Royal Academy and Strathclyde University (MSc and BA Hons in Politics.) Formerly a political researcher for an MEP, she has also done some freelance journalism on European Affairs. She has lectured in the Politics of Health at Paisley University and has served on the Board of Management at James Watt College.

She was elected to North Ayrshire Council in 1995 and was the Council's European Spokesperson and Vice-Chair of the Education Committee. She was Chair of the CoSLA Task Group on Economic and Monetary Union and was one of Scotland's Representatives on the European Committee of the Regions, where she served on the Employment Committee.

She is a member of the European Parliamentary Committee and the Health and Community Care Parliamentary Committee. She is Vice-Convener of the Cross-Party Group in the Scottish Parliament on Tobacco Control and is a member of the Cross-Party Group on Animal Welfare .

Irene Oldfather is a member of NUJ and TGWU.

Cathy Peattie (Labour) is constituency MSP for Falkirk East. Born in 1951, she has worked in the voluntary sector for the last 14 years. She was previously

Convener of the Council of Voluntary Service Scotland and Director of Falkirk's Voluntary Action Resource Centre.

She has held positions in the Labour party and is a past chair of Scottish Labour Women's Committee.

She is a member of the Education, Culture and Sport Parliamentary Committee and the Rural Affairs Parliamentary Committee. She is a member of the Cross-Party Groups in the Scottish Parliament on Women, and on Children and on Oil and Gas.

She is Chair of Linked Work Training Trust–Central and Falkirk Women's Technology Centre Ltd Falkirk. A member of the unions MSF and UNISON, she is also a member of the Co-operative Party.

Nora Radcliffe (Liberal Democrat) is constituency MSP for Gordon. Born in Aberdeen in 1946, she was educated at Aberdeen High School for Girls and Aberdeen University. She pursued a career in hotel and catering until she started a family. She returned to full-time work as an employee of Grampian Health Board in the Community Liaison team, moving to the Primary Care Development team. She is a Justice of the Peace.

A former local councillor for Gordon District (elected in 1988), she served as Vice-Convener of Environmental Health and Vice-Convener of Economic Development. She was involved with the promotion of Scotland's first environmental charters, and is a Founder Member of Gordon Environmental Forum. She has held various positions in the local Party, including Branch Treasurer.

She is Liberal Democrat Parliamentary Spokesperson for Health, Social Services and Community Care. Deputy Convener of the Transport and Environment Parliamentary Committee, she is also a member of the Equal Opportunities Parliamentary Committee. She sits on the Cross-Party Groups in the Scottish Parliament on Women, on Older People, Age and Ageing, on Epilepsy, on the Media; and the Scottish Parliament Renewable Energy Group (SPREG).

Nora Radcliffe is a member of the National Women's Register, Aberdeen Environmental Forum, Saltire Society and Garioch Heritage Society.

Shona Robison (SNP) is List MSP for North East Scotland. Born in Redcar in 1966, she was educated at Alva Academy, Glasgow University (MA in Social Sciences) and Jordanhill College, Glasgow (Post Graduate Certificate in Community Education). She is currently studying part-time for a law degree at Strathclyde University. She previously worked as a Home Care Organiser with the City of Glasgow Council.

Shona Robison has been a member of the SNP since 1988. She has held a number of positions and is currently a member of the National Executive

Committee. She stood as the candidate for Dundee East in the 1997 General Election and contested the same seat in the elections to the Scottish Parliament.

She is SNP Parliamentary Group Secretary and Vice-Convener of the Equal Opportunities Parliamentary Committee. Her interests include community development and equal opportunities.

She is a member of UNISON.

Mary Scanlon (Conservative) is List MSP for Highlands and Islands. Born in Dundee in 1947, she was educated at Craigo Secondary School, Montrose and the University of Dundee (MA Economics and Politics). She also has a Post Graduate Diploma in Personnel Management. She has previously worked as a lecturer in economics and business administration, in Further and Higher Education. A former adviser with the Citizens' Advice Bureau, she has also been a member of Barlinnie Prison's Visiting Committee and has served on the Child Support Agency Appeals Tribunal.

She has previously stood as a Conservative candidate in local elections, and twice contested Westminster constituencies.

She is Conservative Parliamentary Spokesperson on Health (including social work) and is a member of the Health and Community Care Parliamentary Committee. She is also a member of the Cross-Party Groups in the Scottish Parliament on Tobacco Control and on Epilepsy.

Elaine Smith (Labour) is constituency MSP for Coatbridge and Chryston. Born in Coatbridge in 1963, she has an Honours degree in Social Science (Economics and Politics), a Postgraduate teaching qualification, and a Diploma in Public Sector Management. A former secondary school teacher, she worked in local government and in the voluntary sector.

She sits on the Equal Opportunities Parliamentary Committee and is also a member of the Cross-Party Groups in the Scottish Parliament on Women and on Children.

She is member of the T& G Union and the General Teaching Council.

Margaret Smith (Liberal Democrat) is constituency MSP for Edinburgh West. Born in Edinburgh in 1961, she was educated at Broughton High School and Edinburgh University (MA in General Arts). A former Political Organiser for the Scottish Liberal Democrats, she has also worked as a voluntary sector organiser and a civil servant. She is a former Scottish Officer of the United Nations Association.

A councillor for the City of Edinburgh Council from 1995–99, she has held a number of positions within the Party.

She is the Liberal Democrat spokesperson for Health and Community Care. She is Convener of the Health and Community Care Parliamentary Committee and sits on the Public Petitions Parliamentary Committee. She is a member of the Cross-Party Groups in the Scottish Parliament on Children, on Older People, Age and Ageing and Tobacco Control.

Nicola Sturgeon (SNP) is List MSP for Glasgow. Born in Irvine, Ayrshire in 1970, she studied Law at Glasgow University (LLB (Hons) and Diploma in Legal Practice). She is a member of the Law Society of Scotland and most recently worked as a solicitor at Drumchapel Law Centre in Glasgow.

She joined the SNP in 1986. She is a former Convener of the SNP Youth Wing, National Vice-Convener for Youth Affairs and is currently Vice-Convener for Publicity. Before gaining her seat in the Scottish Parliament, she had contested both local and national elections.

She is SNP Parliamentary Spokesperson on Children and Education and is a member of the Education, Culture and Sport Parliamentary Committee. She is a member of the Cross-Party Groups in the Scottish Parliament on Women, on Children and on Epilepsy.

Elaine Thomson (Labour) is MSP for Aberdeen North. Born in Inverness in 1957, she was educated at Aberdeen High School for Girls and the University of Aberdeen (BSc in Pure Science). She is also a certified SAP consultant and has completed other IT courses. Her career has been spent in the oil and gas industry focusing mainly on computing. Until elected she worked for Absoft Ltd, a small information technology consultancy.

She was an external member of Aberdeen Council Women's and Equal Opportunities Committee from 1988–95. She has also been a member of Aberdeen Women's Centre Management Committee. She was Aberdeen campaign co-ordinator of Scotland Forward during the run up to the Scottish Parliament referendum in 1997.

A Labour party member since 1982, she has held various Party positions including Constituency Vice-Chair and Constituency Women's Officer. She has also acted as an election agent in the European elections. Before gaining a seat in the Scottish Parliament she contested a number of local council elections.

She is Deputy Convener of the Finance Parliamentary Committee and a member of the Enterprise and Lifelong Learning Parliamentary Committee. She chairs the Cross-Party Group in the Scottish Parliament on Oil and Gas, and is a member of the Cross-Party Groups on Women, on Animal Welfare and on Older People, Age and Ageing. Her interests include: information technology; economic development; training at work; women's politics; the environment; and issues to do with the older members of society and those with disabilities, particularly learning disabilities.

She is a member of the MSF. She is also a member of Engender.

Kay Ullrich (SNP) is List MSP for West of Scotland. Born in 1943, she was educated at Ayr Academy and Queen's College, Glasgow where she obtained the Certificate of Qualification in Social Work. A court social worker, she took early retirement in 1997. She has previously worked as a hospital social worker (1986–92), a school social worker (1984–86), and a school swimming instructor (1973–81).

An SNP member since 1965, she has held a number of positions in the Party including Vice-President. She stood as a candidate for Cunninghame South in the 1983 and 1987 General Elections and contested Motherwell South in the 1992 General Election. She also stood as a candidate in the Monklands East by-election in 1994.

She is SNP Spokesperson on Health and Community Care and sits on the Health and Community Care Parliamentary Committee. She is a member of the Cross-Party Groups in the Scottish Parliament on Animal Welfare, on Epilepsy and on Oil and Gas.

Kay Ullrich is a member of the union UNISON.

Sandra White (SNP) is List MSP for Glasgow. Born in 1951 in Govan, she was educated at Garthamlock Secondary and Glasgow College. A former Justice of the Peace, she was also a full-time councillor for Renfrewshire and served as Deputy Housing Spokesperson. She was a member of various committees and sub-committees, including: Housing; Leisure Services; Corporate Services; and Civic Functions.

She has held a number of positions in the Party, including Branch Secretary and Political Officer. She contested the 1992 and 1997 General Elections.

She is a Member of the Public Petitions Parliamentary Committee. She is Vice-Convener of the Cross-Party Group in the Scottish Parliament on Older People, Age and Ageing and a member of the Cross-Party Groups in the Scottish Parliament on Women, on Animal Welfare, and on Epilepsy. Her main political interests include social service policies, campaigning against poor quality housing, and encouraging young people to participate in sports and leisure activities.

Currently she is the Press Officer of the William Wallace Society.

Karen Whitefield (Labour) is constituency MSP for Airdrie and Shotts. She is the youngest Labour MSP. Born in Bellshill in 1970, she was educated at Calderhead High School in Shotts and Glasgow Caledonian University (BA (Hons) in Public Administration and Management). She won a scholarship to the US and worked for the Democrats in Congress for a year.

An active member of the Labour Party for 11 years, she was Personal Assistant to Rachel Squire MP from 1992–99, having previously worked as a Civil Servant with the Benefits Agency in North Lanarkshire.

She is a member of the Social Inclusion, Housing and Voluntary Sector Parliamentary Committee. She is also a member of the Cross-Party Group in the Scottish Parliament on Animal Welfare. Her political interests include health and community care, social inclusion and the voluntary sector.

She is a member of MSF union and is involved with the Girls Brigade.

– SCOTTISH PARLIAMENT CROSS-PARTY GROUP ON WOMEN –

– Purpose of the Group –

- to act as a policy forum for discussion and updating on policy impacts on women;
- to share information and expertise on women and gender impact between MSPs;
- to maximise information and expertise from external sources, including the Equal Opportunties Commission (EOC) Scotland, and other statutory, public and voluntary equality organisations which support the aims of this group;
- to act as a forum for networking and support led by women MSPs.

– Members of the Group –

MSPs
Margaret Curran
Helen Eadie
Linda Fabiani
Rhoda Grant
Sylvia Jackson
Cathy Jamieson
Marilyn Livingstone
Lyndsay McIntosh
Kate MacLean
Fiona McLeod
Maureen Macmillan
Mary Mulligan
Cathy Peattie
Nora Radcliffe
Elaine Smith
Nicola Sturgeon
Elaine Thomson
Sandra White

Non-MSPs
Professor Joan Stringer, EOC Commissioner for Scotland
Morag Alexander, Director, EOC Scotland
Angela O'Hagan, EOC Scotland

_ Women at Westminster and the _
European Parliament

– Members of Parliament (MPs) –

Irene Adams (Labour) is MP for Paisley North. She was first elected to this constituency at a by-election in 1990, following the death of her husband Allen Adams, who had previously served as MP for Paisley North. She was born in 1947, and educated at Stanley Green High School, Paisley. She served as a councillor from 1970–84, and on her election to Paisley Town Council in 1970 was the youngest woman ever to become a councillor in Britain. She subsequently served as a councillor on Renfrew District Council and on Strathclyde Regional Council. She is a Justice of the Peace.

Anne Begg (Labour) is MP for Aberdeen South, and was elected in 1997. Born in 1955, she was educated at Brechin High School. She obtained an MA from the University of Aberdeen, and a Teaching Certificate in Secondary Education from the Aberdeen College of Education. She worked as a teacher, and was Principal Teacher of English at Arbroath Academy from 1991–97.

She was a member of the Labour Party National Executive Committee (NEC) from 1998–99.

She is a member of EIS, has served on the EIS National Council, and the General Teaching Council for Scotland.

In 1988 she was named Disabled Scot of the Year.

Lynda Clark (Labour) is MP for Edinburgh Pentlands, and was elected in 1997. She contested North East Fife in 1992. Born in 1949, she was educated at Queen's College, St Andrews (LLB Hons), and the University of Edinburgh (PhD). She worked as a tutor, then lecturer in Jurisprudence at the University of Dundee, then served as an Advocate at the Scots bar from 1977–89, and became a QC in 1989. She was called to the English Bar in 1990.

She was appointed Advocate General for Scotland in 1999.

She has served as a member of the Scottish Legal Aid Board, and of Edinburgh University Court.

Roseanna Cunningham (SNP) is MP for Perth. She was elected to Perth and Kinross at a byelection in 1995. Following a boundary change this became the

Perth constituency, and she was re-elected in 1997. She also contested Perth and Kinross in 1992. She is also an MSP (see MSPs' biographies for further details). She has served as SNP Spokesperson on Home Affairs, Environment and Land Reform, Arts and Broadcasting, Employment, and Women's Issues.

Margaret Ewing (SNP) is MP for Moray, and was elected in 1987. She served as SNP MP for Dunbartonshire East from 1974–79 (as Margaret Bain), and she contested Strathkelvin/Bearsden in 1983. She is also an MSP (see MSPs' biographies for further details).

She is Spokesperson on Europe and Foreign Affairs; Defence; Health; Highlands and Islands; and Gaelic. She has been SNP Parliamentary leader since 1987.

Maria Fyfe (Labour) is MP for Glasgow Maryhill, and was first elected to this constituency in 1987. Born in 1938, she was educated at Notre Dame High School, Glasgow. As a mature student she obtained a degree in Economic History in 1975 from the University of Strathclyde. She subsequently worked as a Senior Lecturer in the Trade Union Studies Unit, Central College of Commerce, Glasgow, until her election to Parliament in 1987. She also served as a councillor on Glasgow District Council from 1980–87, and during this time held the posts of Vice-Convener of Finance, and Convener of Personnel. She was a member of the Labour Party Scottish Executive from 1982–88, and Chair of the Local Government Committee from 1985–87.

She served as Opposition Spokesperson on Women from 1988–91; on Scottish Health and Social Services from 1992–94; and on Scottish Education and Social Work Group from 1994–98.

She chaired the Women's Issues Group of the Scottish Constitutional Convention, and has been an active campaigner for equal representation.

Helen Liddell (Labour) is MP for Airdrie and Shotts. She was first elected to Monklands East at the by-election in 1994 following the death of John Smith, then Leader of the Labour Party. The constituency became Airdrie and Shotts following a boundary change, and Helen Liddell was re-elected in 1997. She also contested Fife East for the Labour Party in 1974. Born in 1950, she was educated at St Patrick's High School, Coatbridge, and at the University of Strathclyde.

She was Head of the Economics Department of the Scottish Trades Union Congress (STUC) from 1971–75, and Assistant Secretary of the STUC from 1975–76. From 1976–77 she worked as Economics Correspondent for the BBC, and then as General Secretary of the Labour Party in Scotland from 1977–88. She was Director of Personnel and Public Affairs for the Scottish Daily Record and Sunday Mail from 1988–92, and Chief Executive of Business Venture Programme from 1993–94.

She was Opposition Spokesperson on Scotland from 1995–97. Since the Labour Government took office in 1997 she has held the posts of Economic Secretary to HM Treasury from 1997–98; Minister of State at the Scottish Office (Minister for Education and for Women's Issues) from 1998–99; Minister for Transport in the Department of Environment, Transport and the Regions 1999; and Minister for Energy and Competitiveness in Europe in the Department of Trade and Industry from 1999. She is a Privy Counsellor.

She has also published a novel, *Elite*.

Anne McGuire (Labour) is MP for Stirling, and was elected in 1997. Born in 1949, she was educated at Our Lady of St Francis, Glasgow. She has an Honours Degree in Politics with History from the University of Glasgow, and a Diploma in Secondary Education from Notre Dame College of Education. She worked as a teacher, then as a manager in the voluntary sector. She was Depute Director of the Scottish Council for Voluntary Organisations (SCVO) prior to her election to Parliament.

She has been a member of the Labour Party Scottish Executive since 1984, and was Chair of the Labour Party in Scotland from 1992–93. She served as a councillor on Strathclyde Regional Council from 1980–82.

Since her election to Parliament she has served as PPS to Donald Dewar MP, Secretary of State for Scotland, 1997–98; and as Assistant Government Whip from 1998.

Rosemary McKenna, CBE, (Labour) is MP for Cumbernauld and Kilsyth, and was elected in 1997. Born in 1941, she was educated at St Augustine's Comprehensive, Glasgow. She holds a Diploma in Primary Education from Notre Dame College of Education and worked as a teacher. She served as a councillor for Cumbernauld and Kilsyth District Council from 1984–96, and during that time was Leader of the Council, Convener of the Policy and Resources Committee, and Provost. She has served as Vice-President and President of the Convention of Scottish Local Authorities (CoSLA). She has also served as a member of Cumbernauld Development Corporation, and on Scottish Enterprise. She has been a member of a number of committees dealing with European issues and with women's issues, including the Committee of the Regions, and the UK and European Standing Committees of Women Elected Members of the Council of European Municipalities and Regions, which she chaired from 1995–98.

She became joint PPS to the Ministers of State at the Foreign and Commonwealth Office in 1999.

She has been a member of EIS, and is a member of GMB.

Ray Michie (Liberal Democrat) is MP for Argyll and Bute, and was first elected to this constituency in 1987. She contested Argyll in 1979, and Argyll and Bute in 1983. Born in 1934, she was educated at Aberdeen High School for Girls; Lansdowne House, Edinburgh; and Edinburgh College of Speech Therapy. Prior to her election to Parliament she worked as a speech therapist for Argyll and Clyde Health Board. She has served as Spokesperson on Transport and Rural Development; on Women's Issues; and on Scotland. On the Liberal Democrat Scottish team she was responsible for Agriculture, Community Care, Rural Affairs, and National Heritage from 1997–99.

She has also served as Vice-Chair of the Scottish Liberal Party, Chair of the Scottish Liberal Democrats, and Deputy Leader of the Scottish Liberal Democrats.

She was a member of the Scottish Constitutional Convention.

She is Vice-President of the Royal College of Speech and Language Therapists, and she is a member of the National Farmers' Union, and the Scottish Crofters' Union.

Sandra Osborne (Labour) is MP for Ayr, and was elected in 1997. Born in 1956, she was educated at Camphill Senior Secondary, Paisley; Anniesland College, Jordanhill College, and the University of Strathclyde. She holds a Diploma in Community Education, and MSc in Equality and Discrimination. She has worked as a community worker, and served as a councillor on Kyle and Carrick District Council and on South Ayrshire Council, where she has served as Convener of Community Services (Housing and Social Work).

She has been PPS to Brian Wilson, MP, Minister of State for Scotland, since 1999. She was Vice-Chair of the the Scottish Regional Group of Labour MPs from 1998–99.

She is a member of Women's Aid. She has been a member of APEX, and is a member of TGWU.

Rachel Squire (Labour) is MP for Dunfermline West, and was first elected to the constituency in 1992. Born in 1954, she was educated at Godolphin and Latymer Girls' School. She has a BA Hons in Anthropology from the University of Durham, and a Certificate of Qualification in Social Work from the University of Birmingham. She worked as a social worker from 1975–81 and as a Trade Union officer from 1981–92. She was Head of the Scottish Labour Party's Task Force on Community Care from 1993–98, is a member of the Labour Movement in Europe, and has chaired the Labour party's Scottish Policy Forum since 1998.

Since her election to Parliament she has served as a Parliamentary Private Secretary (PPS) to Stephen Byers, Minister of State at the Department for Education and Employment (School Standards) from 1997–98, and to Estelle Morris (School Standards) from 1998.

She is a member of UNISON.

– MEMBERS OF THE EUROPEAN PARLIAMENT (MEPs) –

Two female members of the European Parliament represent Scottish constituencies.

Elspeth Attwooll (Liberal Democrat) was elected as a Member of the European Parliament, representing Scotland in 1999. She was born in 1943 in Chislehurst. She is a member of the Group of the European Liberal, Democrat and Reform Party. She sits on the following committees of the European Parliament: Fisheries; Regional Policy, Transport and Tourism; Environment, Public Health and Consumer Policy. She is a Substitute member of the Committee on Employment and Social Affairs and is a Substitute member of the Delegation for relations with Canada.

Catherine Stihler (formerly Taylor) (Labour) was elected as a member of the European Parliament, representing Scotland in 1999. She was born in 1973 in Bellshill. She is a member of the Group of the Party of European Socialists. She sits on the Committee on Fisheries, and the Committee on the Environment, Public Health and Consumer Policy. She is a member of the Delegation to the EU-Hungary Joint Parliamentary Committee.

– SOURCES –

Fuller details may be found from the following sources:
Chambers Scottish Biographical Dictionary
Dod's Parliamentary Companion 1994, 1998, 2000, Hurst Green: East Sussex.
LOBBYcontact MSP Database, Campaign Information Ltd, Bedfordshire
www.politics.co.uk
Scotland on Sunday, Who's Who In The Scottish Parliament, 16 May 1999.
Scottish Parliament website www.scotland.parliament.uk
Who's Who of British MPs, Vol IV.
The European Parliament website wwwdb.europarl.eu.int

Postscript

Whilst this book was in preparation there were two major political reshuffles. These followed on from the resignation of Alex Salmond as leader of the Scottish National party in September 2000 and the untimely death of First Minister and Labour leader Donald Dewar in October 2000.

Women now consist six of the 15 posts in the Shadow Executive led by the new SNP leader John Swinney. They are Roseanna Cunningham (Deputy leader and Justice), Fiona Hyslop (Social Justice and Housing plus co-ordination of policy programme), Nicola Sturgeon (Health and Community Care), Christine Grahame (Social Security), Tricia Marwick (Business Manager) and Kay Ullrich (Chief Whip).

The new First Minister Henry McLeish has appointed four women to his 11-strong Cabinet. Wendy Alexander is Minister for Enterprise and Lifelong Learning (formerly Minister for Communities); Susan Deacon is Minister for Health and Community Care; Jackie Baillie is Minister for Social Justice (formerly Deputy Minister for Social Inclusion, Equality and the Voluntary Sector); and Sarah Boyack is Minister for Transport (formerly Minister for Transport and the Environment). Women comprise two out of nine Deputy Ministers: Rhona Brankin is Deputy Minister for Rural Development (formerly Deputy Minister for Culture and Sport); Margaret Curran is Deputy Minister for Social Justice (formerly Convener of the Social Inclusion, Housing and Voluntary Sector committee of the Scottish parliament).

Information on these and any further changes can be found by consulting the web site of the Scottish parliament at: http://www.scottish.parliament.uk

Bibliography

Arnot, K. (1990), 'Leaving the Pain Behind', in S. Henderson and A. Mackay (eds) *Grit and Diamonds, Women in Scotland Making History 1980–1990*, Edinburgh: Stramullion.

Arshad, Rowena and Mukami McCrum (1989), 'Black Women, White Scotland', in A. Brown and D. McCrone (eds) *The Scottish Government Yearbook 1989*, Edinburgh: Unit for the Study of Government in Scotland, University of Edinburgh.

Aziz, Razia (1997), 'Feminism and the Challenge of Racism: Deviance or Difference?', in Heidi Safia Mirza (ed.) *Black British Feminism*, London: Routledge.

Blake Stevenson (1990) *Women's Consultation Exercise*, Edinburgh: Edinburgh District Council's Women's Committee.

Bain, Margaret (1980), 'Woven by Women', *Chapman*, 27/28, Edinburgh: Chapman.

Bamford, C. (1991), *Local Enterprise Companies and Women: Realising the Potential*, Glasgow: Scottish Enterprise.

Barrett, Michèle (1987), 'The Concept of "Difference"', *Feminist Review*, 26.

Barron, J., C. Crawley and T. Wood (1991), *Councillors In Crisis*, Basingstoke: Macmillan.

Beddoe, Deirdre (1989), *Back to Home and Duty*, London: Pandora.

Bhavnani, Reena (1994), *Black Women in the Labour Market: A Research Review*, Manchester: Equal Opportunities Commission.

Black and Ethnic Minority Infrastructure in Scotland (1999), *Listening to the Voice* (executive summary), Glasgow: BEMIS.

Bochel, Catherine and Hugh Bochel (1998), 'Scotland's Councillors 1974–1995', *Scottish Affairs*, 24.

Bochel, John and David Denver (1992), 'The 1992 General Election in Scotland', *Scottish Affairs*, 1.

Bochel, John and David Denver (1995), 'The Elections for the Shadow Local Authorities', *Scottish Affairs*, 13.

Bochel, John, David Denver and Allan Macartney (eds) (1980), *The Referendum Experience: Scotland 1979*, Aberdeen: Aberdeen University Press.

Bock, Gisella and Susan James (eds) (1992), *Beyond Equality and Difference*, London: Routledge.

Boneparth, E and E. Soper (eds) (1988), *Women, Policy and Power: Toward the Year 2000*, Oxford: Pergamon Press.

Boyne, G., G. Jordan and M. McVicar (1995), *Local Government Reform: A Review of the Process in Scotland and Wales*, London: Joseph Rowntree Foundation.

Braham, Peter, Ali Rattansi and Richard Skellington (1992), *Racism and Antiracism*, London: Sage.

Breitenbach, Esther (1989), 'The Impact of Thatcherism on women in Scotland', in Alice Brown and David McCrone (eds) *The Scottish Government Yearbook 1989*, Edinburgh: Unit for the Study of Government in Scotland, University of Edinburgh.

Breitenbach, Esther (1990), ' "Sisters are doing it for themselves": The Women's Movement in Scotland', in Alice Brown and Richard Parry (eds) *The Scottish Government Yearbook 1990*, Edinburgh: The Unit for the Study of Government in Scotland, University of Edinburgh.

Breitenbach, Esther (1995), *Quality through Equality: Good Practice in Equal Opportunities in Scottish Local Authorities*, Glasgow: Equal Opportunities Commission.

Breitenbach, Esther (1996), 'The Women's Movement in Scotland in the 1990s', *New Waverley Papers*, Edinburgh: Department of Politics, University of Edinburgh.

Breitenbach, E., A. Brown and F. Myers (1998), 'Understanding Women in Scotland', *Feminist Review*, 58.

Breitenbach, E., A. Brown, F. Mackay and J. Webb (1999), *Equal Opportunities in Local Government in Scotland and Wales*, Edinburgh: Unit for the Study of Government in Scotland, University of Edinburgh.

Brown, Alice (1991), 'Thatcher's Legacy for Women in Scotland', in *Radical Scotland*, Apr–May.

Brown, Alice (1991), 'Women in Scottish Politics', paper presented to ECPR Conference, University of Essex, 22–8 March.

Brown, Alice (1992), 'Plans for a Scottish Parliament: Have Women Made a Difference?', paper given at Gender and Power Workshop, ECPR, University of Limerick.

Brown, Alice (1995), 'Plans for a Scottish Parliament: Did Women Make a Difference?', in *Waverley Papers*, Edinburgh: Department of Politics, University of Edinburgh.

Brown, Alice (1995), *In the Name of Democracy: The Fight for Equal Representation in Scotland*, paper presented to Political Studies Association Conference, York, April.

Brown, Alice (1995), 'The Scotswoman's Parliament', *Parliamentary Brief*, April.

Brown, Alice (1996), 'Women and politics in Scotland', *Parliamentary Affairs*, 49 (1).

Brown, Alice (1996), 'Women and Scottish Politics', in Alice Brown, David McCrone and Lindsay Paterson, *Politics and Society in Scotland*, Basingstoke: Macmillan.

Brown, Alice (1997), 'The 1997 General Election in Scotland: Paving the way for a Scottish Parliament?', *Parliamentary Affairs*, 50 (4).

Brown, Alice (1998), 'Deepening Democracy: Women and the Scottish Parliament', *Regional and Federal Studies*, 8, 1, Spring.

Brown, Alice (1998), 'Representing Women in Scotland', *Parliamentary Affairs*, 51 (3), July.

Brown, Alice (1998), 'Women and political culture in Scotland', in A. Howson and E. Breitenbach (eds) *Gender and Scottish Society: Polities, Policies and Participation*, Edinburgh: Unit for the Study of Government in Scotland, University of Edinburgh.

Brown, Alice (2000), 'Politics', in Fiona Mackay and Kate Bilton (eds) *Gender Audit 2000*, Edinburgh: Engender/The University of Edinburgh Governance of Scotland Forum.

Brown, Alice, Esther Breitenbach and Fiona Myers (1994), *Equality Issues in Scotland: A Research Review*, Manchester: EOC.

Brown, Alice and Yvonne Galligan (1993), 'Changing the Political Agenda for Women in the Republic of Ireland and in Scotland', *West European Politics*, 16, 2, April.

Brown, Alice and David McCrone (eds) (1989), *The Scottish Government Yearbook 1989*, Edinburgh: Unit for the Study of Government in Scotland, University of Edinburgh.

Brown, Alice, David McCrone and Lindsay Paterson (1996), *Politics and Society in Scotland*, Basingstoke: Macmillan.

Brown, A., A. Jones and F. Mackay (1999), *The Representativeness of Councillors*, York: Joseph Rowntree Foundation.

Brown, B., M. Burman and L. Jamieson (1992), *Sexual History and Sexual Character Evidence in Scottish Sexual Offence Trials*, Edinburgh: Scottish Office Central Research Unit.

Brown, Usha (1993), 'Women and Power' speech to the Scottish Labour Women's Caucus Conference.

Bruegel, I. and H. Kean (1995), 'The moment of municipal feminism: gender and class in 1980s local government', *Critical Social Policy*, 44/45, Autumn.

Bryson, V. (1992), *Feminist Political Theory*, Basingstoke and London: Macmillan.

Burness, Catriona (1992), 'The Long Slow March: Scottish Women MPs, 1918–1945', in Esther Breitenbach and Eleanor Gordon (eds) *Out of Bounds: Women in Scottish Society 1800–1945*, Edinburgh: Edinburgh University Press.

Burness, Catriona (1995), 'Will Scotland Lead the Way for Women?', in *Parliamentary Brief*, March.

Byrne, P. (1996), 'The politics of the women's movement', *Parliamentary Affairs*, 49 (1).

Carroll, Susan (1992), 'Women State Legislators, Women's Organizations, and the Representation of Women's Culture in the United States', in Jill Bystydzienski (ed.) *Women Transforming Politics*, Bloomington, IN: Indiana University Press.

Chambers, Gerry and Ann Millar (1983), *Investigating Sexual Assault*, Edinburgh: Scottish Office Central Research Unit.

Chambers, Gerry and Ann Millar (1986), *Prosecuting Sexual Assault*, Edinburgh: Scottish Office Central Research Unit.

Chapman, J. (1993), *Politics, Feminism and the Reformation of Gender*, London: Routledge.

Cockburn, Cynthia (1991), *In the Way of Women*, Basingstoke: Macmillan.

Commission for Racial Equality (1997), *Annual Report*, London CRE.

Coote, A., and P. Patullo (1990), *Power and Prejudice: Women and Politics*, London: Weidenfeld and Nicolson.

Coote, Anna and Beatrix Campbell (1987), *Sweet Freedom*, Oxford: Blackwell.

Cosgrove, Katie (1996), 'No Man has the Right', in Chris Corrin (ed.) *Women in a Violent World*, Edinburgh: Edinburgh University Press.

Cosgrove, K. and J. Forman (1995), *Male Violence Against Women in Rural Areas*, report to Strathclyde Regional Council, February.

Cosgrove, K. and J. Macleod (1995), *We Are No Exception: Male Violence against Women with Disability*, report to Strathclyde Regional Council, January.

CoSLA (1991), *Women and Violence*, Edinburgh: COSLA.

CoSLA (1998), *Guidance on Preparing and Implementing a Multi-Agency Strategy to Tackle Violence Against Women*, Edinburgh: CoSLA.

CoSLA/EOC (1999), *Mainstreaming: Integrating Equality into all Council Activities*, Edinburgh: CoSLA, October.

Coyle, A. (1996), *Women and Organisational Change*, Manchester: EOC.

Craig, F.W.S. (1989), *British Electoral Facts 1832–1987*, Aldershot: Parliamentary Research Services.

Crick, Bernard and David Miller, (1991) *Standing Orders for a Scottish Parliament*, Edinburgh: John Wheatley Centre.

Crick, Bernard and David Miller (1995), *To Make the Parliament of Scotland a Model for Democracy*, Edinburgh: John Wheatley Centre.

Cullen, The Honourable Lord (1996), *Public Inquiry into Shootings at Dunblane Primary School on 13 March 1996*, Edinburgh: Scottish Office.

Dahlerup, D. (ed.) (1986), *The New Women's Movement*, London: Sage.

Dahlerup, D. (1988), 'From a small to a large minority: Women in Scandinavian Politics', *Scandinavian Political Studies*, 11 (4).

Denver, David (1994), 'The 1994 European Elections in Scotland', *Scottish Affairs* (9).

Denver, D. and I. MacAllister (1999), 'The Scottish Parliament Elections 1999: an Analysis of the Results', *Scottish Affairs*, 28, Summer.

Dobash, R. Emerson and Russell Dobash (1992), *Women, Violence and Social Change*, London: Routledge.

Dworkin, Andrea (1988), *Letters From A War Zone, Selected Writings 1976–1987*, New York, NY: Secker & Warburg.

Edinburgh Rape Crisis Centre (1988), *Second Report 1978–1988*, Edinburgh: Edinburgh Rape Crisis Centre.

Edinburgh Rape Crisis Centre (1993), *Third Report* Edinburgh: Edinburgh Rape Crisis Centre.

Edwards, J. (1989), 'Local Government's Women's Committees', *Critical Social Policy*, 24, Winter.

Edwards, J. (1995), *Local Government Women's Committees*, Aldershot: Avebury.

Elcock, H. (1996), 'Local Government' in D. Farnham and S. Horton (eds) *Managing the New Public Services*, Basingstoke: Macmillan.

Engender (1993–2000), *Gender Audit*, Edinburgh: Engender.

Engender and Scottish Joint Action Group (1998, 1999), *Women and the Scottish Parliament*, information pack, Edinburgh: Engender/SJAG.

Equal Opportunities Commission (1985), *Women and Men in Scotland; A Statistical Profile*, Glasgow: EOC.

Equal Opportunities Commission (1994), *Equal Opportunities for Black and Ethnic Minority Women in Scotland*, Conference Report, Glasgow: EOC.

European Commission (1996), *Equal Opportunities for Women and Men in the European Union*, Brussels: EC.

Falchikov, N. (1992), *Adolescents' knowledge about, and attitudes to Domestic Violence, summary findings*, report to the Women's Committee Unit, Edinburgh District Council.

Firestone, Shulamith (1972), *Dialectics of Sex: The Case For Feminist Revolution*, London: Paladin.

Freeman, Joreen (1996), 'The Tyranny of Structureless' paper circulated in the 1970s reproduced in *Communities Directory: A Guide to Co-operative Living*, Oxford: Oxford University Press.

Fyfe, Maria (1989–90), 'Womens' Voice – Equal Representation' in *Equal Voice*, Winter.

Galligan, Yvonne (1998), *Women and Politics in Contemporary Ireland*, London and Washington: Pinter.

Galloway, Janice (1991), 'Fearless' in *Blood*, London: Secker & Warburg.

Gelb, J. and M. L. Palley (1987), *Women and Public Policies*, Princeton: Princeton University Press.

General Register Office for Scotland (1993), *1991 Census*, Edinburgh: HMSO.

Government Reply to the Third Report from the Home Affairs Select Committee (1993), Session 1992–93, London: HMSO.

Gray, J. M., A. F. McPherson and D. Raffe (1983), *Reconstructions of Secondary Education: Theory, Myth and Practice since the War*, London: Routledge & Kegan Paul.

Haavio-Mannila, E., D. Dahlerup, M. Eduards et al. (eds) (1985), *Unfinished Democracy: Women in Nordic Politics*, Oxford: Pergammon Press.

Hague, G., E. Malos and W. Dear (1995), *Against Domestic Violence: Inter-Agency Initiatives*, Bristol: University of Bristol.

Halford, Susan (1988), 'Women's initiatives in Local Government: Where do they come from and where are they going?', *Policy and Politics*, 16 (4).

Halford, S. (1992), 'Feminist change in a patriarchal organisation: the experience of women's initiatives in local government and implications for feminist perspectives on state institutions', in A. Witz and M. Savage (eds) *Gender and Bureaucracy*, Oxford: Blackwell.

Hayes, Bernadette and Ian McAllister (1996), 'Political Outcomes, Women's Legislative Rights and Devolution in Scotland', in D. Broughton, D. Farrell, D. Denver and C. Rallings (eds) *British Elections and Parties Yearbook 1995*, London: Frank Cass.

Hedlund, Gun (1988), 'Women's Interests in Local Politics', in K. Jones and A. Jonasdottir (eds) *The Political Interests of Gender*, London: Sage.

Henderson, S. (1998), *Service Provision for Women Experiencing Domestic Violence in Scotland*, Edinburgh: Scottish Office Central Research Unit.

Henderson, S. and A. Mackay (eds) (1990), *Grit and Diamonds*, Edinburgh: Stramullion.

Hersh, M. (1991), 'Women in Campaigning Groups in Central Scotland', in Woman's Claim of Right Group (eds), *A Woman's Claim of Right in Scotland*, Edinburgh: Polygon.

Hills, Leslie (1994), 'Why Engender?', *Chapman*, 76, Spring.

HM Inspectorate of Constabulary (1997), *Hitting Home*, Edinburgh: HMIC.

House of Commons, *Women in the House of Commons*, Factsheet No 5, undated.

Innes, Sue (1994), 'A liberating event for Scottish women' *Scotland on Sunday*, 13 March.

Innes, Sue (1999), *Keeping Gender on the Agenda*, Research Report, Edinburgh: Engender.

Kelly, E. (1992), 'Women's Committees', *Scottish Affairs*, 1, Autumn.

Kelly, Ellen (1992), 'The Future of Women in Scottish Local Government', *Scottish Affairs*, 1, Autumn, pp. 66–77.

Kelly, Ellen (1995), 'Sweeties from the Boys' Poke?': An Examination of Women's Committees in Scottish Local Government, unpublished MSc dissertation, Glasgow: University of Strathclyde.

Kelly, Liz (1988), *Surviving Sexual Violence*, Cambridge: Polity Press.

Kelly, Liz, Sheila Burton and Linda Regan (1994), *Beyond Victim or Survivor: Sexual Violence, Identity and Feminist Theory and Practice*, paper presented to the British Sociological Association Conference, Preston, April.

Kerr, J. B. and P. Jennings (1990), 'Scottish Feminism in the 80s' in S. Henderson and A. Mackay (eds), *Grit and Diamonds*, Edinburgh: Stramullion.

Kinsey, Richard (1992), *Survey of Young People*, Edinburgh: University of Edinburgh.

Kitzinger, Jenny and Kate Hunt (1993), *Evaluation of Edinburgh District Council's Zero Tolerance Campaign: Full Report*, Edinburgh: Glasgow University Media Group/ Edinburgh District Council's Women's Committee.

Kitzinger, Jenny (1995), *Interim Evaluation of Strathclyde Regional Council's Zero Tolerance Campaign*, Glasgow: Glasgow University Media Group.

Lawson, Alan (1988), 'Mair nor a rauch wind blawin' in David McCrone and Alice Brown *The Scottish Government Yearbook 1988*, Edinburgh: Unit for the Study of Government in Scotland, University of Edinburgh.

Lee, Jennie (1981), *My Life with Nye*, Harmondsworth: Penguin.

Levy, Catriona (1992), 'A Woman's Place? The Future Scottish Parliament', in Lindsay Paterson and David McCrone (eds) *The Scottish Government Yearbook 1992*, Edinburgh: The Unit for the Study of Government in Scotland, University of Edinburgh.

Levy, Catriona (1992), 'The Long Slow March: Scottish Women MPs 1918–45' in Esther Breitenbach and Eleanor Gordon (eds) *Against the Grain: Women in the Public Domain in Scotland*, Edinburgh: Edinburgh University Press.

Lieberman, Sue (1989), 'Women's Committees in Scotland', in Alice Brown and David McCrone (eds) *The Scottish Government Yearbook 1989*, Edinburgh: Unit for the Study of Government in Scotland, University of Edinburgh.

Lothian Health/Scottish Women's Aid (1997), 'Evaluation of A Pilot Training Day', Edinburgh: Lothian Health/Scottish Women's Aid, unpublished.

Lovenduski, Joni (1994), 'Will Quotas Make Women More Woman-Friendly', *Renewal*, 2 (1), January.

Lovenduski, J. (1995), 'An Emerging Advocate: The Equal Opportunities Commission in Great Britain' in D. M. Stetson and A. Mazur (eds), *Comparative State Feminism*, London: Sage.

Lovenduski, Joni (1997), 'Gender politics: a breakthrough for women?', *Parliamentary Affairs*, 50 (4).

Lovenduski, Joni and Jill Hills (eds) (1981), *The Politics of the Second Electorate: Women and Public Participation – Britain, USA, Canada, Australia, France, Spain, West Germany, Italy, Sweden, Finland, Eastern Europe, USSR, Japan*, London: Routledge & Kegan Paul.

Lovenduski, Joni and Pippa Norris (eds) (1993), *Gender and Party Politics*, London: Sage.

Lovenduski, J., H. Margetts and A. Abrar (1996), *Sexing London: the Gender Mix of Policy Actors*, Paper to American Political Science Association 92nd Annual Meeting, San Francisco.

Lovenduski, J. and V. Randall (1993), *Contemporary Feminist Politics: Women and Power in Britain*, Oxford: Oxford University Press.

Lyndon, N. and P. Ashton (1995), 'Knocked for six: the myth of a nation of wife-batterers', London: *Sunday Times*, 29 January.

McCrae, R. and U. Brown (1995), *No Voice-No Choice: A Report on Domestic Violence within Black and Ethnic Minority Communities*, report to Strathclyde Regional Council.

McCrone, David, Lindsay Paterson and Alice Brown (1993), 'Reforming local government in Scotland' *Local Government Studies*, 19 (1).

Mackay, Fiona (1995), *The case of Zero Tolerance: Women's Politics in Action?* Edinburgh: *New Waverley Papers*, Department of Politics, University of Edinburgh.

Mackay, Fiona (1996), 'Getting There, Being There, Making A Difference?:

Gendered Discourses of Access and Action in Local Politics', unpublished PhD dissertation, Edinburgh: University of Edinburgh.

Mackay, Fiona (1998), 'In a different voice? Scottish women local politicians and the vocabulary of care', *Contemporary Politics*, 4 (3).

Mackay, Fiona and Kate Bilton (2000), *Learning for Experience: Lessons in Mainstreaming Equal Opportunities*, Edinburgh: Governance of Scotland Forum, University of Edinburgh.

Mackay, Fiona, Esther Breitenbach, Jan Webb and Alice Brown (1995), *Early Days: Local Government Reorganisation and Equal Opportunities Practice*, Edinburgh: New Waverley Papers, Department of Politics, University of Edinburgh.

McKenna, R. (1998), 'Selection Procedures for the Scottish Labour Party Panel for the Scottish Parliamentary Elections', *Scotland Forum*, Edinburgh: HMSO.

Macleod, Jan, Patricia Bell and Janette Forman (1994), 'Bridging the Gap: feminist development work in Glasgow', in Miranda Davis (ed.) *Women and Violence*, London: Zed.

McLetchie, D. (1998), 'Made in Scotland – Scottish Conservatives for the Scottish Parliament', *Scotland Forum*, Edinburgh: HMSO.

Mann, J. (1962), *Woman in Parliament*, London: Odhams.

Mann, L. (1993), *Public Policy and Participation: The Role of Women in the Highlands*, Report to Barail, Easter Ross: Lorraine Mann Research and Consultancy.

Marchbank, J. (1994), 'Nondecision-making . . . A Management Guide to Keeping Women's Interest Issues off the Political Agenda', in G. Griffen, M. Hester, S. Rai and S. Roseneil (eds) *Stirring It: Challenges For Feminism*, Abingdon: Taylor and Francis.

Marchbank, J. (1996), *Going Dutch or Scotch Mist? Making Marginalised Voices Heard in Local Bureaucracies*, Bradford and Ilkley: Centre for Research in Applied Community Studies, Bradford and Ilkley Community College Corporation.

Martlew, C., C. Forrester and G. Buchanan (1985), 'Activism and Office: women and local government in Scotland', *Local Government Studies*, 11 (2).

Metcalfe, B. A. (1984), Note on 'Current Career Concerns of female and male managers and professionals'. An analysis of free-response comments to a national survey in *Public Administration*.

Mitchell, James (1992), 'The 1992 Election in Scotland in Context', *Parliamentary Affairs*, 45 (4).

Myers, Fiona and Alice Brown (1997), *A Research Review Update*, Manchester: EOC.

Nairn, Tom (1994), 'Gender Goes Top of the Agenda', *The Scotsman*, 28 December.

National Inter-Agency Working Party (1992), 'National Inter-Agency Working Party Report on Domestic Violence', *Victim Support*, July.

Norris, Pippa (1993), 'Slow Progress for Women MPs', *Parliamentary Brief*, Nov/Dec.

Norris, Pippa and Joni Lovenduski (1995), *Political Recruitment: Gender, Race and Class in the British Parliament*, Cambridge: Cambridge University Press.

Northern Ireland Office/Department of Health and Social Services (1995), *Tackling Domestic Violence: A Policy for Northern Ireland*, Belfast: NIO/DHSS.

Office of Population Censuses and Surveys/General Register Office for Scotland (1993), *1991 Census of Population*, London: HMSO.

Osmond, J. (ed.) (1994), *A Parliament for Wales*, Ceredigion: Gomer.

Paterson, Lindsay, Alice Brown and David McCrone (1992), 'Constitutional Crisis: The Causes and Consequences of the 1992 Scottish General Election Result', *Parliamentary Affairs*, 45 (4).

Phillips, A. (1995), *The Politics of Presence*, Oxford: Oxford University Press.

Phillips, Anne (1994), 'The Representation of Women', in *The Polity Reader in Gender Studies*, Cambridge: Polity Press.

Phillips, Kate (1989), Letter to *Radical Scotland*, No. 38, Apr/May.

Phizacklea, A. and R. Miles (1992), 'The British Trade Union Movement and Racism', in Peter Braham, Ali Rattansi and Richard Skellington (eds) *Racism and Antiracism*, London: Sage.

Positive Action in Housing (1999), *Scottish Ethnic Minorities Directory*, Glasgow: Positive Action in Housing.

Powney, J., J. McPake, L. Edwards and S. Hamilton (2000), *Gender Equality and Lifelong Learning in Scotland*, Manchester: EOC.

Public Services Privatisation Research Unit (PSPRU) (1992), *Privatisation: A Disaster for Quality*, London: PSPRU, March.

Radical Scotland (1989), 'Getting it Together', *Radical Scotland*, 38, Apr/May.

Radical Scotland (1989), 38, Apr/May.

Randall, V. (1987 2nd edition), *Women and Politics*, Basingstoke: Macmillan.

Randall, V. (1992), 'Great Britain and Dilemmas for Feminist Strategy in the 1980s, in Jill Bystydzienski (ed.) *Women Transforming Politics*, Bloomington, IN: Indiana University Press.

Rhode, Deborah (1995), 'The Politics of Paradigms: Gender Difference and Gender Disadvantage', in Gisella Bock and Susan James *Beyond Equality and Difference*, London: Routledge.

Riddoch, Lesley (1994), 'Zero Tolerance: the Second Wave', *Harpies and Quines*, 12, March.

Roddick, Jackie (1989–90), 'Women and Voting Systems', in *Radical Scotland*, Dec/Jan.

RoSA!! (1999), *Speaking for Ourselves* (pamphlet), Glasgow: Racism on the Scottish Agenda.

Rosen, B. and T. H. Jerdee (1974), 'Sex Stereotyping in the Executive Suite', *Harvard Business Review*, 52.

Ross, Jennifer (1990), *Equal Voice*, Glasgow: STUC.

Rowbotham, S., L. Segal, et al. (1979), *Beyond the Fragments*, Newcastle: Newcastle Socialist Centre and Islington Community Press.

The Scotland Act 1998.

Scottish Conservative & Unionist Central Office (1966), *The Year Book for Scotland 1966*, Edinburgh: Scottish Conservative & Unionist Central Office.

Scottish Constitutional Commission (1994), *Further Steps: Towards a Scheme for Scotland's Parliament*, October, Edinburgh: CoSLA.

Scottish Constitutional Convention (1989), 'Women and a Scottish Parliament', in *Towards Scotland's Parliament, Consultation Document and Report to the Scottish People*, October, Edinburgh: CoSLA.

Scottish Constitutional Convention (1990), *Towards Scotland's Parliament, A Report to the Scottish People*, November, Edinburgh: CoSLA.

Scottish Constitutional Convention (1992), *Electoral System for Scottish Parliament*, February, Edinburgh: CoSLA.

Scottish Constitutional Convention (1995), *Scotland's Parliament, Scotland's Right*, November, Edinburgh: CoSLA.

Scottish Executive (1999), *Domestic Abuse – there's no excuse* (leaflet), Edinburgh: Scottish Executive.

Scottish Executive (2000), *Towards an Equality Strategy: Consultation on the Development of the Strategy*, Edinburgh: Scottish Executive.

Scottish Liberal Democrats' Women's Commission (1990), *Report of the Scottish Liberal Democrats' Women's Commission*, November.

Scottish National Party (1995), *Programme for Government*, Edinburgh: SNP.

Scottish Needs Assessment Project (1997), *Domestic Violence*, Glasgow: SNAP.

Scottish Office (1997), *Scotland's Parliament*, Cmnd. 3658, July, Edinburgh: HMSO.

Scottish Office (1997), *Reaching Women in Scotland*, Edinburgh: HMSO.

Scottish Office (1998), *Shaping Scotland's Parliament*, Report of the Consultative Steering Group on the Scottish Parliament, December, Edinburgh: HMSO.

Scottish Partnership on Domestic Abuse (2000), *National Strategy to Address Domestic Abuse in Scotland*, Edinburgh: Scottish Executive.

Scottish Trades Union Congress (1999), *General Council Report*, Glasgow: STUC.

Scottish Women's Aid (1987–1998), *Annual Report* (1987–1998), Edinburgh: Scottish Women's Aid.

Scottish Women's Aid (1992), *Women Talking to Women: A Women's Aid Approach to Counselling*, Edinburgh: Scottish Women's Aid.

Scottish Women's Aid (1999), *Women's Aid in Scotland: 25 years of Listening to Women*, Edinburgh: Scottish Women's Aid.

Scottish Women's Co-ordination Group (1995), Report and Recommendations to the UN 4th World Conference on Women, Beijing 1995.

Scottish Women's Liberation Journal (1977), 'The Scottish Convention of Women', *Scottish Women's Liberation Journal*, 3.

Shelton, Anita (1999), 'Black and Minority Ethnic Women', *Gender Audit 1998/99*, Edinburgh: Engender.

Simpson, Emma (1990), ' "Mainly Manly": The Scottish Constitutional Convention and the implications for women's representation', unpublished Politics Honours dissertation, University of Edinburgh,

Sinclair, Maggie (1989), 'Feminism in the Eighties', *Radical Scotland*, No. 36, Dec/Jan.

Stacey, M. and M. Price (1981), *Women, Power and Politics*, London: Tavistock.

Stedward, Gail (1987), 'Entry the System: A Case History of Women in Scotland', in

J. Richardson and G. Jordan (eds) *Government and Pressure Groups in Britain*, Oxford: Clarendon.

Stone, I. (1988), *Equal Opportunities in Local Authorities*, London: HMSO.

Strachan, Yvonne and Sutherland, Lesley (1989), 'Women in Trade Unions in Scotland', in Alice Brown and David McCrone (eds) *The Scottish Government Yearbook 1989*, Edinburgh: Unit for the Study of Government in Scotland, University of Edinburgh.

Strachey, Ray (1979 reprint), *The Cause*, London: Virago.

Sudbury, Julia (1998), *'Other Kinds of Dreams': black women's organisations and the politics of transformation*, London: Routledge.

The Guardian (1990), 25 July.

The Guardian (1991), 12 July.

The Scotsman (1918), 10 December.

The Tribune (1991), 12 April.

Turner, E., S. Riddell and S. Brown (1995), *Gender Equality in Scottish Schools: The Impact of Recent Educational Reforms*, Glasgow: EOC.

Vallance, Elizabeth (1988), 'Two cheers for equality: Women candidates in the 1987 General Elections' *Parliamentary Affairs*, January.

Wainwright, H. (1987), *Labour: A Tale of Two Parties*, London: The Hogarth Press.

Warner, G. (1994), 'Time to give Zero Tolerance to the Sex Warriors', *Sunday Times Scotland*, 9 October.

Weir, A. and E. Wilson (1984), 'The British Women's Movement', *New Left Review*, 148 Nov/Dec.

Woman's Claim of Right Group (1989), 'A Scottish Woman's Claim of Right', unpublished submission to the Scottish Constitutional Convention.

Woman's Claim of Right Group (eds) (1991), *A Woman's Claim of Right in Scotland*, Edinburgh: Polygon.

Women's Support Project/*Evening Times* (1990), *Report on Responses from 1503 Women to the Survey on Violence Against Women*, March, Glasgow: Women's Support Project/*Evening Times*.

Young, I. M. (1990), 'The Ideal of Community and the Politics of Difference', in L. J. Nicholson (ed) *Feminism/Postmodernism*, London: Routledge.

Young, K. (1990), 'Approaches to Policy Development in the Field of Equal Opportunities', in W. Ball and J. Solomos (eds) *Race and Local Politics*, Basingstoke: Macmillan.

Zero Tolerance (1995), Briefing paper, 'Canadian Initiatives on Violence Against Women', Briefing paper, 'Making Z-Way': Ayrshire Zero Tolerance Conference, 6 March.

Index

Thatcher, Margaret, 17, 27, 182–3, 184,
203, 214–15, 222
Thomson, Elaine, 272, 274
'thresholders', 6, 7, 9, 55–8, 66
trade union movement, 232
see also Scottish Trades Union Congress
training, 58, 71, 97
see also education
Training 2000, 97
Turnbull, Karen (Karen Gillon), 261
Tweedsmuir, Lady, 181
twinning, 222, 242, 246n, 252
'Tyranny of Structurelessness, The', 84

UK parliament see Westminster parliament
under representation rates; see also MPs
Ullrich, Kay, 273, 280
UN see United Nations
UNISON, 111
Unit for the Study of Government in
Scotland, 234–5
United Nations, 17
Beijing Conference on Women, 207,
226n, 235–6
Charter on the Rights of Women, 208
International Women's Year, 183
Urban Aid, 36, 70–1
USA, 20, 197, 227n

values, 75–6, 137
verdicts, 72–3
victim language and images, 73, 109
violence against women see male violence
and sexual violence
'votes for women' as still an unattained
goal, 168, 180
voting, 168, 169

WAFE (Women's Aid Federation of
England), 65
Wages Councils, 28
Wainwright, Hilary, 84
Wales, 150, 199, 246n
see also Welsh National Assembly
Wallace, Jim, 237, 242
Warner, Gerald, 138, 142–3
WAVAW conference, 72
Webb, Janette, 160n, 161n
Weir, Angela, 78
Welsh National Assembly, 21n, 65, 246n,
249
Welsh Women's Aid, 65

West, Rebecca, 96
West Lothian, 150
Westminster parliament see under
representation rates; see also MPs
WFS see Women's Forum Scotland
White, Sandra, 273, 274
Whitefield, Karen, 273–4
Wilson, Elizabeth, 78
wives, necessity for councillors, 95
Woman's Claim of Right Group, 82–5, 87,
165–9, 173, 183, 184–5, 204, 217
women
barriers to political participation see
under political participation
organisations and, 64
representation of see representation and
representation rates
situation of, 27–8, 95, 100–2, 166–8,
186, 201
value placed on, 38, 166
Women Against Violence Against Women
conference, 72
Women Against Violence Europe, 65–6
Women in Scotland Consultative Forum,
20, 51–2, 236, 239–40, 245
women-only space, 10, 43–5
Women's Agenda for Scotland, 239
Women's Aid, 6–7, 8, 55 66, 86, 87, 120
Code of Practice, 57
local authority support for, 155
refuges, 49, 59–60, 63
Scottish Parliament and, xiii–xiv
as social movement, 81
and Zero Tolerance campaign, 109, 117,
125, 134, 139–40
women's centres, 10, 43–5
women's committees
local government see under local
government
STUC see under Scottish Trades Union
Congress
Women's Co-ordination Group see Scottish
Women's Co-ordination Group
Women's Forum Scotland, 231, 233, 235,
239–40
Women's Issues, Minister for, 237
Women's Advisory Group to, 236, 237
Women's Legal and Financial
Independence Campaign, 86, 183–4
Women's Liberation Movement, 3, 80, 86–
7
conferences, 86, 87